ANTAGONISTICS

ANTAGONISTICS

GOPAL BALAKRISHNAN

VERSO

London • New York

First published by Verso 2009
© Gopal Balakrishnan 2009
All rights reserved

1 3 5 7 9 10 8 6 4 2

Verso
UK: 6 Meard Street, London W1F 0EG
US: 20 Jay Street, Suite 1010, Brooklyn, NY 11201
www.versobooks.com

Verso is the imprint of New Left Books

ISBN-13: 978-1-84467-268-4 (hbk)
ISBN-13: 978-1-84467-269-1 (pbk)

British Library Cataloguing in Publication Data
A catalogue record for this book is available from the British Library

Library of Congress Cataloging-in-Publication Data
A catalog record for this book is available from the Library of Congress

Typeset by Hewer Text UK Ltd, Edinburgh
Printed in the US by Maple Vail

Contents

Introduction

Originally published as reflections on a number of books offering broad theorizations of past and present, the essays collected in this volume form a chronicle of the second decade of the post–Cold War status quo. In terms of topical variety, the works under consideration offer vantage points from which to bring the historical moment into sharper relief. Only a few words on this larger context are in order, as these exercises in reconstruction and criticism hopefully speak for themselves.

Over a seven-year period, a provisional totalization of the times took shape in these essays around the theme of 'neutralization'. What does this term signify? Carl Schmitt understood it to be the foreclosure of an epochal contention that leaves behind a political and intellectual field, initially devoid of a primary, structuring antagonism.[1] So conceived, it captures many of the defining contours of the world ideological scene that emerged after the late twentieth-century collapse of Communism and anti-colonial nationalism. A new historical situation arose out of the demise of revolutionary politics, soon followed by a vast slackening of reform, as this term was once understood. Rounding out this picture, the withdrawal of anti-systemic states and movements opened up new regions for the consolidation and expansion of capitalism and, for a brief moment, the march of liberal civilization seemed to extend

1 Carl Schmitt, 'The Age of Neutralizations and Depoliticizations', in *The Concept of the Political*, Chicago: University of Chicago, 1996, p. 80.

indefinitely into the future. But it did not take long for the age of imperial peace to shift into a more chaotic phase, one that has made it increasingly difficult to forecast the shape and direction of things to come. It would appear as if the same social logic that neutralizes the power to build new hegemonies is generating dimensions of disorder and change beyond intelligible totalization.

This condition of historical disorientation has some approximate precedents. The realization that inherited concepts of politics and war were losing their purchase on emerging zones of conflict, and that capitalism was undergoing a fateful structural mutation, first surfaced in a now remote inter-war era. Bringing these developments to a head, the advent of fascism seemed to impart a tangible form to this estrangement of the historical milieu. The writings of Antonio Gramsci and Carl Schmitt are in-depth explorations of the unfamiliar landscape that emerged out of this effacement of narrative coordinates and conceptual distinctions. For both, accounts cast in terms of older oppositions—state and society, revolution and reform, war and peace, and so on—were failing to bring into focus some of the unsettling peculiarities of the period. Arguably, the most successful theorizations of that time captured what was unprecedented by registering the limits and plasticity of the classical terms. Our situation differs from theirs. Although the words 'state', 'revolution' and 'war' are still very much with us, they are little more than faded tokens of the historical names they once were. Have these categories been neutralized as the ordering forms of political existence? The state as a repressive apparatus distinct from society, holding in place its order of property and privileges; revolution as a qualitative transformation of this dispensation through the seizure and reconstitution of political power; war as a legitimate instrument of settlement between sovereign communities—these definitions encapsulate the historical experiences of a past which now persists only in vestiges and aftermaths. The inter-war context in which these concepts still appeared indispensable and absolute, was, paradoxically, a time when the present could be experienced as a transition to another form of society, for such sharply defined terms signalled their own historicity, holding open the space for their negation, abolition, or withering away. This experience is no longer immediately available to us. The political concepts that made this overcoming intelligible have ceased to seem binding in either politics, or, for that matter, in the writing of history. One might go so far as to say that the epochal schemas of past, present and future, within which some basic mental and material conditions of possibility could come into view, have lost much of their status as objectively valid thought-forms. In an attempt to register the consequences of this conceptual erosion, many of these essays ask the question, what does 'anti-war' mean when the phenomenon of 'war' itself has been dissolved into a nebulous region of arbitrarily classified, asymmetrical violence?

This waning experience of the finitude of modes of life and thought—stalked by the prospect of their transcendable nature—is often regarded as part of a larger decline of metaphysical absolutes, the onset of a condition in which History can no longer claim to be the whole, and politics is reduced to a dialogue over values. While attenuated notions of public life have characterized 'bourgeois society' from its inception, the field of opinion formation no longer seems able to support a more elevated stage of properly 'historical' action. In *Politics as a Vocation*, Max Weber conjoined the more prosaic to the loftier level of political choice in a memorable account of the predicaments of modernity that moves from postgraduate careers to the ethos of ungrounded conviction. While such 'anti-foundationalism' eventually became a familiar liberal trope, Weber wrote at a time when it still seemed to invite resolute leaps of faith for heroic causes of collective struggle. In the 'tragic vision' of German sociology, modernity is the fragmentation of the meaningful whole into ever more disconnected, warring sectors and perspectives, periodically regrouped by mytho-political totalizations. History makes its appearance as a momentary upsurge of meaning.

My own view is that the age in which we live can be made at least partly intelligible as a story of the origins and expansion of capitalism. Of all the classical categories of social thought, only this one has acquired a newfound, indeed omnipresent actuality. But comprehending a basic direction of historical change does not settle the essential question of whether a politics oriented toward the long-term tendencies and limits of capitalism is still possible. The time lines of capital are intertwined with a number of relatively autonomous histories—an occasionally volatile region of thought and subjectivity, a once slow-changing, customary order of family life and gender relations, a now uncertain trajectory of state formation and war and, finally, a deep time of the species and its habitats. How could such discontinuous temporal orders be made commensurable with one another in a single historical horizon? The current inconceivability of thought and politics on this scale is a consequence of the defeat and exhaustion of those subjective agencies that once sought to inflect and integrate the vectors of structural change in line with revolutionary and reformist agendas. Over the last several decades, the *Standpunkt* of an emancipation from all remediable unfreedom and want—from which wave after wave of the 'ruthless criticism of all that exists' once poured forth—has been abandoned for the security of political settlements that shelter an endless, more or less heated conversation over the values that distinguish today's shades and poles of opinion. For better or worse, this is the world of opinion and thought we inhabit, and *Antagonistics* is a survey of a segment of it.

Such general remarks are offered, not as a report on the historical context of their genesis, but rather as an explanation of the approach to criticism that informs each of these essays. As I understand it, criticism is a reconstruction of the overall argument of a work, which explores the possibility that its logical, empirical and even stylistic failures arise from ideologies embedded in its framework. Many of the authors addressed here have political alignments very far from my own, ranging from post-Marxism all the way over to an older world of the Right. The symbolic logic that classifies positions in these terms is still powerful, and makes true impartiality difficult. Carl Schmitt once wrote that 'all political concepts, images and terms have a polemical meaning'—a disquieting reminder of the obstacles that confront any attempt to articulate objective judgments in a sphere so inescapably ideological. But measuring the relative intellectual value of political stances need not be an exercise in neutrality, for not everything is thinkable from every point of view. Recognizing this elementary fact requires that criticism contain a coefficient of polemic. But how could polemics ever be a form of thought, distinct from the milieu of mere vehement opinion? The answer to this question perhaps is to be found in a literary form of indirect attack, focusing on the intellectual vices that stem from an ideological entanglement. But I would go further to maintain that political commitments grounded in thought can be distinguished from opinion and ideological attachments by their capacity to subsume the authentic insights of opposed conceptions of the world. 'To understand and evaluate realistically one's adversary's position and his reasons (and sometimes one's adversary is the whole of past thought) means precisely to be liberated from the prison of ideologies'—so wrote an imprisoned Antonio Gramsci. *Antagonistics* is meant to evoke an older notion of rational polemics bound by a critique of political—*that is to say over-politicized*—reason. But the neologism is also meant to index a historical moment in which some of the presuppositions of criticism—most vitally the test of and passage to action—are missing. Regardless, in every successive phase of modern capitalism and state formation, from the era of classical liberalism and early social-ism, through the inter-war age of extremes, to the 'postmodern' present, a measured, historically comparative reflection on the prospects for a rational transformation of the order of human things has been the *sine qua non* of any intellectually consequential opposition. These essays are all attempts to develop a form of writing, and position-taking, that might further this goal.

What are the themes of this collection? Its first section consists of essays on recently published macro-histories of the centuries-long co-evolution of capitalism and the inter-state system. As the introductory paragraphs of several of these essays indicate, their publication often coincided with one or another episode in that great arc of American military interventions that began with the end of the Cold War, but escalated to unsettling levels of strategic ambition in the aftermath of the *attentats* of 9/11. Although the relationship of Atlantic statecraft to neoliberalism was a widely addressed topic during the previous decade, the terms of this discussion remained, by and large, within the parameters of globalization discourse, even when occasionally enlivened by trenchant exposés of the gap between the facts and the normative rationales of humanitarian warfare. The terrorist thunderbolts that struck downtown Manhattan changed the terms of this discussion immediately. While the rhetoric surrounding that event has been of a predictable quality, heated dispute over the rationality of America's subsequent course of action has resulted in a renewed interest in Grand Strategy and, in some quarters, a sharper focus on the outstanding problems of conceptualizing the structural nexus between war and capitalism. Although several of these works were conceived before 9/11, their publication in this period contributed to a more vivid delineation of the limits of older traditions of International Relations realism, historical sociology, and Marxist conceptions of imperialism. The desire and capacity to narrate large-scale historical change has undoubtedly faded in the milieu of postmodern, post-political societies. Yet some of the theoretical ferment surrounding the current conjuncture of neo-imperial statecraft stems from an estrangement, a dissipation of the haze of familiarity that surrounded the inter-state realm in all the canonical accounts of modernity, beginning with Marx. The entrenched vestiges of an old regime of war and diplomacy perhaps begin to take on a different appearance with the realization that no major state has waged open war with another for over a half century. There is an obvious Hegelian trope of retrospection that might account for this emerging depth dimension, as a long history of intertwined state formation and capital accumulation from the early modern era to the present— and an even longer one of the history of violence itself—enters a new, uncertain phase. In both its reviews and editorials, *New Left Review* has been at the forefront of the reclamation of this terrain, and *Antagonistics* is but a sample from an ongoing internal discussion on the strategic, legal and moral rationales behind the latest campaigns of Pax Americana. My own view, iterated in the concluding paragraphs of many of these essays, has been that, rationales to one side, the post–Cold War reflation of American power was ultimately based on unsustainable world economic imbalances and speculative bubbles. These would eventually unravel, precipitating a global downturn of intractable, if not inter-war proportions, and the onset of a new season of political surprises. The first part of this prediction seems to have been lately confirmed.

The next set of essays in this collection might be subsumed under the rubric of 'politics' in the classical sense of the genesis, internal identity and motives of state. If the first group of authors consisted disproportionately of Americans by extraction or education, the second comprises a clear European majority, although exceptions in both sets dilute this suggestive contrast. This second section, moreover, embraces writers of incomparably higher renown, corresponding, in part, to the older vintage of the problems they address. At issue for several of them was the question of what stance to take toward 'democracy', today the *summum bonum* of a complacent political universe, but then an advancing condition of mass entitlement, menacing Old Europe with the spectre of permanent revolution. One descent line of the conservative liberalism that currently rules the roost extends back to a counter-revolutionary problematic whose contours took shape in turning points between the Orleanist France of Alexis de Tocqueville and the Weimar Germany of Carl Schmitt. Even now, when democracy means little more than the electoral legitimation of responsible, market-friendly policy—and the occasional recrudescence of a less domesticated populism causes so much elite wailing—the terms of these older controversies persist. The entwinement of popular sovereignty with unstable notions of collective identity remains at the centre of disputes surrounding the long-term historical viability and necessary quotient of homogeneity required of today's nation-states, occasioning some troubled afterthoughts on what forms of solidarity, if any, might take hold in the multicultural cosmopolis to come. Radicalizing spirals of ideas and praxes that generate new modes and orders have yet to break out. Accompanying several of these diagnoses of the period are some thoughts on the clash of fundamentalisms. My own inclination is to make no concessions to an overwrought hysteria before today's 'existential enemies' of the West, and to harbour no illusions regarding their anti-systemic significance. Finally, *Antagonistics* concludes with two reflections on Machiavelli, the first, in a review on posthumous work by a man broken by the political outcomes of the last century, aptly entitled *Machiavelli and Us*. The second is not a review, but a more free-standing essay that offers notations on a figure to whom I have turned in order to comprehend the defeat of revolutionary causes and the prospect for their renewal, 'without hope or fear'.

(2008)

I

Concepts of the Geopolitical

1

Arms and Accumulation

According to conventional wisdom, 1648 marks the moment of creation: the inauguration of the modern inter-state system.[1] The Peace tortuously negotiated in the Westphalian towns of Münster and Osnabrück—while half-starved mercenary armies, spurred on by France or Sweden, Austria or Spain, continued to ravage the farms, towns and villages of the German principalities—famously recognized the territorial sovereignty of the 300-odd states of the Holy Roman Empire. Their princes were freed from the imperial yoke, empowered to contract treaties with each other and with outside powers, sole rulers of their own dominions. French absolutism appears at the centre of this story, as the power that secured the diplomatic recognition of this pluriverse of sovereign states.

For Benno Teschke, in this ambitious if uneven work, the textbook narrative contains completely erroneous assumptions about when and where modernity began: 'Periodization is no innocent exercise, no mere pedagogical and heuristic device to plant markers in the uncharted flow of history. It entails assumptions about the duration and identity of specific epochs and geopolitical orders.' The very title of the book signals the importance of representing the transition to capitalism and modern statehood in a narrative form, organized around landmark dates. Undaunted

---

[1]   This article first appeared in *New Left Review* 2: 26, March–April 2004, and is a review of Benno Teschke, *The Myth of 1648*, London: Verso, 2003.

by the sheer number of events that have been posited as definitive starting points of modernity—in politics, economics, religion and even philosophy—Teschke maintains that the moment of inception was, in fact, the consolidation of parliamentary rule in England in the aftermath of the Glorious Revolution. For it was then and there that the first properly capitalist state in world history was constituted.

Teschke sees this development rather than the Peace of Westphalia, forty years before, as the point of departure for the modernization of the European inter-state system. The eighteenth-century expansion of English capitalism set into motion the crisis of the European *ancien régime*, and eventually created the conditions for a new world order based on global capitalism. Understanding the genesis and expansion of capitalism as a process of modernization brings into focus the overarching historical trend-line. During the course of this long transition, the old predatory game of war and diplomacy broke down, and was replaced by another order. Capitalism is a social system in which the role of force in accumulating wealth has been eclipsed by the power of money invested in the means of production. The expansionary dynamic of this system should, over the long term, he argues, re-programme the prime directives of states towards the more or less peaceable promotion of economic development.

The Myth of 1648 takes aim at a series of international-relations models. A prime target is the Realist view that an anarchic system of strategic action, structured around the balance of power, emerges whenever states must fend for themselves or perish. From this Hobbesian perspective, the maxims of war and diplomacy have undergone no fundamental changes since the era of the Peloponnesian War. The transhistorical outlook of this school is resumed in Kenneth Waltz's observation: 'The enduring character of international politics accounts for the striking sameness in the quality of international life through the millennia.' Teschke aims to replace the static analytics of Realism with a historicism that comprehends a succession of qualitatively distinct geo-political orders from the Carolingian age to the present. His study distinguishes itself from a number of contemporary sociological critiques of Realism that offer their own versions of the origins of geopolitical modernity yet remain, he argues, beholden to a mystifying schema of periodization structured around the inaugural moment of 1648.

While orthodox Realism cannot even acknowledge this transformation, Teschke argues that international-relations theories that seek to be historical are eclectic. Such accounts can only comprehend the advent of modernity as the coincidental confluence of bureaucratic rationalization, the recognition of absolute property rights, a new economic ethos and the spread of commerce. The syncretistic methodology of Max Weber lies behind these parables of modernization:

> Any reconstruction of European history will therefore have to retrace the independent developmental logics of different social spheres (political, economic, legal, religious etc.) that never stand in any necessary relation of co-constitution but may or may not form 'elective affinities'.

A 'coincidental conjuncture of an expandable list of contingencies' merely describes aspects of this multi-level transition, however, without explaining how it was possible. Any such explanation must take the form of integrating all these series into a single developmental logic.

Teschke's account of this epochal transformation relies heavily on the work of Robert Brenner, whose essays on the origins of agrarian capitalism and socio-political history of the English Revolution are arguably the definitive contributions to long-standing debates surrounding both topics. Brenner's theoretical contribution is a rigorous clarification of how social-property relations determine the conditions of access to the means of subsistence, and thus the long-term developmental dynamics of entire societies. *The Myth of 1648* is an attempt to explain the formation and crisis of geopolitical orders from the quotidian requirements of reproduction dictated by these social-property relations. For Teschke, 'changes in property regimes restructure the identity of political communities and their distinct forms of conflict and cooperation.'

These property regimes set the terms for the production and appropriation of resources, and thus determine the agents and stakes of armed conflict. They are the 'deep generative grammar and transformative logic of international relations'. Following Brenner, Teschke assembles the basic conditions of survival in a world of the plough and sword—with an emphasis on the specificities of European feudalism—and the pattern of cooperation, crisis and conflict that emerged from them. In his account, peasant households possessed the means of their subsistence and sought to produce the full range of their necessities themselves, rather than maximize their income. As a result of this lack of specialization, productivity remained low and the food supply uncertain. The systemic persistence of low levels of agricultural productivity, in turn, limited sustainable population growth, yet peasant households were compelled to have numerous children as security. This led to rising land/man ratios, the subdivision of plots, rising food prices and deteriorating levels of subsistence. These limits could be surmounted through colonization and reclamation of new lands but, as extensive expansion continued, ever less fertile land was brought into cultivation, exposing a growing population to diminishing returns and crop failure.

Because peasants possessed the means of production, a surplus could only be appropriated from them through coercion. Even when innovations to improve productivity could be implemented on a local scale, relying on coercion was an invariably cheaper and safer way to extract surplus. Predatory competition between the lords who possessed the means of coercion compelled the latter to form groups whose survival hinged upon building up an increasingly effective organization of tribute collection. This superincumbent weight of exploitation compounded the natural subsistence predicament generated by population growth, subdivision and soil exhaustion, leading to catastrophic socio-demographic crises.

The problem is to explain how this stagnant Malthusian world eventually mutated into the dynamic international market society of the nineteenth century. Brenner has persuasively demonstrated how distinct property regimes emerged out of the class struggles between lords and peasants in different regions of Europe. He argues that it was the unusual resolution of the late-medieval English class struggle that sealed off its social evolution from the iron laws of warlordism and subsistence agriculture prevailing on the continent. Teschke characterizes this development as a secession from a multi-actor geopolitical civilization, whose remote origins he reconstructs in a striking central chapter. The starting point for this continental order is the millennial collapse of Charlemagne's empire which, at its zenith, embraced Gaul, western and southern Germany, the northeastern Iberian peninsula and Lombardian Italy. 'Intra-ruling class struggle among late Frankish lords under outside pressure precipitated the implosion of the Carolingian Empire during the Feudal Revolution of the year 1000.' As this bucolic edifice crumbled, banal lordship—the right to levy fees and exact fines—tumbled downward from the imperial aristocracy to regional counts, and then finally to local castellans and manorial micro-lordships. The old Carolingian light cavalry and peasant infantries eventually gave way to heavy cavalry quartered in a new network of small stone castles. Swarming to these rural fortresses, motley crews of retainers formed a new layer of lesser nobles, 'trapped between impoverishment and adventure':

> Armed, pretentious and poor, the knights clung to their stoned off space, talking of weapons and deeds, of strikes, of demands; of lucrative stratagems more than management or incomes.

Feudal society was organized as a ladder of conditional tenures contractually stipulating obligations of armed assistance between overlords and vassals. These political communities were not public orders but fluid ensembles of lordships, held together by their campaigns and through distribution of the spoils of war. The prizes at stake were estates picked up through feuds and inheritance, comprising an assortment of rent-generating rights over far-flung territories. Teschke highlights the private nature of feudal political power: 'Every lord was his own conflict unit.'

In this age of marauding chivalry, the European peninsula—previously the most backward zone of Eurasia—underwent an enormous material transformation as 'woods, marshes, swamps, wastelands, alluvial lowlands, and even lakes and parts of the sea vanished to make room for ploughland'. European development also involved extensive military gains on the peripheries of the old Frankish empire: the reconquest of the Iberian peninsula; the colonization of the Slavic-Baltic east by German lords, peasants and townsmen; the crusades that established the ephemeral principalities of Syria; the Norman conquest of England. Domination of these terrestrial peripheries resulted in the establishment of a maritime ascendancy over the Baltic, North Atlantic and Mediterranean.

Relentless political competition between feudal bands formed a field of selection in which 'the main causes for survival, transformation or decline have to be sought in the nexus between internal revenue extraction and productivity, i.e. in class relations'. This was because the outcomes of class conflict between lord and peasant determined the surpluses available for building up an effective war machine, vital for survival and expansion at the expense of competitors.

The need to attract and reward followers with gifts, equipment and fiefs stimulated the demand for artisanal crafts, purchased with part of the surplus taken from producers of food and raw materials. But the increasingly sophisticated urban commercial system that emerged from the expansion of this basic circuit did not dissolve systemic barriers to economic development, because marketable surpluses could only be garnered by squeezing taxes and rents from peasant cultivators for unproductive consumption and war. Although this commercialization hastened the decline of decentralized banal feudalism in Western Europe as villages secured their personal freedom in the aftermath of the late-medieval demographic collapse, outside of England it did not lead to the development of capitalism but rather to more centralized monetary forms of coercive surplus extraction.

On this landscape of micro-warfare, the boundaries between communities of vassals had been fluid and precarious. The subsequent consolidation of royal authority led to the incipient differentiation between the domestic and the military-diplomatic spheres of politics, and thus the reconstitution of anarchy on a more recognizably inter-state basis. Although this process has seemed to many the beginning of a Europe-wide transition to sovereign statehood, Teschke argues that radically different dynamics of state formation were unfolding under the cover of this common geopolitical development. In fact, his entire narrative assumes that the onset of social and inter-state modernity can be told as a story of an ever-widening divergence between capitalist England and absolutist France. He argues that, while post-fourteenth century French society had ceased to be feudal, it was not moving towards capitalism, or even towards modern bureaucratic administration. The Kingdom of France emerged as a court-centralized system of the fiscal exploitation of independent peasants. As private feudal lordship eroded, venal office-holding came to replace it as the tap root of family fortunes.

By contrast, the centralized lordly community installed by Norman conquerors withstood the erosion of serfdom, enabling lords to hold onto large holdings of land, even while they lost the coercive power to extract surpluses from their now largely free tenants. The old apparatus of lordly rule and the village community dissolved simultaneously, leading to the formation of property relations in which individual landlords and tenant farmers were dependent on the market for their inputs and incomes, and thus compelled to compete, specialize and invest. This set into motion a post-Malthusian 'virtuous cycle' of economic development which outstripped population growth, as an increasingly efficient agriculture sustained an ever-larger population, producing the manufactured inputs—purchased from rising farm incomes—that went into a progressive lowering of costs and increasing of yields.

But despite this striking long-term divergence of social structures, Teschke concedes that membership in a common European system of military and diplomatic competition led to an isomorphic convergence of institutional forms: military revolutions, monopolization of the means of legitimate violence, mercantilism and colonial slavery redefined the conditions of ruling and profiteering on both sides of the Channel. But while acknowledging these developments he is insistent that, in identifying the nature of states, institutional forms are separable from social content:

> while the French state formation resulted in absolutist sovereignty, the cornerstone of the Westphalian state-system, English state formation resulted in capitalist sovereignty, the cornerstone of the post-Westphalian, i.e. modern state-system.

The problem with various contemporary attempts to historicize international relations, Teschke contends, is that they conflate absolutist with modern sovereignty. Having persuasively maintained that the agrarian social structures of France and England were developing along different paths towards distinct constitutional orders, he burdens his case with the drastic conclusion that France and England were 'incommensurable social totalities', unlike 'in all dimensions of society, economy and political organization'. Such assertions stand in an uneasy relationship to the parallels he registers. The narrative formula of modernization generates, at this point, a peculiar antinomy: the 'early modern' is left stranded as an anomalous sociotemporal category without any determinate relation to what follows.

His argument is on stronger ground when it avoids the pitfalls of this temporal schema, and establishes empirical criteria of classification. Weber's sociology of political institutions provides a clarifying distinction: 'All states may be classified according to whether they rest on the principle that the staff of men themselves own the administrative means, or whether the staff is "separated" from these means of administration.' The step towards a modern bureaucracy was not taken in France because an entrenched market in venal offices prevented the formation of a true public domain. French absolutism was less a state than a hierarchical racket of sinecures to be pawned, sublet and divided upon inheritance. Teschke understands modernity to be a socio-juridical condition in which the political is *separated* from the economic. By this standard, the *ancien régime* was an early-modern dead end, lacking even the preconditions for a later transition to national capitalism. Gesturing towards its undeniable subsequent emergence, he suggests that 'the deeper preconditions for the state's withdrawal from direct economic exploitation', leading to the division of public and private, would not arise until some unspecified point in the nineteenth century.

The fiscal pump of this tax-office polity was constantly being tested in the arena of cabinet war and diplomacy, a system organized around the patrimonial pursuit of family fortunes. One could say that, of the two bodies of the king, Teschke only recognizes the private. '[The] basic units of international politics were not states but persons and associations of persons, who literally owned their respective realms and dominions.' He concludes that the geo-politics of the eighteenth century were not modern because the leading absolutist monarchies all strove for the medieval chimera of universal monarchy and the elimination of their adversaries, as opposed to a balance of power (with which, it appears, geo-

political modernity can be equated). The evidence he adduces for
this absence of an inter-state balancing mechanism is the extremely
atypical case of the Polish partitions, for aside from that, no state
of even modest size was eliminated from the map in this period—
unlike the one that followed.

The historical viability of French absolutism was fatally
diminished by the mounting costs of war with parliamentary
England, generating an irreversible fiscal crisis that culminated
in terminal bankruptcy. A stagnant agrarian social foundation
of small peasant households could no longer sustain the costs of
war on three continents. But for Teschke, the Great Revolution
that erupted out of the meltdown of the *ancien régime* had little
independent significance in the constitution of the modern state
system: not just 1648 but, implicitly, 1789 as well is removed
from this story of an exclusively English road to modernity. The
unsettling deflation of this event follows from conclusions that
some students of Brenner seem to have drawn from his account of
absolutist society: a bourgeoisie of venal office holders, merchants
and lawyers was merely the untitled rung of a plutocracy of rentiers
living off the peasantry; its revolution amounted to a liquidation
of clerico-aristocratic privileges, leaving the essential relationship
of state to agrarian society more or less intact. It seems that such
moments of revolutionary transformation are judged solely on the
basis of whether or not they lead to the formation of capitalist civil
societies, as if the term 'modernity' could now be purged of any
association with other transitions, along less plotted directions.
(Although Teschke claims that class struggles are the motor of
the historical process, after the property settlements of the late
Middle Ages their importance seems to recede dramatically.) The
domestic legacy of the Revolution is summarized in the following
awkward and evasive formulation:

> Although the institutional structure of the absolutist state, whose
> centralizing advances were radicalized by Napoleon, was the historical

condition in which French capitalism would develop in the nineteenth century it was not logically necessary for its development.

Perhaps not surprisingly then, the Revolutionary and Napoleonic Wars that transformed the map of Europe and set into motion its numerous subsequent national reconstructions are en bloc demoted to a mere manifestation, albeit indirect, of the geo-economic ascendancy of the United Kingdom.

After bold assertions of the categorical opposition between epochs and the states that epitomize them, Teschke equivocates as to whether England was, after all, the singular locus of the transition to (capitalist) modernity—or, alternatively, simply a highly distinctive participant in concurrent transitions unfolding across the *jus publicum europaeum*. At times he seems inclined to accept the latter, more plausible, option, asking whether we should 'refine this simplified perspective by arguing the case for a series of transitions between and among distinct geopolitical orders whose cumulative effect was the contemporary geo-political configuration?' But his account of these processes more often seems to presuppose that the isolation of England's socio-political evolution from the wider European inter-state field was a necessary condition of its subsequent transformative impact upon it. Logically, of course, this does not follow. 'International military pressure had no influence on the English social revolution and little influence on the English political revolution.' It should be said that there is little in Brenner's account of the emergence of capitalist property relations or of the seventeenth-century English constitutional crisis to warrant such cut-and-dried formulations.

A more compelling explanation of the peculiar position of England within the absolutist system of war and diplomacy would take into account the geographical situations that generate the enduring strategic predicaments of state formation. Others have argued that an expensive build up of troop strengths was an indispensable condition of survival for the Renaissance monarchies on the mainland. The insular situation of the Tudor state freed it from this imperative, enabling its propertied classes to stave off the emergence of a tax-office court at a time when the most powerful states were assuming this form. For most of the early modern era England was simultaneously marginalized as a terrestrial force on the continent, yet relatively secure from naval attack. As a result, Parliament's limiting power shifted the direction of this build up towards Atlantic sea-power and settler colonialism.

Relatedly, Teschke fails to register the relationship between the seventeenth-century political crisis in England and the Europe-wide civil–religious wars that formed its context of historical possibility. Politics is a sphere in which strategic projects directed at enemies take shape. The militant Protestantism of the parliamentary class was directed at the domestic and foreign bulwarks of Counter-Reformation absolutism. It was this strategic mediation that linked the domestic to the international. The characterization of early modern geopolitics as pure dynastic strife ignores the fault lines of the confessional war running through the leading states of the era, detonating many of its central friend–enemy oppositions.

Teschke's account of the transformative impact of the British regime on the European state-system focuses on the eighteenth century, when disputes over inheritance provided the typical occasion for hostilities. He suggests that this period simultaneously witnessed the inconspicuous beginnings of Albion's disengagement from a policy of territorial aggrandizement, and a drift towards its later commitment to off-shore balancing and colonial empire building. The crux of the narrative is the unintended geopolitical fall-out of the United Kingdom's mounting fiscal superiority as a mercantile–military polity over its absolutist adversaries and allies: 'In the eighteenth century Britain was bellicose, militarized, and on a near permanent war footing, like any other comparable European power.' Although he does not specify the mechanism, it seems that it was through military pressure—not the pressure of market forces—that capitalism 'came to universalize its logic of political organization and international relations in the pluriverse created by absolutist state formation'.

Teschke sees this coexistence of qualitatively distinct social formations, subject to common standards of geopolitical competition, as an eighteenth- and early nineteenth-century story of the 'gradual crisis-ridden internationalization of the British state/society complex'. But the fact that the European pluriverse of antagonistic sovereign states was forged in the era of absolutism, and yet survived as the inter-state matrix of the core zone of world capitalism, strongly suggests that the struggle for power between states is not easily aligned to a logic of accumulation. This difficulty becomes acute when geopolitics becomes *separated* from the logic of accumulation, as Teschke thinks happened with the advent of capitalism. Under these conditions, it is arguable that the standard for determining the distribution of sovereign power acquires an autonomy as a force field of combined and uneven development, coercively mediating the inter-relationships between different social systems.

British naval victories in the Napoleonic Wars destroyed the mercantilist empires of France and Spain, establishing the conditions for an open world market based on the freedom of the seas: 'This new free trade regime brought with it forces that undermined the ancient logic of commercial capitalism during the nineteenth century, inaugurating the era of the emergent world market.' For Teschke, post-Westphalian modernity arrives with Britain's stabilization of a balance of power between European states, undergoing more or less successful structural adjustments to the world market. But the inter-state conventions of this first era of 'globalization' collapsed in the next century: why then are they canonical for understanding the relationship between capitalism and geopolitics?

At this point, we should recollect that Teschke proposed to 'historicize anarchy'—that is, provide an explanation of the formation of the conditions of possibility for this Realist schema.

This raises the question as to whether he thinks Realism is wrong simply because it eternalizes 'modern' inter-state anarchy, or wrong about the dynamics of the modern inter-state system as well. *The Myth of 1648* focuses entirely on the first question, without specifying the stakes of inter-state rivalry in the era of world capitalism. This leads to an enormous lacuna at the end of the narrative: from the Victorian era it leaps to the 1990s, bypassing World Wars, Fascism, Communism, the Cold War and decolonization, as if these episodes of state formation did not complicate the relationship Teschke seeks to establish between modern geopolitics and the formation of the world-market. The gap between his account and the empirical record is mentioned in a single paragraph.

After confidently asserting that social-property relations generate geopolitical orders, he seems to acknowledge that the problem has not been solved and asks:

> If capitalism and a system of states are not genetically co-constitutive and co-emergent, and if capitalism did not develop simultaneously in all early-modern states, what was the relation between capitalism and the inter-state system?

It is apparently hard to determine whether a plurality of sovereign states is a good or bad thing for capitalism as a system—assuming such a calculation could even be made. But the more intractable difficulty does not concern plurality, but antagonism. The conclusion to the millennial story Teschke tells strongly implies that the withdrawal of coercion from the internal sphere of economic relations resulted in the withering away of the apparatus of externally directed coercion—but this, of course, never happened. How then can the social-property relations of capitalism explain the persistence of war as a recognized means of settlement between states, long after it has ceased to be a systemic means of accumulation? Recognizing the problem that his conception of capitalism raises, he hesitantly offers the long-term forecast that 'since capitalism is not predicated on the logic of domestic political accumulation, we should expect it to bring about the decline of external geopolitical accumulation that defined the war-driven international conduct of the feudal and absolutist ages'.

But no account that raises such expectations without even addressing the historical record can be considered adequate. The actual pattern of regime change and reform that began in the nineteenth century in response to the discipline of various, increasingly capitalist markets, is better explained in terms of an adaptive process of the specialization of functions within the state apparatus. Although European parliaments in this age successfully redefined the mandate of government in matters of taxation, justice, infrastructure and education, this process of administrative reorganization did not result in the demise of geopolitics, but rather its formal rationalization. The diplomatic and military staffs of the *ancien régimes* became the modern bureaucratic elites of the classical bourgeois states of the long nineteenth century. According to Michael Mann, 'the foregoing also enabled war risks and means to be calculated more precisely, and the calculations could be inserted into a rational geopolitical diplomacy.' He notes that, accordingly, 'this was the age of theorist-generals and diplomats'.

This observation raises a question which should have been at the centre of Teschke's theorization of the post-Westphalian situation: when do the costs and benefits of war make it a rational policy, for states refashioned under the economic discipline of capitalism? Put this way, it is obvious that any estimate must take into account exponential increases in the destructiveness of war, as this qualitatively changes the terms of the calculation. An adequate theorization of the history of inter-societal violence would address the evolution of force structures and weapon systems.

The formal rationalization of statecraft was a consequence of the bureaucratic specialization of state functions. The separation of the political from the economic was accompanied by a bifurcation of the strategic imperatives of foreign policy from the domestic imperatives of economic growth and social stability. Mann again provides a compelling explanation for this structural division between the rationality operative in these separate fields:

> Diplomacy is far less regulated, routinized and predictable than are major domestic politics. Diplomacy involves a number of autonomous states among whom there are few normative ties, yet continuous recalculations of the main chance.

Is there a central *Staatsraison* that integrates these distinct imperatives? How, by whom, and against whom, is this integration achieved as a strategic project? Gramsci's scattered reflections on politics provide intriguing sketches of the historical cases that could potentially answer such questions. The concept of hegemony he developed brought into focus a range of political practices conjoining the ongoing maintenance of domestic power positions to the improvisational pursuit of specific strategic aims in the geopolitical field. However incomplete, it at least provides a point of entry into areas that do not even register in Teschke's problematic.

Near the beginning of this work he acknowledges that an adequate international-relations theory would have to take into consideration the 'mentality and self-understandings of collective actors'—what he calls 'the culture of war'—but the suggestion is never subsequently taken up. Bracketing this theoretical area, Teschke's study only addresses the abstract problem of capitalism's compatibility with the plurality of sovereign states, without any attempt to conceptualize the latter as a strategic field. But as long as war remains a possibility between the leading states of the world system, a theory of international relations has to be able to explain the specific rationality of this sphere, whose standards of success and failure stand in a loose, indeterminate relationship to the imperatives that determine the aggregate fortunes of a national economy in the world market. Realism is the spontaneous representation of this field from the perspective of the outwardly turned apparatus that embodies the entire state in its relations to other states. However fictional this representation, it is an objectively operative fiction.

The penultimate chapter suggests how capitalism might bring about, somewhat belatedly, the demise of Grand Strategy: 'It follows that the key idea of modern international relations is . . . the multilateral political management of global capital's crisis potential and the regulation of the world economy by the leading capitalist states.' Thus Teschke arrives at a conclusion reached by Karl Kautsky at the beginning of the First World War. It should be remembered that Lenin rejected Kautsky then not because he thought that this scenario was incompatible with the abstract social logic of capital. This was, he argued, beside the point. Even today, his pamphlet on imperialism reminds us that the massively uneven and violently cyclical pattern of capitalist economic development makes any future euthanasia of military-diplomatic statecraft highly unlikely. For Lenin the definitive separation of the political from the economic never takes place.

Where do we stand now 'in the flow of history'? Teschke's modernization narrative is an attempt to explain its 'direction and meaning'. He rejects what he takes to be the prevailing view outside of the Realist camp, that 'the modern, territorially bounded sovereign state, is being replaced by a post-territorial, postmodern global order', but only because he objects to the term 'postmodern'. After many centuries of transition, he announces that 'modern international relations may just have arrived'.

But none of the proposed inaugural moments of modernity turn out to be definitive, as the geopolitical trend-line is periodically deflected from its anticipated course. After striking down the myth of 1648, Teschke pauses to reflect on the antinomies of periodization. It turns out that 'no single event or date can be unequivocally singled out as the decisive system-wide caesura of inter-state modernity. There was no "structural rupture" that divided premodern from modern inter-state relations.'

The oscillations of this place-holder term 'modernity' at numerous points in the narrative seem to confirm the assessment of Fredric Jameson that 'there is something fundamentally unrepresentable about such moments of radical structural change, of the break or transition, in the first place.' Long downturns, competition for liquid capital, debt-driven expansion, one meltdown after another, looming fiscal insolvencies: what geopolitical transformations will emerge out of this mounting global turbulence? Suddenly the direction is unclear. Taking stock of this situation requires dispensing with 'modernity'—a narrative category that no longer comprehends the military, economic and cultural vectors of the latest phase of capitalism.

2

Virgilian Visions

Over the last decade, a series of works offering a comprehensive vision of the state of the world after the end of the Cold War have enlivened the tenor of mainstream intellectual life.[1] These have sought to capture the experience of American victory over Communism, and lesser adversaries at home and abroad. Conceived in the spirit of monumental portraits of old, depicting a princely commander gazing reflectively out of the canvas, a still-smoking battlefield in the far background, the genre has been a speciality of the American Right (or indistinguishable Centre). Its various practitioners—Fukuyama, Nye, Huntington, Luttwak, Friedman, Brzezinski—have seized the opportunity to survey the full extent of the field of US hegemony in geopolitics, economics and mass culture. That was to be expected. Yet what is often most striking in this body of work is not so much its crass triumphalism—in some cases, an exaggerated charge—as the sporadically brutal candour with which it registers the harsh realities of the incoming American Century. A sub-tone of foreboding—a still hint of *sic transit*—lurks in the depths of the canvas. In varying degrees, it is the dangers of relaxation or hubris that are typically the leitmotif of concluding chapters.

---

1   This article first appeared in *New Left Review* 2: 5, September–October 2000, and is a review of Michael Hardt and Antonio Negri, *Empire*, Cambridge, MA: Harvard University, 2001.

Comparable totalizations from the Left have been few and far between; diagnoses of the present more uniformly bleak. At best, the alternative to surrender or self-delusion has seemed to be a combative but clear-eyed pessimism, orienting the mind for a Long March against the new scheme of things. In this landscape, the appearance of *Empire* represents a spectacular break. Michael Hardt and Antonio Negri defiantly overturn the verdict that the last two decades have been a time of punitive defeats for the Left. After years of living in French exile, Negri is now serving out the sentence he received in Italy in the early eighties, during the crack down on the Far Left, writing as an inmate of the Roman prison system that once held Gramsci under fascism. But the work he and Hardt have written owes very little to the precedent of the *Prison Notebooks*. Few messages could be further from that harsh strategic reckoning than the argument of *Empire*. Its burden is that, appearances to the contrary, we live in a springtime of peoples, a world overflowing with insurgent energies. In a period where others merely cast about for silver linings, Hardt and Negri announce a golden age.

Empire develops its rousing theme in an attractive variety of registers. The collaboration between American literary theorist and Italian political philosopher has produced a strange and graceful work, of rare imaginative drive and richness of intellectual reference. Theoretically, and to some extent architectonically, Hardt and Negri situate themselves in the line of Deleuze and Guattari's *Thousand Plateaux*. Their work freely crosses disciplinary boundaries, venturing reflections on law, culture, politics and economics with a repertoire of concepts ranging from the canon of European classical philosophy to the findings of contemporary American social science and cultural studies, not to speak of side-lights from Céline or Kafka, Herman Melville or Robert Musil. However counter-intuitive its conclusions, *Empire* is in its own terms a work of visionary intensity.

Hardt and Negri open their case by arguing that, although nation-state-based systems of power are rapidly unravelling in the force-fields of world capitalism, globalization cannot be understood as a simple process of deregulating markets. Far from withering away, regulations today proliferate and interlock to form an acephelous supranational order which the authors choose to call 'Empire'. The term, as they use it, refers not to a system in which tribute flows from peripheries to great capital cities, but to a more Foucauldian figure—a diffuse, anonymous network of all-englobing power. Hardt and Negri claim that the sinews of this phantasmic polity— its flows of people, information and wealth—are simply too unruly to be monitored from metropolitan control centres. Their account of its origins adds a few striking nuances to a now familiar story. An older, statist world of ruling class and proletariat, of dominant core and subject periphery, is breaking down, and in its place a less dichotomous and more intricate pattern of inequality is emerging. 'Empire' could be described as the planetary *Gestalt* of these flows and hierarchies. The logic of this volatile totality evades and transgresses all the inherited divisions of political thought: state and society, war and peace, control and freedom, core and periphery; even the distinction between systemic and anti-systemic agency is blurred beyond recognition. The advent of this Empire is thus not merely a momentous episode in world history, it is an event of considerable ontological importance, heralded here in the voice of impassioned prophecy.

The political order of this latest stage of capitalism has a universal mission of pacification, comparable to those Empires of the past that strove to embrace the known world. Virgil is cited to convey the sheer magnitude of the change: 'The final age that the oracle foretold has arrived; the great order of the centuries is born again.' While Hardt and Negri discern a clean break between this system and the state-based colonialisms that preceded it, they place great stock in more ancient genealogies for this postmodern Empire. Those who want to understand the new universe should look to the writings of Polybius, who sought to explain to stupefied contemporaries how it was that Rome had risen to become master of the Mediterranean world. Polybius held that Rome had transcended the unstable cycles of the classical polis because its constitution mixed monarchy, aristocracy and democracy in proportions that checked the degenerative potential inherent in any unalloyed form of government. Hardt and Negri argue that the new world order can be envisaged as an analogous structure, in which US nuclear supremacy represents the monarchical, the economic wealth of the G7 and transnational corporations the aristocratic, and the internet the democratic principle—Bomb, Money and Ether composing the contemporary version of the constitution of the Roman Republic, on the morrow of its defeat of Carthage. But if this use of Polybius suggests an Empire at the threshold of centuries of ascendancy, other classical allusions—Montesquieu or Gibbon—imply eclipse or decline: tropes not just of universal order, but of decadence, transvaluation and crumbling *limites*. In this register, Hardt and Negri liken potential revolutionaries of today to Christians of the later Roman Empire, witnessing the inexorable hollowing out of the terrestrial order of things, and the beginnings of a new, rejuvenating era of barbarian migrations. Parallels with the Ancient World, central to the rhetorical strategy of *Empire*, oscillate between alternative meanings: do they point to the rising or the falling fortunes of global capitalism?

Overall, the book suggests the latter. Empire, its authors insist, did not emerge out of the defeat of systemic challenges to capital. On the contrary, its existence stands as a resounding, if paradoxical, testimony to the heroic mass struggles that shattered the Eurocentric old regime of national states and colonialism. Running through the work is the fervent belief that contemporary capitalism, although seemingly impervious to anti-systemic challenge, is in fact vulnerable at all points to riot and rebellion. The increasing importance of immaterial, intellectual labour in high value-added sectors of the economy is shaping a collective labourer with heightened powers of subversion. An ineradicable plebeian desire for emancipation is stoked by the increasingly apparent malleability of all social relationships and permeability of all borders. This global multitude, embracing all those who work, or are just poor, from computer scientists in Palo Alto to slum-dwellers in São Paulo, no longer imagines communities as integral nations. But mere heteroglossia or hybridization offer no trenchant alternative. For the ideology of Empire has become a supple, multicultural aesthetic that deactivates the revolutionary possibilities of globalization. Far from being oppositional, academic enthusiasts for diversity articulate the inclusive logic of a spontaneous order that no longer depends upon a metaphysics of natural difference and hierarchy.

Multiculturalists are not the only ones on the Left to be bluntly disabused. Hardt and Negri also question the notion that even the most blameless NGOs are agencies of a global civil society pitted against the established powers. Rather they can be compared to the Dominicans and Franciscans of late feudal society, functioning as 'the charitable campaigns and mendicant orders of Empire'. Media-staged crusades by Amnesty International or *Médecins Sans Frontières* play an essential role in mobilizing public opinion behind humanitarian interventionism. It is no surprise that their critique of its jargon relies heavily on the writings of Carl Schmitt:

> The traditional concept of just war involves the banalization of war and the celebration of it as an ethical instrument, both of which were ideas that modern political thought and the international community of nation-states resolutely refused. These two traditional characteristics have reappeared in our postmodern world . . . Today the enemy, just like war itself, comes to be at once banalized (reduced to an object of routine police suppression) and absolutized (as the Enemy, an absolute threat to the ethical order).

Empire is a world order in a 'permanent state of emergency and exception justified by the appeal to essential values'. Although powerful and succinct, the formulation is difficult to reconcile

with Hardt and Negri's insistence that Empire is a coherent
constitutional structure, a self-enclosed legal system of the sort
imagined by Hans Kelsen. A constitution engulfed in a permanent
state of exception cannot form a self-enclosed legal system and
is, in fact, only nominally a juridical order. But the attempt to
define Empire as a constitutional system poses a second, even
graver problem. What constituent power brought it into being,
or decides how international law is to be interpreted, and when it
can be suspended? It is generally thought that if the contemporary
world system can be described as an empire, it is because of the
overwhelming concentration of financial, diplomatic and military
power in American hands. Hardt and Negri, however, reject
any idea that the United States can be described as an imperialist
power. For Empire in the upper-case sense, with no definite article,
excludes any state-based imperialism. Although they acknowledge
that the US is at the top of the international power hierarchy, they
conjure away the significance of this fact with a series of dubious
assumptions: a denial that the 'metaphysical' concept of sovereignty
has any purchase in the postmodern era of Empire, coupled with
a claim that a political system without a centre of decision may
be plausibly called an empire; and finally, a declaration of faith
that, contrary to all appearances, the constituent power of Empire,
the force that brought it into being and empowers its manifold
networks of control, is the 'multitude', that is to say, the wretched
of the earth. Not in the form of a 'people' or a 'nation'—these
being metaphysical figments of statism—but scattered, speaking
no common language, and locked into job-cages: it is in this
condition that the multitude is all powerful. The world's poor,
its omnipresent have-nots, form an already existing collective
subject, but are not cognizant of it. How, in that case, they could
have constituted an Empire is not explained.

It is a reasonable conjecture that the messianic streak in this
vision derives from an Italian past rather than an American
present. Around the mid-seventies Negri came to the conclusion

that the industrial working class was no longer an agent of social revolution. Out of a mounting ultra-Left frustration in the face of deadlocked class struggles he drew an innovative re-reading of Marx's *Grundrisse*, which dissolved any hard proletarian core into a broader pool of the dispossessed and disaffected. The latter, he contended, were just as essential to the reproduction of capital, and more prone to volatile upsurges. His prediction that a new social worker was taking shape, although more attuned to reality than certain Marxist orthodoxies of the time, also encouraged a headlong flight forward into a drastically simplified conception of revolutionary strategy as a violent test of strength with the state. The failure of this attempt 'to transform the poor into proletarians and proletarians into a liberation army' did not lead Negri down the path of resignation. What seems to have happened instead is that he eventually came to reject any residual conception of politics as a strategic field. In the age of Empire, revolutionaries no longer need to distinguish tactics and strategy, position and manoeuvre, weak links and invulnerable ones; they can now rely on a pervasive, if diffuse, popular desire for liberation and an episodic intuition of friend and enemy.

While older class and national liberation struggles sent long-lasting shock waves across the inter-state system, in the optic of *Empire* contemporary intifadas are of brief duration, media dependent, and do not fan out across national, let alone global, worlds of labour. In this celebrated age of communication, struggles have become all but incommunicable. Such a penetrating and sombre image of serialized outbursts of class anger warrants in-depth treatment. But Hardt and Negri dispel it, with a rousing vision of two, three, many Los Angeles riots. In this sense, their book reproduces the horizons of today's new activist counter-cultural scene, where a paralysing cynicism has been banished, but often at the expense of the ability to make a dispassionate assessment of the balance of forces at large, let alone conceive of a path to power. Hardt and Negri suggest such Leninist concerns are irrelevant to rebellions against Empire, which successfully capitalize on the symbolic logic of postmodern politics. In this alternative space, world history unfolds as a sequence of nearly magical serendipities. For happily, although local struggles no longer trigger off horizontal, upwardly spiralling revolutionary sequences, they can now immediately catapult up to the global level as unforeseen media events. By this more direct vertical route, the virtual centre of Empire can be attacked at any point.

For just because Empire is a media-steered system of political publicity, it is permanently vulnerable to the impact of destabilizing, marginal events that slip out of the control of those who manufacture consent. Empire is a society of the spectacle, seemingly powered by the pursuit of happiness—but in reality based on the mobilization of desires that are intimately wedded to the fear of failure, exclusion and loneliness. Intriguingly, Hardt and Negri suggest that this spectral social order, sustained by false promises and a distracted, vicarious mode of being in the world, is a void for the future. In an excursus on Machiavelli, they maintain the time has come to compose great manifestos which pry open an empty space for transformative intervention, and beckon the multitude to surge through. Taking their cue from Althusser, they maintain that Machiavelli invoked the masses in the transcendent form of an ideal prince because he assumed that collective action could only be imagined in the mediated form of a singular agent; but the task now is to demystify these ossified mediations— leaders, parties and unions—and reclaim their absconded power for the multitude. This is the politics of the society of the spectacle, in which the masses seek only the most immediate experiences of empowerment and agency, even if these are only ever episodic.

An epigram from Spinoza encapsulates the goal of the book: the prophet creates his own people. Machiavelli's thoughts on prophecy strike a different note, far from the comforts of any liberation theology, old or new:

It must be considered that there is nothing more difficult to carry out, nor more doubtful of success, nor more dangerous to handle, than to initiate a new order of things. For the reformer has an enemy in all those who profit by the old order, and only lukewarm defenders in all those who would profit from the new order, this lukewarmness arising partly from fear of their adversaries, who have the laws in their favour; and partly from the incredulity of mankind, who do not believe in anything new until they have had actual experience of it.

We scarcely need to be reminded of the conclusion: all armed prophets have conquered, and unarmed ones failed.

In the seventies, Negri might have understood this passage as a clarion call to frontal collisions with the state. Decades later, *Empire* offers by contrast an optimism of the will that can only be sustained by a millenarian erasure of the distinction between the armed and the unarmed, the powerful and the abjectly powerless. It is not till near the end of the book that Hardt and Negri spell out what they take to manifest the primal power of the helpless multitude: Empire, seemingly in control everywhere, is unable to bridle the planetary flow of workers seeking jobs and a better life in rich countries. Reshaping social relations everywhere, immigration on this scale reveals both the hostility of the multitude to the system of national borders and its tenacious desire for cosmopolitan freedom. 'The multitude must be able to decide if, when and where it moves. It must have the right also to stay still and enjoy one place rather than being forced constantly to be on the move. The general right to control its own movement is the multitude's ultimate demand for global citizenship.' In keeping with its ontological background, *Empire* does not develop any sustained programme for the injured and insulted of the world. Logically, however, its most distinctive proposal (the right to a guaranteed basic income occupies second place) is for abolition of all immigration controls: *papiers pour tous!* For Hardt and Negri, this is a demand that opens up the possibility of rejuvenating the politically stagnant core of global capitalism.

But the desire to live, work and raise families in more affluent lands arguably finds its true manifesto in the inscription at the foot of the Statue of Liberty, holding out the promise of entirely prosaic freedoms.

In *The Lexus and the Olive Tree*, Thomas Friedman argues that globalization brings democracy in its wake in part because it feeds on a now irresistible desire of consumers and would-be consumers—his version of the multitude—to be a part of the system, in a dialectic that subjects democracy to an ever tighter market-discipline. *Empire* can be read as *The Lexus and the Olive Tree* of the Far Left. Both books argue that globalization is a process powered from below. Friedman portrays a ubiquitous dispensation buoyed by pension-fund speculation, credit-card profligacy and the universal appeal of the American way of life. Crude and exaggerated, the book effectively portrays social realities that are not always more subtle, in its own fashion demystifying saccharine pieties of the hour. From an incomparably higher cultural level, Negri and Hardt often fail to achieve this level of realism, and end up recasting some of the mythologies of American liberalism. Friedman leaves not the smallest doubt about the paramount power of the United States as global banker and gendarme; indeed he rubs in with chauvinist relish what Hardt and Negri would metaphysically sublimate. But while they downplay the mailed fist of the US in the global arena, they grant America a more gratifying centrality as a laboratory of domestic political innovation. As they see it, both the apogee and the antithesis of Empire lie in the inclusive, expansive republicanism of the US Constitution, which long ago shed the European fetish of a homogeneous nation. In this spirit, Hegel is cited—'America is the country of the future, and its world historical importance has yet to be revealed in the ages which lie ahead . . . It is the land of desire for all those who are weary of the historical arsenal of old Europe'—and Tocqueville congratulated for deepening him, with an exemplary understanding of the significance of American mass democracy. There is an echo of old illusions here. *Empire* bravely upholds the possibility of a utopian manifesto for these times, in which the desire for another world buried or scattered in social experience could find an authentic language and point of concentration. But to be politically effective, any such reclamation must take stock of the remorseless realities of this one, without recourse to theoretical ecstasy.

3

Algorithms of War

As the Napoleonic Wars came to an end, the French liberal Benjamin Constant envisioned a new age of commerce, legality and representative government, in which the traditional war-making powers of the state would wither away. The militarism of the old regime and its revolutionary nemesis had proved ineffectual before a polity based on sound credit and unbridled money-making. As the returns to conquest in the European theatre sharply declined, societies would come to insist on taxing themselves in parliaments and settling their scores on the market. Comparable predictions were offered after the resounding Western victory in the half-century Cold War. The transition to an international order based on capitalism, elections and human rights seemed to form a global trend-line extending into the far future. In this scenario, however, the obsolescence of military force was never seriously considered. The US would preserve the hegemony it had won in the struggle against Communism by protecting the entire zone of affluence against sundry threats in the coming era of globalization. Neutralization of Russia as a great power through NATO encirclement and financial inducements; regulation of China's entry into the world market through checkpoints at the WTO and the Taiwan straits; effortless direction of the IMF and World Bank by the Treasury Department; stepped up harassment of rogue regimes, with or without UN enabling clauses; even hostile takeovers of crony capitalisms by Wall Street—all were welcomed by Western opinion, as stock in America soared to all-time highs, under a president who explained that the time of power politics had passed.

This feel-good dictum, however far from the realities of the Washington Consensus, conveyed the relaxed tone of unchallenged primacy. The arrival of a new Republican administration in 2001 altered the atmosphere: although posting at the outset no far-reaching departures from the doctrinal innovations of the Clinton era, its harsh deviations from a familiar script grated nerves in allied capitals. Then came the thunderbolt of 9/11, transforming—to all appearances—the domestic and international scene. A global spectre had materialized, conveniently replacing the galvanizing power of the Soviet threat; and one over which easy victories could be scored to plebiscitary acclaim. Stoking anti-terrorist panic, an invigorated executive team proceeded to implement a replay of the Reagan revolution: massive tax cuts, a new arms build-up, and a determined effort to shift the centre of gravity of the whole political system at home yet further to the right. Abroad, outright military conquest has regained its lustre, as American arms have swept to Kabul and Baghdad, and strikes against Tehran and Pyongyang are contemplated as sequels.

Washington's new 'unilateralism' has naturally aroused disquiet in the ranks of traditional allies and clients, reduced with few exceptions to the role of impotent onlookers. In the eyes of its critics, this is an administration that lives entirely off the momentum of the fortuitous conjuncture of 9/11, and seeks to institutionalize it. From its inception the coherence and viability of this audacious enterprise has been the subject of an ongoing controversy amongst pundits, journalists, academics and anti-war demonstrators around the world. For many, the policies of the Bush regime represent a fundamental and bewildering break with the—on balance, rational and benign—international role played by America since 1945, whose achievements came to full fruition in a post–Cold War setting under the last Democratic administration. Typically, in this perspective, Clinton's rule is looked back at longingly, as the halcyon days of a humane and responsible Pax Americana, whose abandonment since has been a brutal disappointment. But—so runs the reassuring message—a return to earlier norms of leadership, a multilateralism more respectful of traditional allies and international institutions, can be expected over time as the sense of domestic emergency fades away, or practical difficulties mount overseas. The current adventurism should be seen as an unsustainable spasm, a neo-conservative coup alien to the underlying spirit of the republic.

Philip Bobbitt's *The Shield of Achilles* gives little comfort to such hopeful prognoses.[1] Its aim is to situate contemporary developments in a long saga unfolding from the Renaissance to the present, whose turning points are periodic revolutions in military affairs that throw constitutional forms into flux, as warring states confront unprecedented strategic alternatives. In excess of 900 pages, the book was probably conceived in the mid-90s when the author—a constitutional lawyer doubling as a deterrence theorist—began to formulate a sweeping critique of the force structure inherited from the Cold War, in contentions over what was to be done with this awesome arsenal after the historic adversary it was designed to overwhelm had ceded the field. *The Shield of Achilles* offers, among other things, a panorama of the debate in Washington over the aims, priorities and instruments of American foreign policy from Desert Storm to Enduring Freedom.

The identity of its author is of more than incidental significance. Bobbitt is not a Republican but a Democrat, and no ordinary Democrat at that. A nephew of Lyndon Johnson, whose father ran LBJ's radio stations, he is a scion of a Texan political elite that has produced such bi-partisan insiders as John Connolly, Lloyd

---

1   *The Shield of Achilles: War, Peace and the Course of History*, foreword by Michael Howard, New York: Knopf, 2002; henceforward *SA*. This chapter originally appeared in *New Left Review* 2: 23, September–October 2003.

Bentsen or Robert Strauss. His career has been an effortless spiral
between academic and political appointments, tracing the profile
of a figure at the highest reaches of overlapping establishments.
Holder of a chair in constitutional law and international relations at
the University of Texas, not to speak of concurrent appointments
in history at Oxford and war studies at King's College, London,
Bobbitt is also a member of the American Law Institute, the
Council on Foreign Relations, the Pacific Council on International
Policy and the International Institute for Strategic Studies. In
Washington, he served successively as associate counsel to
the president under Carter, counsel to the Senate Iran-Contra
Committee under Reagan, counsellor on International Law at the
State Department under Bush Senior, and director of Intelligence
on the National Security Council under Clinton.

The Clinton catalyst

If Bobbitt's opinion of such various masters of the American state
is uniformly glowing,[2] one stands out for especial admiration.
Clinton, although at first slow to grasp the issues at stake before
him, and at times ill-served by his speech-writers, was the
statesman who steered the United States towards an entirely new
conception of international relations, a change 'of a magnitude
no less than Bismarck's'. The turning point in this revolution
was the president's decision to intervene, first in Bosnia and
then in Kosovo, overriding the anachronistic fetishes of national
sovereignty, and the un legalisms enshrining them, in the higher
interests of humanity and the Western community. Bobbitt

2　See the revealing interview with Bobbitt by Andrew Billen in the *Times*, 24
June 2002: 'Perhaps we should be reassured that having spent so long so close
to power, he has concluded that it is, in the main, wise and benign, that Gerald
Ford was "just a wonderful man", Carter not the vacillating indecisive president
portrayed and Reagan—from Bobbitt's access to his private correspondence—a
master of detail.'

devotes a passionate chapter of his book to these episodes, in which he was evidently an ardent actor behind the scenes. He has since explained how he proposed to Clinton a doctrine justifying such operations on a global scale. 'The US would intervene when the threat to our vital strategic interests was overwhelming and imminent; or when significant strategic interests and humanitarian concerns coincided; or, when a vital strategic interest was absent, humanitarian concerns were high and strategic risks were low.'[3]

In offering the most systematic theorization of American imperial interventions to date, *The Shield of Achilles* makes clear that the major ideological innovations powering them are the creation of the Clinton, not of the Bush, presidency. Here the key development was the proclamation of the legitimacy of military intervention—regardless of national sovereignty or absence of aggression—to defend human rights, to stamp out terrorism, or to block nuclear proliferation. In the name of the first, Clinton launched a full-scale war on Yugoslavia; of the second, bombed Sudan, Iraq and Afghanistan; and of the third, came within an ace of unleashing a preemptive attack on North Korea in 1994 (holding off only for the reasons that have so far also restrained Bush—fear of the consequences for Seoul). The Republican administration, for all its glaring contrasts of style, has essentially operated within the same framework. The principal difference has been tactical—the lesser extent to which it has acted in concert with its European allies—rather than juridical: the degree to which it has cast aside previous constraints of international law.

It is in keeping with his role under Clinton, therefore, that Bobbitt should have been an eloquent apologist for the invasion of Iraq by Bush, since in his view the Ba'ath regime richly merited attack by just the criteria he had laid down at the time of Bosnia. Saddam was at once an arch-violator of human rights, a seeker of nuclear weapons, and—crucially—a holder of strategic assets

---

3   'What's in it for us?', *Guardian*, 7 June 2003. See further *SA*, p. 339.

vital to the us. 'The West's interest in prising Iraqi oil out of
Saddam's hands was at least as important a motivation to the
US/UK as making the benefits of oil pay for ordinary Iraqis,'
he has explained. 'It was Saddam's great wealth, derived from
oil revenues and put in service of his relentless pursuit of WMD,
that made his removal so imperative.'[4] Temporarily out of office
in Washington, Bobbitt thinks the Bush administration would
have done better to insist more openly on the preemptive nature
of its assault on Baghdad—to prevent rather than destroy Iraqi
nuclear weapons—and should have appointed some distinguished
Democrats to cabinet positions, to manifest national unity in the
war against terrorism.[5] Meanwhile, basing himself in London
where his numerous academic stints have afforded him contacts at
all levels of the local establishment, he has been tireless on behalf of
the Blair government, in broadsheets, talk shows and on websites,
firming up British opinion for Operation Iraqi Freedom. The role
of informal adviser and courtier at Downing Street is curiously
apposite, since the living embodiment of the unity of the Clinton
and Bush periods is the UK's social-democratic prime minister, an
eager apostle of the war aims of both presidents.

Poetry and piety

If such is the political significance of the career, what is the
intellectual character of the work that has been its fruit? *The Shield
of Achilles* sets out to present the military interventions of the post–
Cold War decade as the latest chapter in the history of civilization.
The literary pretensions of the work are striking enough—the title

---

4   *Guardian*, 7 June 2003.
5   Talking of the War on Terror last summer, he complained: 'We are not
treating it as a war. If we, in America, were treating it as a war there would be
Democrats in the War Cabinet. One of the first things Roosevelt did was bring
in Henry Stimson and Frank Knox to be Secretary of War and Secretary of the
Navy.' Interview with Billen, *The Times*, 24 June 2002.

refers to the ekphrastic passages from the Iliad in which an archaic world of epic strife is presented in microcosm on a hero's shield. The author subscribes to that ancient dictum: 'War is the father of all things'—or, as he puts it in more modern idiom, 'No less than the market and law courts, with which it is inextricably intertwined, war is a creative act of civilized man, with important consequences for the rest of human culture.'[6] If the pathos of the battlefield permeates the book, projecting a heroic vision of war without end, the lyre delineates its structure. Poems, set in italics, introduce each of its six parts. Their relationship to the arguments that follow is quite adventitious, their rhetorical function lying elsewhere. The selection is preponderantly Eastern European, comprising an anthology of despair on the ravages of modern fanaticism, interspersed with an occasional patriotic ode. The scent of an older *Kulturpessimismus* wafts from these pages. The historian Michael Howard, amidst an otherwise extravagant encomium that prefaces the work, at one point incautiously compares it to Spengler's *Decline of the West*. But Bobbitt's is a more upbeat text. Milosz, Holub, Brodsky, Herbert, Szymborska, alongside a dollop or two of Larkin and Auden, are there to raise the tone. They do not get in the way of a sturdy inventory of the world-historic victories of the West, and the contemporary means of extending them.

The extraneous poetry does little, in fact, to conceal the author's cultural limitations: though French and German phrases occasionally decorate its pages, the bibliography of *The Shield of Achilles*—some three hundred items—is, with a handful of unlikely exceptions, monolingual. Nor do the oddities of the book stop there. While his depictions of an emerging imperial *Machtpolitik* are typically lucid and dispassionate, Bobbitt can also lapse into the most florid sermonizing: the same author who burns with indignation over the fate of Sarajevo contemplates nuclear first strikes with detachment. The resulting rhetoric is a disconcerting

---

6   *SA*, p. xxxi.

combination of American jingoism and cold-blooded diagnostics. The piety is of the Baptist persuasion, the faith that brought Clinton to his genuflections of atonement with the Reverend Jackson, and continues to inspire his successor. Bobbitt displays it in dedications of a flamboyance that belongs to another epoch. *The Shield of Achilles* is dedicated:

> To those by whose love God's grace was first made known to me and to those whose loving-kindness has ever since sustained me in His care.

An earlier work, *Constitutional Fate*, opens with the words:

> I would like to say 'This book is written to the glory of God', but nowadays that would be chicanery, that is, the trick of a cheat, for it would not be rightly understood. I mean simply that it came at the end of another's suffering and is intended to serve a value I cannot name that is other than mere self-regard. Insofar as I have failed to be in harmony with this value, my book will fall short of the vision it is an attempt to express.

Such flourishes of postmodern unction sit uncomfortably with a pagan militarism. But *The Shield of Achilles* suffers from graver defects than its value dilemmas, or faults of taste. It is a work, to put it mildly, of uneven historical literacy. Purporting to offer a scholarly narrative covering the past five hundred years of (exclusively) Western history, it is in fact a sequence of stylized facts selected to illustrate a lesson or an argument. The real form of the book is that of so many parables—edifying or minatory as the case may be—from the past, after the fashion of popular writers like Barbara Tuchman rather than serious historians in the tradition of Hintze or Bloch. Symptomatic of this mode are uplifting portraits of great, neglected figures whose lives can offer moral inspiration to present actors. Two of these are picked out for such *Boy's Own Paper* treatment in *The Shield of Achilles*, each a lengthy excursus occupying space wildly disproportionate to the ostensible purposes of the analytic scheme: Castlereagh and Colonel House. The first features, logically enough, as the clairvoyant architect of the counter-revolutionary settlement at the Congress of Vienna, whose lonely wisdom lights a beacon to contemporary statesmen in the aftermath of the twentieth century's Waterloo.

The second, Woodrow Wilson's palace familiar, was less successful at Versailles, but nonetheless helped steer America towards its future global destiny. In this case, the role model is closer to home. For House too was a Texan, operating half in the political daylight of electoral machinations, half in the shadows of diplomatic intrigue, yet possessed of a visionary attachment to a 'world made of law' according to US specifications. Bobbitt dwells with especial admiration on The Inquiry, the secret body of 126 experts assembled by House in the wake of the October Revolution, 'to collect the data that would provide the factual and analytical basis for an American-directed settlement' in Europe. What the United States needs today, he explains, is a comparable 'Vision Team', also to be convened in secret, but now including not just lawyers and scientists as in Wilson's day, but also business executives, to offer true strategic guidance to the Presidency.[7] The candidate for House's position is not hard to guess.

Digressions like these might be bracketed as quirks, however revealing, in a text whose force of argument lies elsewhere. A more serious difficulty is posed by the structure of *The Shield of Achilles*, the general organization of which is opaquely jumbled and overextended. The contrast with John Mearsheimer's recent *Tragedy of Great Power Politics*, a model of clarity and economy, is stark in this respect, as in others.[8] Despite being divided into two parts, 'States of War' and 'States of Peace', the book obeys no

7   SA, pp. 339, 315.
8   See Peter Gowan's essay on this important work, 'A Calculus of Power', *New Left Review* 2: 16, July–August 2002.

coherent logical or chronological order. It starts with a section on the period 1914–1990; recedes to 1494–1914; jumps forward again to the 1990s and future prospects; swerves sideways to Colonel House and then skips to Bosnia; wheels back to the early sixteenth century; and works forward once again to the present—finally topping off the menu with imaginary scenarios for the twenty-first century, complete with an epilogue on the Twin Towers which reiterates George VI's prayers to the Lord in 1939: 'May that Almighty Hand guide and uphold us all.' Bobbitt explains he originally intended to write two volumes, then decided to amalgamate his themes into one. The result is an overweight construction, in which the individual sentences are lucid, even elegant, but their sum becomes corpulent and flabby—a dropsical mass more likely to deter than to attract or impress its target readership.

Strategy and legality

The Shield of Achilles is not, however, reducible to its many weaknesses and eccentricities. As a theoretical work, it possesses one core strength that sets it apart in the strategic literature of the current period. Bobbitt's unusually varied background—as constitutional lawyer and weapons expert—has allowed him to combine two perspectives that, as he notes, are normally dissociated: the internal legal—and social—order of states, and their external military and diplomatic constellation. The originality of his book lies in its attempt to address the problem of how to conceptualize the state as, simultaneously, an inwardly and outwardly tested concentration of legitimate public force. In itself, the merit of this enterprise is plain. Bobbitt's way of negotiating it is the most significant criterion for judging the book. Here the architrave on which his account of the succession of modern state-forms as a coherent series depends— the notion that allows him to unify their inner and outer fields as a single system—is that of 'constitution'.

Domestically, of course, this is a familiar part of the political lexicon, denoting the juridical framework of state power within any given social order: in premodern societies, accepted by custom or tradition; in nearly all modern ones, codified in written charters. Bobbitt's key move is to extend its application from the intra-state to the inter-state arena. *The Shield of Achilles* posits a succession of international legal regimes that established the norms of war and diplomacy from late-medieval times to the twentieth century:

> It is my premise that there is a constitution of the society of states as a whole: that it is proposed and ratified by the peace conferences that settle the epochal wars previously described, and amended in various peace conferences of lesser scope; and that its function is to institutionalize an international order derived from the triumphant constitutional order of the war-winning state.[9]

Bobbitt conceives of these historic peace conferences—Augsburg, Westphalia, Utrecht, Vienna, Versailles—as constitutional conventions following protracted violent conflicts, where the signatories agree to accept the fundamental precepts, over which they will then contend during the next Long War. The conferences that set the rules for this game sanction the strategic doctrine of a hegemonic state whose internal arrangements have proven themselves as the most effective mode of mobilizing and deploying forces.

Two features of this theoretical construction should be noted at the outset. The first is a fundamental equivocation at the level of historical causality. Do strategic—that is, military—revolutions typically give rise to new legal configurations, first within states and then between them? Or is it rather the emergence of juridical innovations within states that ultimately ensures victory on the battlefield? Formally, Bobbitt—viewing the *raison d'être* of state power as in constant movement between the intertwined

---

9   *SA*, p. 483.

imperatives of domestic order and foreign dominance—appears to allow for either possibility, without concerning himself to establish any particular dialectic between them. On closer inspection, however, a basic contradiction in his construct becomes clear. On the one hand, he asserts the primacy of internal developments: 'over the long run, it is the constitutional order of the state that tends to confer military advantage by achieving cohesion, continuity and, above all, legitimacy for its strategic operations'—hence 'international law is a symptom of the triumph of a particular constitutional order within the individual states of which that society consists.'[10] On the other, he insists that it is the external matrix that is decisive: 'The reason epochal wars achieve in retrospect an historic importance is because however they may arise, they challenge and ultimately change the basic structure of the state, which is, after all, a war-making institution'—hence 'an epochal settlement recognizes and legitimates the dominant domestic constitutional order because that archetypal order has been forged in the conflicts that are composed by the peace settlement.'[11]

So formulated, the two postulates are incompatible. In the narrative they unchain, there is little doubt which has the upper hand. Although Bobbitt's primary background, and the bulk of his previous writing, is in constitutional law rather than deterrence theory, in *The Shield of Achilles* it is war and its outcomes that hold front stage. The central claim of the book is that 'constitutional' authorizations periodically mutate in a remorseless geopolitical field of selection, whose history is a sequence of Long Wars, lasting anywhere from thirty to eighty years. The pressure to adopt the latest military innovations leads to a shift in the domestic epicentre of decision-making to those who can most effectively mobilize the newest weaponry, altering the inherited norms of rulership and

---

10   SA, pp. 209, xxix.
11   SA, pp. 333, 502.

warfare to their advantage. From the early modern inception of the era of warring states, governments have sought to emulate those innovations that seem to explain the success of their ascending rivals.

This *Primat der Aussenpolitik* is qualified, but not rescinded, by the acknowledgment that domestic revolutions can redefine the strategic goals of states within this field. Aspiring powers seek to emulate the constitutional prototype of the hegemonic state. Weighed down by an older constitutional inheritance, most fail to adopt the winning strategic innovations of an era, and are either annexed, neutralized, or drop back in the race. In each designated period, the author spotlights only those states that represent the sleek line of historical advance, relegating the rest to irrelevance. Constitutional history unfolds as a sequence of decisive attributes of legitimate force—'princely', 'kingly', 'territorial', 'state-national' and 'national-state'—which ultimately comprise a stylized genealogy of the contemporary neoliberal militarism onto which the narrative will debouch.

In this procession, weaponry and diplomacy are what matter. They, not jurisprudence, institute a new legitimacy. Bobbitt accompanies his main story with a perfunctory subplot that promises to track the evolution of theories of international law across the same five hundred years. Vitoria, Suárez, Gentili, Grotius, Wolff, Vattel, Austin are passed in hasty review as so many exemplifications of their periods. Just how unserious this sideline in the book is, in fact, becomes clear when it reaches modern times—the inter-war period of the twentieth century. At this point Bobbitt manages to discuss Kelsen without apparently being aware of *Das Problem der Souveränität und die Theorie des Völkerrechts* and Schmitt without having heard of *Der Nomos der Erde*, the classic study of epochal epistemes in international law, supposedly his topic here—instead floundering out of his depth in divagations on the Frankfurt School. It would be unfair to make too much of the crassness of such sections. For what these glosses on jurists from Salamanca to the New Haven School suggest is a rather modest role for this tradition in defining the terms of statecraft. Perhaps this is because Bobbitt ultimately regards the precepts of international law not as valid norms, binding on Great Powers, but as a repertoire of elastic formulae, idioms and rationalizations—essentially a loosely scripted, diplomatic language game. Revealingly, he asks at one point, 'would the history of the twentieth century have been any different if there had been no international law?', noting—if not endorsing—the caustic judgment of Dean Acheson that 'the survival of the state is not a matter of law'.[12]

Ambiguating constitutions

If violence and legality are thus by no means on an equal footing in Bobbitt's account of inter-state relations, how does the latter fare in the domestic evolution of states? Here an anomaly immediately strikes the eye. In no country in the world does the constitution loom larger than in the United States. But for American history to fit Bobbitt's schema, there would have had to be at least three successive constitutional orders—juridical transformations corresponding to the state-nation, the nation-state and today's market-state. Even were the Founders to be credited with inaugurating a nation-state proper, skipping the first stage (a line of argument Bobbitt's account of the Civil War appears to disallow), a second constitution would still seem to be in train, or in order, as the market-state takes form. This would certainly be an incendiary thought for a culture in which the charter of 1787, give or take its handful of subsequent amendments, is treated as a virtually sacred document. Bobbitt hastens to disavow it.[13] The Constitution is not, after all, to be touched.

What this reveals, of course, is that Bobbitt's usage of the term 'constitution', at home no less than at large, is essentially tactical

---

12   *SA*, pp. 642, 654.
13   'I should emphasize that such a transformation does not mean that the present US Constitution will be replaced': *SA*, p. 213.

and metaphorical. It refers to no tangible charter of rights or firm principles of law, but to dispositions of another kind. Beneath the rhetor ical surface of the text, an abrupt dismissal of normative illusions suggests a preference for a more concrete jurisprudence. Bobbitt's conception of a constitution collapses the distinction between hard facts and legal norms. In *The Shield of Achilles* the term refers in practice to a mode of distributing power, wealth and status—a 'regime' in the Aristotelean sense—whose telos can be expressed in the form of a legitimating maxim. But it loses nothing by illicit association with its traditional meaning. The slippage from one to the other is integral to the progression of the book.

From the Renaissance to the Great War

Bobbitt begins his historical narrative proper in the prelude to the so-called 'military revolution' from 1560 to 1660. This period witnessed a tenfold increase in the size of armies, the introduction of musket-armed infantry, new schemes of recruitment and drilling, an improvised financial apparatus for the raising and provisioning of troops, and fiscal centralization to keep up with runaway costs. The great monarchies of the sixteenth century began this arms race by emulating the post-feudal miniature polities of the Italian peninsula, earning them, in Bobbitt's account, the Machiavellian title of 'princely state'. Although attributing the rise of the latter to the secular ethos of the Renaissance, he nonetheless has the Counter-Reformation Hapsburgs epitomize its constitutional form. Loosely grounded in its core state territory, this Austro-Hispanic dynasty vied for European primacy with its Valois counterpart for a half century before being forced to a partition of its inheritance and an abandonment of the most grandiose imperial ambitions at the Treaty of Augsburg in 1555.

The next era of inter-state war erupted along the front lines of continent-wide religious strife. Bobbitt sees the battlefields of the Thirty Years War as the testing grounds of an emerging 'kingly state' whose canonical status was eventually ratified at the Treaty of Westphalia. The powerful, separate branches of the Hapsburg clan, residing in Madrid and Vienna, fall out of view, as does the Dutch Republic, whose heyday is transferred, implausibly, to the following century. The seventeenth-century revolutions of the United Provinces and England do not perturb the author's image of an age of ascendant absolutism. Richelieu and Gustavus Adolphus are the two heads of this emerging world, whose constitutional formula is cuius regio, eius religio. The subsequent reign of the Sun King is regarded as the apogee of this kingly state—in Bobbitt's typology, a dynastic regime fused to a core state territory, clamping down on confessional strife, and practising a predatory fiscalism. The wars of the coalition that contained the military and dynastic aggrandizement of Louis XIV established, in turn, the constitutional form of the 'territorial state' whose vested interest in the balance of power was recognized as a fundamental norm of war and diplomacy at the Treaty of Utrecht of 1713. Eschewing the courtly pomp and dynastic ambitions of Versailles, states defined by Bobbitt as 'territorial' were distinguished by their tolerance, legal rationality and growth-promoting mercantilism. In the classical decades of cabinet warfare, the triumvirate of Great Britain, the United Provinces and Prussia held the fort against a slowly declining Bourbon monarchy.

The constitutional innovations that moved states up the European power hierarchy in the next era of international relations were the legacy of republican upheavals. The French Revolution forged a model of government-orchestrated mass mobilization, subsequently adopted by the most innovative states to re-emerge from Napoleonic occupation. The Hegelian–Clausewitzian figure of 'the state-nation', arising from a drastically pruned old European state-system, claimed to be the ethical embodiment of a historic people. Bobbitt rehearses the story of the Congress of Vienna as a diplomatic convention contending over the security rights and obligations of the Areopagus of Great Powers, in a concerted effort torn between restoration and reform. The story of Castlereagh is a moving tale of a visionary statesman at odds with blinkered contemporaries unwilling to abandon the status quo ante. Bobbitt's figure is a conceit of a certain genre of history in which the author ventriloquizes some improbable colossus of world history, comparable in this respect to Kissinger's Metternich, or Calasso's Talleyrand.

Expatiation on his misunderstood genius cannot, however, entirely conceal the aporia of the narrative at this point. Supposedly enshrining the state-nation as the legitimate constitutional form of the new era, in reality, of course, the Congress of Vienna sealed the crushing of its most advanced embodiment—which ought, according to Bobbitt's scheme, to have been the victor—in France, and the triumph of its negation, dynastic legitimism, across the larger part of the Continent, from Alexander I at one end to Ferdinand VII at the other. What these rulers would have made of their presumptive dedication to the 'state-nation' can be left to the imagination.

For Bobbitt, the transition to the next stage of the 'nation-state' is an artefact of the mid-century industrial revolution that brought the landscapes of Manchester to the US and the European continent. Suddenly widening discrepancies in the velocity of troop transport, firepower and scale of provisioning proved decisive in a series of wars of national unification won by Prussia, Piedmont and the Union. These constitutional settlements became the mould for an emerging political universe in which statehood eventually became a populist project of welfare promises, mass education and universal conscription. But the full package only came together in a slide towards total war, as the official state nationalisms of the Great Powers moulted into more militant creeds. Out of the First World War there then sprang the Russian Revolution and Mussolini's March on Rome, as well as Wilsonian idealism, opening a historic conflict between drastically different models of legitimate nation-statehood.

Guilty Germany

The introduction of this axis of division breaks, however, the coherence of the narrative a second time, and more critically. In his accounts of earlier peace conferences, the legitimating norms of the inter-state order were invariably settled not too long after the genesis of the ascendant constitutional paradigm. But at Versailles this constitutive power fails to materialize because of the presence of irreconcilable *ideological* divisions, between regimes belonging to the same populist family. Liberal democracy, Communism and Fascism were the three faces of the twentieth-century nation-state: as opposed to the constitutions that precede it, there are no concrete universals that embody this ideologically divided genus. As a result of the intensity of this internecine struggle, the entirety of the twentieth-century Long War—from 1914 to 1990—unfolded without a foundational international settlement. In history according to *The Shield of Achilles*, consensual norms of 'nation-state' sovereignty only become system-wide with the conclusion of this Long War at the Peace of Paris in 1990—and then immediately begin to dissolve. Or so it would seem. The discrepancy in the narrative is not registered, let alone addressed by the author.

In this story, Wilsonian internationalism is taken to epitomize the liberal-democratic conception of a nation-state based world order. Bobbitt claims that the purity of American motives was never more in evidence than in Wilson's decision to intervene, which turned back the German offensive of 1918; even more than the later anti-Hitler coalition, this was a moral enterprise par excellence. Now is the moment for Colonel House to emerge from the wings. Bobbitt recounts with gusto how, circumventing traditional diplomatic channels, Wilson's confidant was dispatched to uplift the Old World. He does not allow any Jamesian irony to spoil the tale of this bustling American envoy. The story repeats a lesson from an earlier chapter: just as Castlereagh had sought to coax the Holy Alliance towards the emerging norms of the semi-parliamentary state-nation, so now House attempted to move them to an understanding of the highest ideals of the new nation-state. But myopic European belligerents clung to their obsolete prerogatives, disfiguring the future envisioned by Wilson.

Historians who adopt this view usually fault the victorious Entente for abandoning the historic convention of diplomatic amnesty, and attaching unsustainable war-guilt charges to the terms of defeat. By contrast, Bobbitt seeks to conjoin the noble preambles of Wilson to the wintry ultimatums of Clemenceau: in his view, not only had Germany started the Long War, it was destined to remain an essentially criminal aggressor until it met with crushing, punitive defeat. The most bizarre single feature of *The Shield of Achilles* is its resurrection of a 1914-vintage scarecrow of the Huns. Bobbitt's judgments on the Prusso-German Reich consist of a series of astonishingly ignorant assertions. Chief amongst them is the claim that this state was already fascist in 1871. Hence, he solemnly informs the reader that: 'the basic continuity in German history between 1871 and 1945 lay in its substantive goal: the defence of a fascist constitutional system against liberalism and socialism'.[14] Thus he suggests that had the victors not imposed such heavy burdens on the Weimar Republic, the Nazis would simply have come to power at an earlier date, and so enjoyed a decisive advantage in the inevitable war to come. The notion that the Weimar Republic collapsed in part due to the harsh terms of the Versailles Treaty warrants scarcely even a dismissal.

Anachronistic as it seems, this animus towards German militarism, in a work that otherwise treats the assorted rapacities and manoeuvres of the Great Powers with sang-froid, has a contemporary resonance. One need only think of the rhetorical usages of appeasement, designed to make the equation between Hitler and Saddam Hussein. Embedded coverage of German

---

14   SA, p. 26.

history constitutes the low point of *The Shield of Achilles*. Elsewhere Bobbitt is quite capable of intellectual independence. He has no difficulty, for example, in acknowledging that the United States was consistently on the offensive against a weaker Soviet Union during the Cold War, and finds that record wholly commendable, praising, for example—though here perhaps family loyalties come into play—his uncle's war in Vietnam and the invasion of the Dominican Republic as meritorious episodes in the battle against Communism.[15] Although where necessary he allows himself to be moved by officially sanctioned victimologies, they never entirely bewitch his judgment, as he often alternates these with the harshest nostrums. Indeed he confesses to be looking forward to a near future in which the norms justifying great-power intervention will no longer have to be couched in the language of defence—the now obsolete idiom of the sovereign nation-state.

Dawn or dusk at Paris?

Bringing a close to the pre-history of the present, Bobbitt portrays what he calls the Peace of Paris—the 'Charter for a New Europe' adopted by the CSCE in late 1990—as the diplomatic stage upon which the liberal-democratic constitutional norm of the victorious West finally achieved the universal recognition it missed at Versailles. The importance of this moment for the architecture of Bobbitt's narrative is decisive: it is the true hinge of contemporary history, on which the present continues to turn. Yet just at this crux, the third and most fundamental aporia in his construction breaks open. For on the one hand, the Peace of Paris signals a new constitution of the society of states, based on worldwide legitimation of democracy, human rights and the market economy. As such it provides the empowering charter for military

---

15   The Vietnam War 'contributed to the ultimate Alliance victory'; the intervention in the Dominican Republic was 'one of the most successful pro-democracy acts of the period': SA, pp. 9, 59, 474.

interventions to secure these norms wherever they are too grossly defied. As Bobbitt puts it:

> The Peace of Paris ought to settle this constitutional question for the society of states: no state's sovereignty is unimpeachable if it studiedly spurns parliamentary institutions and human rights protections. The greater the rejection of these institutions—which are the means by which sovereignty is conveyed by societies to their governments—the more sharply curtailed is the cloak of sovereignty that would otherwise protect governments from interference by their peers. US action against the sovereignty of Iraq, for example, must be evaluated in this light.[16]

So too, he adds, the Peace of Paris strips the mantle of national sovereignty away from any government seeking nuclear weapons that fails to conform to its norms, warranting preemptive strikes against the delinquent.[17] In this register, the Charter of 1990 appears as the lineal successor of the Congress of Vienna, setting the terms of legitimate diplomacy and war for an entire epoch, the period ahead.

The briefest glance at the text of the charter, however, makes clear that the 'Peace of Paris' bears no relation to this construal. It expressly rules out the actions Bobbitt would have it endorse. 'In accordance with our obligations under the Charter of the Nations and commitments under the Helsinki final act,' declared its signatories, 'we renew our pledge to refrain from the threat or use of force against the territorial integrity or political independence of any state, or from acting in any other manner inconsistent with the principles or purposes of these documents. We recall that

---

16 *SA*, p. 680.
17 'No state that does not derive its authority from representative institutions that coexist with fundamental rights can legitimately argue that it can subject its own people to the threat of nuclear preemption or retaliation on the basis of its alleged rights of sovereignty because the people it thus makes into nuclear targets have not consented to bear such risks. At a minimum, the Peace of Paris stands for this': *SA*, p. 680.

non-compliance with obligations under the Charter of the United Nations constitutes a violation of international law.'[18] That this was no mere *clause de style* can be seen from the reaction of the figure who was, historically speaking, its most significant signatory—given that most of the document was standard boiler-plate for Western politicians—namely Gorbachev, who denounced both NATO's attack on Yugoslavia and the Anglo-American invasion of Iraq.

But if even the most tendentious reading could not make the Peace of Paris into an open-ended Enabling Law, empowering the US to maraud at will in the name of human rights and the prerogatives of the nuclear club, can it really be the dawn of the new international system the epoch requires? At other moments, no doubt sensing its limitations, Bobbitt offers a very different diagnosis, casting the charter of 1990 in precisely the opposite light. In this version, far from defining a new world order at the end of History, the contracting parties at Paris would have ratified the international norms of a constitutional framework in decline. For at the very hour of its triumph, the bell was tolling for the liberal-democratic nation-state. An entirely new political form, the market-state, has since arisen to supplant it. Bobbitt underscores the drastic nature of this mutation, expressing the difference between the two in a simple, icy formula: the market-state ceases to base its legitimacy on improving the welfare of its people.[19]

Instead this new form of polity simply offers to maximize opportunities—to 'make the world available' to those with the skills or luck to take advantage of it. 'Largely indifferent to the norms of justice, or for that matter to any particular set of moral values so long as law does not act as an impediment to economic competition',[20] the market-state is defined by three paradoxes. Government becomes more centralized, yet weaker; citizens increasingly become spectators; welfare is retrenched, but security

18   See 'Charter of Paris for a New Europe': www.osce.org
19   *SA*, pp. 222ff.
20   *SA*, p. 230.

and surveillance systems expand. Bobbitt etches the consequences imperturbably. The grip of finance on electoral politics may become so tight as to erase the stigma of corruption. Waves of privatization will continue to roll over the state, eventually dissolving large parts of it into a looser, shifting ensemble of subcontracted and clandestine operations. (Recalling his stint as an advisor to the Senate investigation of the Iran-Contra Enterprise, Bobbitt calls for a jurisprudence more discerning of the fine lines separating capitalism from crime.)

Public education will implode as parents seek to augment the human capital of their children with early investments in private school. Inequality and crime could grow to Brazilian proportions. Civil liberties will have to be reconceived to accommodate far-reaching anti-terrorist dragnets. Some of the fictions of citizenship will gradually give way to more realistic weighted voting systems. Representative government itself will become increasingly nominal as media plebiscites openly assume the function of securing the consent of atomized multitudes. National security spin doctoring will become so pervasive as to engender a new epistemology of managed opinion.

Travails of the market-state

As the end point of his demi-millennial narrative, the market-state sets the stage for Bobbitt's prescriptions for the West today. But though he depicts it graphically enough, he offers no coherent explanation of its origins. Five factors, we are told at the outset, have given a quietus to the nation-state: human-rights norms, weapons of mass destruction, transnational pestilences, global finance and the internet. In another enumeration 'environmental threats, mass migration, capital speculation, terrorism and cyber interference' are the challenges that phased it out.[21] Elsewhere, Bobbitt remarks that 'the market-state is a

---

21 *SA*, p. xxii.

constitutional adaptation to the end of the Long War and to the revolutions in computation, communications and weapons of mass destruction that brought that to an end'—only to withdraw the claim as hastily as it is made: 'I have not argued, and do not wish to argue that the State has changed in the precise ways it has *because* of strategic challenges to itself.'[22]

The transition to the market-state is thus simply invoked: no real effort is made to explain it as feedback from a revolution in military affairs. Nor, on the other hand, is there any attempt to account for it in terms of the world economic upheavals of the last thirty years, the fiscal crisis of the welfare state, or the ideological sea change brought on by the defeat of Communism. Nowhere, in fact, is the underlying slackness in the causal joints of *The Shield of Achilles* more apparent than here, at the most critical point in its exposition.

Even the chronology of its origins remains curiously vague. If any two architects of the market-state were to be named, Thatcher and Reagan would be the obvious choices—the pioneer of privatization, and the unleasher of financialization on a world scale. In the United States, the agenda of the Reagan administration to reflate American power through rearmament and a vast shakedown of organized labour was no mere paroxysm of the late Cold War: the employer offensive and militarism of the eighties signalled the advent of a new political order in which we are still living today. For Bobbitt, however, 'President Reagan and Prime Minister Thatcher were among the last nation-state leaders', because their legitimacy still rested on their claim to improve the welfare of their peoples. In scrapping this relic, by contrast, 'Bush and Blair are among the first market-state political leaders'.[23]

On this reading, no symbol could have been more apt than

22 *SA*, pp. 228, 234.
23 *SA*, p. 222. Elsewhere, in keeping with the overall oscillation of his account at this point, he pays due tribute to the founder: 'Within the most prominent market-states, the groundwork was laid by Margaret Thatcher and Ronald Reagan, who did so much to discredit the welfare rationale for the nation-state': p. 333.

Thatcher's fall from power at the very moment she was signing the Charter for a New Europe in Paris in November 1990, when she was ignominiously ousted in her absence by her own party in London. Of the two antithetical accounts of the Peace of Paris that Bobbitt musters, there is little doubt which informs more of the narrative. The media splash of that month, soon forgotten, was not the inauguration of a new constitutional order, but the passing of an old one.[24] In short order, a series of post–Cold War crises and disasters dissipated its illusions, creating states of emergency in which the US not only claimed the sovereign right to decide on the interpretation of international law, but increasingly to make and break it at will. The first Gulf War, with its rhetoric of American leadership in the international community, looked as if it would be the inaugural event of the coming era, but ultimately turned out to be a false dawn.

For in the Balkans, the UN proved a broken reed, and the homilies of Paris offered scant guidance. Far from displaying any united purpose, the newly minted market-states fell into lamentable disarray. Bobbitt's account of the Yugoslav crisis shifts the focus from the axial relationship of social structure and strategy to the *mise en scène* of Western public indignation over the fate of Bosnia—that is, from hard to soft power. Although keenly aware of the plebiscitary nature of modern governance, Bobbitt often collapses the world into its journalistic representation. His selective reconstruction of the break-up of Yugoslavia rehashes the official lessons of Atlantic internationalism. It is a story of European appeasement, American hesitation and international indifference in the face of genocide, exposing the incompatibility of human rights and nationalism. In this myth of origins, the villainous Boutros-Ghali—impertinently pointing to the far

---

24   A glance at Plate III, which offers a heraldic diagram of successive international orders, each pivoting at mid-point on its respective peace treaty, makes it clear that the 'Peace of Paris', situated far to the right of the axis of modal settlement, does not fit the series: *SA*, p. 346.

greater enormities of Rwanda—expresses the shocking sophisms of a dying inter-state order. Western collusion in those events is passed over with unruffled composure.

Fortunately, in the end Clinton saw the light and acted to check Milošević. Thus in practice the turning-point was Rambouillet rather than Paris. Not the pieties of the Concert of Powers, but an ultimatum by the United States was the moment at which the international architecture inherited from the Cold War started to be reshaped.[25] Since then, the field of manoeuvre of the American state has steadily widened. The limits of the possible are still being boldly redefined. In Bobbitt's terms, the American regime is the detonator of an expanding legal universe of market-states, bursting asunder an old international order based on the nominal recognition of the sovereignty of all nation-states. The norms of twentieth-century treaty and alliance structures are thus in flux. This disorder is not, however, the transitional manifestation of a constituent power at work, but a new, protean mode of imperial authority that is dispensing with the very form of universal legal rules and adopting a jurisprudence based on flexible strategic guidelines.

American supremacy

In that sense, treaty conferences are mere chapter headings in the annals of history: their meaning comes from what follows. Since the declarations of Paris, the US, as the undisputed champion of the neoliberal market-order, has had to take the lead in rewriting the rules of property, war and peace. This has entailed exposure to the risk of being held accountable to the rules of one's own making. But Bobbitt believes that the problem can easily be circumvented by a prudent insistence on flexibility and exemptions.

---

25 See *SA*, p. 468, though Bobbitt appears not to register the contradiction in his account.

Treaties on land mines, a human-rights court, chemical and biological weapons, anti-ballistic missiles and emissions that do not sufficiently safeguard America's interests, should be discarded without qualms. 'The United States is simply not in the same position as other states, at least as long as it continues to assume global security responsibilities, and therefore should not be shamed by charges of hypocrisy when it fails to adopt the regimes that it urges on others.'[26] In contrast to those who see in the contemporary imperialism a freak storm brought on by neo-conservative hubris, Bobbitt vividly sketches the long-term logic of American expansion.

The United Nations is only one pillar of a now tottering international dispensation: in this age of creative destruction, the World Health Organization, the World Bank, the IMF, the OSCE, the European Union and even NATO itself will either be reformed, or decline into irrelevance. The emerging world of market-states mirrors its domestic social shape: it is openly run by highly selective clubs in which rank is apportioned in strict accordance to financial and military clout. The legitimating maxim of these planetary oligarchies is 'to each according to his abilities'. Although Bobbitt occasionally rehearses some of the mantras of globalization, the age we are entering is portrayed as a scene of gated affluence surrounded by immiseration, violence and epidemic disease, with little alleviating Homeric joy. The characteristic promise of the age of nation-states was economic development for backward, 'late-coming' regions, but Bobbitt suggests that this too is now being rescinded. The terms of trade between advanced and backward regions are at present as bad as they were during the Great Depression; the possibility of leapfrogging development under conditions of protection is now closed off.

In this landscape, the US now enjoys uncontested supremacy. How long will it last? Bobbitt is at pains to dispel the suspicion that

---

26   SA, p. 691.

the constitution of all market-states must be modelled to American specifications. Europe and Asia currently have their own variants, expressing different cultural lineages and slightly divergent public priorities. Thus there are at present, he suggests, a trio of market-state forms—'entrepreneurial', 'managerial' and 'mercantile'— that represent the familiar dominants of the OECD: the Anglo-Saxon street, the Rhenish stakeholder model, and Japan Inc. Here each is graced with its own verdant image: the meadow (US), the park (Germany) and the garden (Japan). Bobbitt sketches their respective traits with an air of impartiality, as if all were of equal standing, and any might ultimately prevail over the others.

But, as one might expect, this is little more than a gesture. The mercantile and the managerial variants, Japan and Germany, divide the legacy of the nation-state; the first retaining a traditionalist ethos of group responsibility, the second, interest-group cooperation and social justice. Only the entrepreneurial version—the US— approaches the pure model of the market-state, and therefore is set to out-compete the others. 'Its multiculturalism, its free market, and its diverse religious make-up—all of which resist the centralizing efforts of the nation-state—and, above all, its habit of tolerance for diversity give it an advantage over other countries in adapting to this new constitutional order.'[27]

This, of course, is far from capturing the unique position of the United States in the international system, where Washington can use its massive military advantages to forestall the verdict of the world market on the increasingly unstable economic foundations of its primacy. In the inter-war era, major European states were willing to accept American arbitration of their affairs in large part because they were massively in debt. The US exercised an awesome creditor veto on any international debt settlement that would have brought an end to this destabilizing circulation of

---

27   *SA*, p. 242. Moreover, 'the entrepreneurial model offers the United States the best chance of developing, marketing and "selling" the collective goods that will maintain American influence in the world': p. 292.

money in the world economy. Today the situation is reversed. If American hegemony is accepted by potential rivals, it is in part because however poorly most national economies have fared in the past thirty years, the affluent of all countries have shared in the bounties of unbridled financial markets, and continue to look to American capitalism as the horizon of the future.

But more fundamentally, they have reason to fear that in practice they have little choice in the matter. For however 'irresponsible' its macroeconomic policies may be, the difficulties and risks of trying to impose fiscal discipline on the US look prohibitive, since American deficits now form the principal source of the demand that drives the world economy. The US market is the key to the export economies of the rest of the world. For the moment, this is the basic check on the tendency of an anarchic inter-state system to throw up balancing coalitions against what might otherwise be a destabilizing concentration of power at the apex of world politics.

Bobbitt's concerns lie elsewhere. Economic calculations surface only desultorily in *The Shield of Achilles*, and the typology of the market-state has little incidence on its argument. The historical narrative it constructs is essentially an erratic, grandiose prologue to contemporary strategic debates in Washington. At this point, the discussion moves to the canonical national-security briefs that defined the aims of the American state at moments when it confronted the option between fundamentally different stances towards competitors and enemies; and surveys the alternatives that are now circulating inside the Beltway. Here Bobbitt's account is terse and controlled, setting out with exemplary clarity the range of doctrines currently on offer: a new nationalism (Buchanan), a new 'internationalism' (Brzezinski), a new realism (Kissinger), a new evangelism (survivors of Clinton), and 'the new leadership' of the sole remaining superpower (Krauthammer). Reproaching each with proposing only a set of policies for the US state, Bobbitt calls for a more long-term paradigm to define the strategic outlook in the twenty-first century. But in practice, his recommendations differ little from the 'new leadership', the most aggressive of all agendas for contemporary American empire.

This position has the merit of candour. Bobbitt has no time for customary hypocrisies about international law or the United Nations. 'The universal view of international law is flawed in two important respects,' he writes. 'It mixes the equality of states, a legal concept, with the decision to use force, a strategic concept, in a way that is fatal to both.' Were the UN General Assembly ever to demand 'economic concessions and constitutional reform consistent with a universal mandate', the result would either be contradictory, since the Security Council retains the character of a Concert of Great Powers, or perilous, because of the demagogy of vast majorities.[28] Like the League before it, the UN has spawned a 'second generation of failures, that is, a new wave of crimes shielded by sovereignty'. The future lies rather with another Congress, like Utrecht or Vienna, to create 'a constitution for a society of market-states that will resemble those of corporations, which allow for weighted voting based on wealth'.[29] But that time is still far off. Meanwhile, the United States must act as it can, to 'devise a strategy of long-term dominance over peer competitors that will enable it to prevail in conventional confrontations as well as to field expeditionary forces'.[30]

Recent Bush administration strategy is based on the expectation that vigorous mobilizations of American-led coalitions of the willing, followed by earth-shaking victories, will periodically replenish the stock of political pressure available for strong-arming the reluctant and recalcitrant at all negotiating tables. For the moment, the environment appears favourable enough to such designs. Although Washington has sharpened the tone against France and Germany, it has taken an extremely accommodating line towards Japan: recognizing that while Japan subsidizes America's

28   SA, pp. 361, 475.
29   SA, pp. 472, 475, 777.
30   SA, p. 302.

massive and growing debt, conveniently it has no capacity or will to use that leverage. For all the Washington bluster directed at them, the political classes of Paris and Berlin are for the moment quite unwilling to invest in the very costly and risky business of attempting to construct an independent centre of gravity in world politics—and this will continue to be the case unless they are forced down this path. Russia's slow-motion decline appears to require only a modicum of encouraging speeches, encirclement and periodic emergency loans; and unlike the old Soviet Union, China is thoroughly integrated into an American-dominated world market, in which it seeks only to expand, without excessive disruption.

Adversaries

But this very freedom from external balance-of-power constraints contains the danger of a wilful exaggeration of threats and a casual underestimation of obstacles. The discipline that a nuclear-armed Soviet Union once imposed on America's rulers has evaporated. The rhetoric of the Republican administration is an ominous anticipation of what might happen in the event of a world economic downturn. Yet even an escalation of hostilities between the US and China or Russia, or Europe or Japan, would be unlikely to reverse one of the central sociological trends of the post–Second World War era: the decline of mass militarism in Western Europe and Japan after forty years of heavy-casualty warfare, a process that eventually reached the US during the high point of its Indochinese operations. The enormous conscript citizen armies of the Great Power nation-state were either destroyed in the immediate aftermath of the war or discredited in the last decades of colonialism. The raising of overarching nuclear umbrellas, the advent of consumerism, the cultural neutralization of nationalist pathos in public life, the final collapse of rural social strata from which both officers and soldiers were recruited and the break-up of traditional gender roles sealed the fate of an older Great Power politics. The only military interventions now capable of soliciting domestic acclamation are those that demand no heavy sacrifices of the home front. It is now well understood, as ballooning American deficits testify, that under no circumstances can the social segment extending from the wealthy to the super-rich be asked to bear the costs of empire.

Bobbitt recognizes this irreversible change, although confessing ambivalence towards it—a nostalgia which 'I feel more than most'.[31] *The Shield of Achilles* can in part be read as the swan song of this older militarism of state-nations and nation-states. But it is also a distinctively postmodern call for yet another heroic age. The book repeatedly, if inconclusively, raises the question of whether we should brace ourselves for wars between the American, European and Japanese variants of the market-state in the twenty-first century, like those between liberal democracy, Fascism and Communism in the twentieth. Two years into the First World War, Lenin declared that imperialism was not simply a policy, it was the structural logic of world-market competition refracted through the field of Great Power rivalry. Bobbitt never goes so far, but there are hints in *The Shield of Achilles* that the neoliberal 'constitutional' upheaval of the last two decades may now be assuming its true geopolitical form, not in the utopias of peaceful Free Trade, but in an abrupt sharpening of inter-state tensions at the top tier of the world power hierarchy.

Here, in a volume whose horizon is otherwise undeviatingly Atlantic—all of whose narrative landmarks take their names from European cities—the focus of anxiety is Pacific. The prospect of Japan acquiring nuclear weapons is, in Bobbitt's eyes, far more dangerous than that of North Korea. Indeed, he argues, it might be necessary to tolerate the latter in order to avert the former:

31 'The Long War of the nation-state is over, having destroyed every empire that participated in it, every political aristocracy, every general staff, as well as much of the beauty of European and Asian life': SA, pp. 242, 805.

It would be a tragedy for the world if, in order to extirpate a North Korean nuclear force with which Japan has learnt to live, we plunged the Korean peninsula into a war that led to the mobilization of Japan's energy and wealth on behalf of its armed forces. Already the Japanese, with less than 1.5 per cent of GDP, field the world's third largest defence establishment, and there is no NATO-like institution that links this establishment with the forces of surrounding states.[32]

By contrast, China, which looms large in Mearsheimer's analysis of potential future threats to the United States, is—rather mysteriously— accorded scant attention by Bobbitt.

The need to check the ambitions of would-be rivals, expressly set out for the first time in the Pentagon's Defense Planning Guidance of 1992, and since enshrined in the National Security Strategy proclaimed by Bush in 2002, occupies first place in Bobbitt's global prospectus, which ranks enemies in terms of the dangers they pose to the US, and aims to adjust the force structures made possible by the Revolution in Military Affairs to counter them. Adversaries can be classified in an ABC table. The 'A' group consists of peer competitors: Bobbitt lists Germany, France, Japan and Russia. 'B' comprises mid-level powers on the verge or just beyond WMD potential: Pakistan, India, Iran, Iraq, North Korea. 'C' embraces a comparatively motley category of minor rogue states (Libya, Serbia, Cuba), terrorists, criminals and insurgents. China is left unclassified. *The Shield of Achilles* makes no bones that the top priority is to ensure military superiority over the A-powers. 'The greatest threats to American security will come from powerful, technologically sophisticated states—not from "rogues", whether they be small states or large groups of bandits.'[33] In keeping with this conviction, Bobbitt has recently expressed his reservations about the 'Axis of Evil' and, true to his Cold War métier, asserts

---

32   SA, p. 261; see also p. 687.
33   SA, p. 315; see also pp. 306, 309.

that facing the challenge of A-list states is a matter of maintaining nuclear primacy over them, by integrating them under the American shield.

Though ultimately less menacing to the US, because they do not actually threaten the American homeland, B targets pose more immediate risks of nuclear proliferation, and should be dealt with accordingly. In this respect the signature innovation of the last decade is the doctrine, of which Bobbitt has been a foremost champion, foreseeing preemptive strikes against states on the threshold of developing weapons of mass destruction. It is on these grounds that he has applauded the conquest of Iraq. But he anticipates continuing pressure towards proliferation in the B list to compensate for America's overwhelming conventional superiority, and concludes that the use of nuclear weapons will be more likely in the future. No treaties to neutralize the arms races to come are foreseen.

What, then, of C targets? Here a further anomaly becomes visible. The challenges that command Bobbitt's survey of potential dangers to American hegemony, at force-levels A and B, have virtually nothing to do with the imputed novelties of the market-state. Nuclear weapons were a creation of the Second World War, and the centrepiece of the Cold War, which saw them spread not only to Britain, France and China, but also to Israel and South Africa. They belong to the epoch of the nation-state. It is really only at level C, the least significant, that specifically market-state considerations enter into play. At once artefact and agent of 'globalization', the strengths and weaknesses of the market-state arise from its exposed, porous borders. These are the frontiers across which a fanatical terrorism can snake and strike, dissolving the line separating foreign policy from homeland surveillance.

In his considered inventory of the perils confronting the US, no doubt composed during the Clinton administration, Bobbitt consigned such threats to a residual category, at the bottom of the ABC hierarchy. But, perhaps sensing the disjunction between his diagnostics of the 'new constitutional order' and his predictions of the rather traditional turbulence awaiting it, he seems to have felt it necessary to up the stakes of jeopardy specific to the market-state, by tacking onto his work a series of lurid futurological scenarios. Supposedly, the inspiration for these came (a suitably market-state touch) from managerial deliberations within Royal Dutch Shell, but in fact they are closer to the pop fantasies of Tom Clancy. Terrorist explosions in the Chunnel and Chartres Cathedral, devastating Water Wars in the Subcontinent, raging pandemics in Africa, chemical attacks on South Korea, world economic collapse, preemptive strikes in Central Asia, race riots in Washington—the pages are littered with assorted disasters and death tolls.

None of the theories Bobbitt develops in the book is demonstrated or tested in these phantasmagorias, which even admirers have regretted. But such apparently extraneous flights of fancy have their function. They ratchet up what Mike Davis has called 'the globalization of fear', with images that create the right psychological atmosphere for a draconian doctrine of armed preemption at home and abroad.[34] In such panic-mongering, *The Shield of Achilles* gives a narrative shape to the nightmares that plague the market-state, rendering them as the cinematic scenery of a heroic twilight of the West.

But like Spengler's version before it, which foresaw the— possibly ominous—arrival of a new Caesar to save a dying civilization, this one too ends with a stoic posture. The West cannot avert the epochal war to come, but it may hope to shape it. The attacks of 9/11 provide the United States with a 'historic opportunity' to awaken its citizens to the tasks before them. 'War is a natural condition of the State, which was organized to be an

---

34 A passage from Aristotle's *Politics* captures the political dynamics of this hyperbole: 'When danger is imminent, people are anxious and they therefore keep a firmer grip on their constitution. All who are concerned for the constitution should therefore create anxieties, which will put people on their guard, and will make them keep watch like sentinels on night-duty. They must, in a word, make the remote come near.' *Politics*, Book v, Chapter 8.

effective instrument of violence on behalf of society. Wars are like deaths, which, while they can be postponed, will come when they will come and cannot finally be avoided.'[35] Adorno's observation that, for all its obvious intellectual crudity, Spengler's thesis stood unrefuted, should be kept in mind.

Addendum

Bobbitt's latest work *Terror and Consent* comes five years after the publication of *The Shield of Achilles*, and more than redresses the latter's apparently inopportune scanting of asymmetrical challengers. In the new book, the great power adversaries that preoccupied him in the nineties have simply vanished. In a belated adjustment to post–9/11 realities, the author has now taken stock of a myriad of forces—once relegated to threat level C— that menace the precariously open societies of the market-state world. It turns out that the wars of the twenty-first century will not be between the American, European and Japanese variants of this new constitutional order. The Long War that has just begun is a struggle between the entire world order of pro-globalization states, led by the West, and the forces of chaos that threaten to destabilize it. Bobbitt calls the former 'states of consent', and the latter 'states of terror'—a catch-all for today's most spectacular forms of disaster. 'Terror' is a far broader phenomenon than Islamic jihad. It encompasses everything that poses an existential threat to these affluent yet vulnerable societies, forcing them to trade a certain amount of liberty for security. Not just bombs, but pandemics and natural disasters belong to this vast continuum of violence. So conceived, 'terror' becomes a more formidable long-term adversary, but what is the historical precedent or rationale for waging war against such a miscellaneous assortment of threats?

---

35   *SA*, p. 819.

Bobbitt has written *Terror and Consent* to counter the numerous sceptics—mostly mainstream realists and constitutionalists— who eventually came to see the War on Terror as a disaster for American power, legitimacy and liberties. Although reluctant to condemn a standing US president, he confesses that he has often felt indignant at the sheer arrogance and incompetence with which this war has been prosecuted and legitimized, and looks forward to a commander-in-chief of greater stature. In making his case, Bobbitt suggests that wholly new modes of thought might be required to confront the challenges that lie ahead. Along these lines, he proposes that his latest work be read as a contribution to 'political philosophy', hinting that Western military planners may have to abandon the static ontology of Parmenides, and contemplate 'whirlpools of reason':[36]

> We think terrorists will attack; so they think we think terrorists will attack; so they think we shall intervene; so they will attack; so we must.[37]

Anglo-American intelligence agencies have yet to attain this level of reflexivity. Today's statesmen need to be better versed in the art of finding the facts and presenting the arguments that lay the groundwork for preemptive strikes. Making the case for these military interventions need not always be controversial, as most Westerners are coming to terms with the ambiguities that arise in the course of policing the nations of the world. For better or worse, 'we live in a world of casual deceit', in which our occasional solicitude for the victims of disaster assists in the day-to-day deceptions.[38]

How does 'the war on terror' fit into the constitutional epic of state formation and military revolutions that was presented in

---

36   Philip Bobbitt, *Terror and Consent: The Wars for the Twenty-First Century*, New York: Knopf,, 2008, pp. 551, 10; henceforward *TC*.
37   *TC*, p. 10.
38   *TC*, p. 386.

the previous work? *Terror and Consent* introduces an interesting twist to the narrative that traced a succession of legal–strategic orders from the early modern princely state to its postmodern market-state incarnation. Whereas previously the focus was on inter-state wars between contending variants of the same civilizational principle, Bobbitt now proposes that each age of warring states was also haunted from below by the spectre of a specific form of anti-civilizational chaos that, as he sees it, can quite simply be equated with terrorism:

> In each era, terrorism derives its ideology in reaction to the raison d'etre of the dominant constitutional order, at the same time negating and rejecting that form's unique ideology but mimicking that form's structural characteristics.[39]

Bobbitt not only attempts to insert this principle of negativity into a roster of constitutional forms that stretches back to the Renaissance, he documents human rights abuses from even more remote times, going so far as to put the Persian Empire onto his list of historic terrorist organizations. (Notwithstanding this capacious scope, the ravages of colonialism and African slavery are left out of his discretionary catalogue.) From the mercenary rabble and pirates thrown up by early modern absolutism, to the anarchist assassins and guerilla movements who took up arms against the modern state forms of the nineteenth and twentieth centuries, Bobbitt's tale culminates in a survey of the contemporary landscape of danger. In whose crosshairs do we now live?

The US and UK have been openly at war with terrorism for seven years, and Bobbitt is astonished that there is still no clear definition of the enemy. Not only has this state of affairs exposed the US and UK to charges of hypocrisy and worse; more importantly, it has made

---

39   *TC*, p. 26.

it difficult for either states to articulate its long-term objectives in this epochal war. Disorientation has resulted in demoralization. In order to rectify this situation, Bobbitt proposes the following definition of the terrorism specific to the era of market states:

> Terrorism is the pursuit of political goals through the use of violence against noncombatants in order to dissuade them from what they have a lawful right to do.[40]

The proposal that the term should be expanded to embrace the calamities of nature itself has simply been dropped. But even when retracted to the political realm, his definition proves as nebulous and question-begging as the ordinary usage: what of the fire bombing of Dresden, or attacks on Israeli settlers in illegally occupied territory? The author ponders this inevitable and apparently impertinent line of inquiry and momentarily wavers, conceding that what is called 'terrorism' in the US or UK may be a discriminatory term. But no degree of moral and conceptual indeterminacy should deter us from crafting an operational notion of nemesis that makes sense by market-state criteria, even if this leads to judgments deemed unfair from the perspective of older norms of statehood. The question of who has the right to decide on such matters is best not thrown into the whirlpool. Ditto for all the other criteria by which friend and foe are to be labelled and judged.

Where do the wars of today fit in to the longue durée of international relations? 'A war on terror' obviously introduces a striking anomaly into the pattern of history, for no other epoch but ours is defined by its campaigns against its primitive rebels; the latter were only ever a secondary problem of order and conflict. Bobbitt makes a lame attempt to conceal the slippage by elevating networks of Islamic affiliates to the status of 'states'—indeed turns them into structural caricatures of the world's increasingly

---

40   *TC*, p. 352.

privatized 'market-states'. This is a tacit concession to the fact that
great power wars of the kind that were foreseen in *The Shield of
Achilles* are presently beyond the horizon of what is strategically
conceivable. But even the possibility of regime-changing
expeditions against states like Sudan, North Korea and Iran seems
to have receded of late. The invasion and occupation of Iraq failed
to establish a compelling precedent for follow-up operations against
roughly comparable states. As a consequence, even the previously
designated B level of potentially WMD-possessing regimes is no longer
at the forefront of Bobbitt's account of this conjuncture of war. The
time of rogue states has passed. Unlike terrorists of the Al-Qaeda
variety, they uphold an older, superseded nation-state conception
of closed, or 'opaque sovereignty'. It would seem to follow that the
threat they represent as revisionist states will increasingly be eclipsed
by their role as anti-systemic sanctuaries for networks of terrorist
privateers. Against such regimes and their proxies, Western states
of consent are divided in their legal–strategic thinking between an
Anglo-American notion of immediately rescindable 'transparent
sovereignty', and an Old European one of a 'translucent sovereignty',
qualified by international legal norms. Bobbitt repeatedly expresses
his preference for the morality of the former in bitter recollections
of how Schroeder, Chirac and Zapatero undermined the efforts of
the coalition.

What evidence is there that 'terror'—even in a loose definition—
has emerged from the underworld to become the primary adversary
of today's leading states? Bobbitt reproduces some questionable
figures in an effort to show a dramatic spike in the incidence and
savagery of terrorist attacks since 9/11. This might suggest that the
war on the nebula of non-state actors is backfiring. But who is to
say that the number of casualties wouldn't have been even higher
had it not been for America's heroic efforts of pree-mption? After
all, 'there are no "killer facts".'[41] No stranger to literary licence,

41   *TC*, p. 339.

Bobbitt once again tries his hand at drafting the kind of scenarios that have become standard fare in the popular American culture of the period: ticking time bombs present and correct among other harbingers of the end.

But why should a world that is in the process of becoming an 'Edenic paradise' of 'immense prosperity' be tottering perpetually on the edge of catastrophe?[42] The question is out of bounds. Bobbitt belongs to that large segment of mainstream American opinion that still considers it inappropriate to dwell on the causes of Islamic terrorism. Certainly, to this group, the idea that it has anything to do with US support for Israel and other regional clients can be summarily dismissed. In any event, jihadi violence is only the first manifestation of the blowback to arise from globalization, and so there would be little use in focusing on the motivations of Islamic terrorists.

For Bobbitt, this raises new problems at the interface of law and strategy. The first is how to craft a jurisprudence in which 'the aggressive use of informants, surveillance, wiretaps, searches, interrogations, and even group-based profiling must be measured not only against the liberties these practices constrict, but also with respect to the liberties they may protect.'[43] Sympathetic to the problems posed by illegal combatants, Bobbitt insists that the black holes into which these people have been thrown can be turned into grey areas, more in keeping with our traditions. The second problem is how to develop a strategic doctrine in the tradition of Monroe and Truman that could impart long-term direction and legitimacy to American policy in the coming time of troubles. It is only by the light of such doctrines that peoples this side of the thin blue line can develop benchmarks of success in the war against the horrors that threaten to erupt with the slightest lapse of vigilance.

However overwrought Bobbitt's prophesies of chaos turn out

---

42   *TC*, p. 94.
43   *TC*, p. 245.

to be, the idea that they might indict the present course of capitalist civilization is, of course, never entertained. The subsumption of the entire planet under its laws is now approaching completion with the incorporation of the last outlying zones. But the future course of what now appears inexorable—'globalization'—is manifestly overdetermined by a structural impasse of classical forms of war and collective politics, not to mention a human and ecological finitude that may or may not be transcendable. A status quo of capital, legitimate violence and natural limits seems to be drifting towards disintegration, and yet actively breaking with it still seems impossible. Perhaps, in this sense alone, terrorism is the proper name for negations that do not yet have a name.

4

Battleground of the Spectacle

The greatness of an estate, in bulk and territory, doth fall under measure; and the greatness of finances and revenue, doth fall under computation. The population may appear by musters; and the number and greatness of cities and towns by cards and maps. But yet there is not any thing amongst civil affairs more subject to error, than the right valuation and true judgment concerning the power and forces of an estate.

—Francis Bacon

At the turn of the century, it seemed unlikely that American strategic planners would contemplate any course of action that might disrupt a number of exceptionally favourable international trends. All the main ones seemed to point to the dawning of another American century: an unopposed encroachment of NATO into the void opened up by the elimination of the USSR, the apparent reversal of a quarter-century of economic decline in a climate of explosive speculation, the deft deflection of Europe back into the Atlantic fold, the deepening synergy with China as the low-wage supplier of the world market, and a compliant attitude at the UN Security Council before the step-wise progression of US revisionism. Washington was allowed the exemptions and privileges of a super-state on the plausible assumption that it had committed its power to the protection and expansion of the zone of globalization. This accommodating hegemonic formula seemed to obviate the need for big and medium powers to have to concern themselves with the arduous task of balancing against the American 'hyperpower'. Indeed, the two potential nuclear adversaries of this democratic peace—rising China and declining Russia—exhibited little interest in an alliance, seemingly convinced of the pointlessness of security competition with the great enforcer of Open Door capitalism.

On the peripheries of this volatile circuitry of market forces, tightened neoliberal conditions of access to Western investment, aid and moral legitimation resulted in a far-reaching attenuation of the sovereignty of weak and failing states. Washington's initiatives against small rogue regimes in the name of human rights and WMD interdiction appeared to have consigned to the past traditional statecraft based on great power rivalries. The new strategic doctrines authorizing US and Western interventions in violation of the UN Charter derived their legitimacy from a vague but widely held assumption that the period was a transitional state of exception laying down the foundations of an international community to come. This assumption offered some consolation to liberals on both sides of the Atlantic, who rapidly embraced an airbrushed version of it as the credo of a new cosmopolitanism.

The scrambling of this picture in the aftermath of 9/11 has created a historical context whose elements have yet to settle into an intelligible pattern. In trying to determine whether 9/11 signals the beginning of a new era of international politics, it is necessary to begin by asking whether the aggressive 'unilateralism' of the US response to this event has been an atavistic regression from previously more 'multilateral' norms of neoliberalism, or, alternatively, their continuation by other means. It is here that the Retort group's striking recent intervention, *Afflicted Powers*, poses a series of fundamental questions.[1] This is an intricate piece

---

1   Retort [Iain Boal, T. J. Clark, Joseph Matthews, Michael Watts], *Afflicted Powers: Capital and Spectacle in a New Age of War*, London: Verso, 2005; hereafter *AP*. This chapter originally appeared in *New Left Review* 2: 36, November–December 2005.

of work, interconnecting the three constituents of its subtitle—capital, spectacle and war—at a remarkable level of imaginative intensity. In what follows, I will consider the principal themes of the book in turn, and end by offering some reflections of my own on certain of the wider issues it raises.

Primitive accumulation?

Afflicted Powers sets out, in the first instance, to examine the adequacy of certain Marxist concepts to the current geopolitical situation and ask if this can be made more intelligible by locating it within the historical pattern of capitalist development. One of the keys to understanding the sudden darkening of the horizon, its authors maintain, is Marx's conception of 'primitive accumulation'—the earth-shaking use of force to create or restore the social conditions of profitability. In the tradition of historical materialism, the periodization of eras in the history of capitalism has typically involved controversial narrative conjunctions of political and economic developments. Lenin's explanation for the outbreak of an inter-imperialist world war as an effect of the passage from free-market to monopoly capitalism is a famous example. The attempt to do this today puts into question the ability of the term 'liberal-democracy' to capture the latest, emergent features of advanced capitalist polities: indeed, not so long after it had been declared to be the culminating point of history, Philip Bobbitt went so far as to argue that the convergence of powerful trends in markets, media and warfare was spawning a new type of polity in the West. For Bobbitt, the line of historical development points to a national security regime committed to market freedoms, pre-emptive strikes against human rights violators and unauthorized WMD holders, and stage-managed televisual plebiscites.[2]

---

2   *SA*; for reflections on this ambitious work, see my 'Algorithms of War', *New Left Review* 2: 23, September–October 2003, pp. 5–33.

By contrast, Retort's analysis attempts to offer an explanation of the continuities of American foreign policy in terms of the general logic of capitalism, without reference to the structure and history of the capitalist, or more specifically, the American state. *Afflicted Powers* presents post–9/11 American 'unilateralism' as a response to the sputtering out of the first round of neoliberalism with the end of the stock market bubble and its boom of the nineties. But the story its authors tell by and large avoids any emphasis on the crisis dynamics of capitalism and the distinct periods to which these can be said to give rise. That, they dismiss as the outmoded preoccupations of an older generation. This is a more than questionable judgment, as even a cursory familiarity with the contents of a business magazine would demonstrate. Economics to one side, however, they cannily put their finger on a sudden change in the realm of appearances. In but a few years, the figures typifying contemporary capitalism have shifted from silicon to oil, guns and steel. This is happening, they claim, because neoliberalism is 'mutating from an epoch of "agreements" and austerity programmes to one of outright war . . . those periodic waves of capitalist restructuring we call primitive accumulation'.[3] This conception of the role of force in jump-starting and lubricating accumulation comes from Rosa Luxemburg, although the name goes unmentioned. In effect, Retort wholly subscribe to Luxemburg's definition of imperialism as 'the political expression of the accumulation of capital in its competitive struggle for what remains still open of the non-capitalist environment'.[4] For them, this is no demarcated stage, but a continuous process in history since the dawn of capitalism. 'Sweating blood and filth with every pore from head to toe' characterizes not only the birth of capital but also its progress in the world at every step.[5]

3 *AP*, p. 52.
4 Rosa Luxemburg, *The Accumulation of Capital*, London: Routledge, 1951, p. 453.
5 Ibid., p. 446.

Retort give this Luxemburg-derived account a further, Polanyian twist: the violence that marks the history of capitalism has typically taken the form of coercive enclosure of 'the commons'—i.e. the appropriation of myriad forms of common wealth embedded in the non-market environment upon which capitalism feeds. This claim is a striking example of a near-universal tendency on the part of Marxists to understand the relationship between capitalism and war in terms of a systematic logic. I will question the degree to which capitalism has a geopolitical logic at all. In evaluating the plausibility of Retort's argument—or alternative accounts which make this same assumption—three signal contemporary developments need to be borne in mind. There has been a quarter-century of protracted structural adjustment whose main indices are wage stagnation, heightened job insecurity, speed-up and lengthening of work hours, burgeoning debt service, and levels of inequality not seen since the 1920s. Accompanying it has been a major internal expansion of markets through privatizations over the same period. In the last fifteen years, there has been a huge external expansion of capitalism, with the collapse of the Soviet bloc, and the more or less complete incorporation of China into the world market.

The key question in any assessment of the central thesis of *Afflicted Powers* is that of the role, if any, that politico-military coercion played in enforcing this wide-ranging transformation at the expense of labour and other strata, on the one hand, and opening up and determining the conditions of access to new areas of capital development, on the other. Scepticism is appropriate here. Firstly, most of this domestic restructuring of society for the benefit of investors, owners and rentiers has unfolded from the early eighties without any significant bouts of organized violence from above—certainly when measured against comparable periods in the past when police, Pinkertons and fascist squads were crucial agencies of labour discipline. Secondly, unlike conditions in the era of colonialism, the semi- and non-capitalist environment is now organized on a nation-state basis that impedes the open use of military coercion to acquire or retain spheres of influence. It seems rather unlikely that the new round of imperial wars and occupations is securing the conditions for the ongoing expansion of capitalism, as they claim. In practice, *Afflicted Powers* itself shows some uncertainty here, oscillating between depictions of military force as a way of breaking down barriers standing in the way of the expansion of neoliberalism, and characterizations of it as a product of ideological fixations and delusions peculiar to an impasse of neoliberalism.

The particularity of the United States

In attempting to theorize the relationship between capitalism and military power, Retort equates the US with 'the state' generically conceived, without regard to the sui generis character of the former. Carl Schmitt argued, by contrast, that the extension of America's manifest destiny from the Western hemisphere into the Old World was transforming the geo-spatial order of territorial statehood, altering the very meaning of the terms 'sovereignty', 'war' and 'international law'.[6] The entry of the US into the Eurocentric old regime of sovereign states was accelerating the erosion of its classical norms of war and diplomacy. The *jus publicum europaeum*, he argued, was a concrete diplomatic order in which war was a legitimate instrument of settlement between fully sovereign states able to measure each other's relative power positions in a geopolitical environment structured by the homogeneity of state forms and aims. But once a field of relatively homogeneous rival powers vanishes, the very meaning of balancing becomes problematic, while the theories based on this assumption become correspondingly less realistic. Confirming this assessment, the final destruction of Axis empires

---

6   See, in particular, *Völkerrechtliche Grossraumordnung, mit Interventionsverbot für raumfremde Mächte*, Berlin and Vienna: Duncker & Humblot, 1939.

at the opposite ends of Eurasia did in fact result in a far-reaching reconstruction of the inter-state matrix of the core capitalist zone, precluding any restoration of a traditional system of separate regions and balances.[7]

But the consequences of this radical departure from the security concepts of an older world of war and diplomacy were not entirely apparent during the Cold War, because superpower rivalry, based on a rough symmetry between the main contenders, imposed an overarching bi-polar logic onto the political, military and ideological heterogeneity of a vastly expanded state system. Arguably, the specificity of the US relationship to the inter-state order became evident in the aftermath of the Cold War, when American strategic planners scotched any talk of returning to the Western hemisphere after their victory over the last great contender for Eurasian hegemony.[8] The narrower security concepts of *Realpolitik* cannot explain the historical pattern of this transformative and expansionary agenda. The attempt to account for the change was the rational kernel of Hardt and Negri's conception of Empire as an open polity transcending the coordinates of closed sovereign states. It could be said that the US differs from other states, because it is the paradigmatic capitalist regime, geared, like the system it promotes, for unlimited

---

7   Peter Gowan, 'A Calculus of Power', *New Left Review* 2: 16, July–August 2002, p. 64.

8   John Mearsheimer, *The Tragedy of Great Power Politics*, New York: W. W. Norton, 2001, p. 34. The great merit of Mearsheimer's conception of realism is that it provides a framework for analysing the strategic logic of high-risk Great Power geopolitics. The anomalies that its basic assumptions generate when applied to contemporary US foreign policy are therefore especially noteworthy, as they point to a crisis in the realist problematic itself. While the author of this theory of 'offensive realism' has no trouble reconstructing, in these terms, the strategic calculations that went into the enormously risky Japanese decision to bomb Pearl Harbor, his assessment of the post–Cold War scene often falters: while the theory predicts that underdog powers will take a chance to enhance their security through bold aggression, it follows that the most powerful—thus most secure—state in the world should stick to the status quo.

expansion. In contrast to the authors of *Empire*, the Retort collective seems more cognizant of the fact that the American Republic is still very much a particular state, vigilantly pursuing its particular strategic interests, while articulating these interests within a wider project of universalizing capitalism by enabling regime changes, from gunboat and dollar diplomacy to shock therapy in both core and periphery. 'Each military intervention is intended to serve an overall strategic project of pressing American power—and the potential for Western capital entrenchment in "emerging markets"—ever further into vital regions of the globe.'[9] Although *Afflicted Powers* pays little attention to the structure of the inter-state system, its general line of argument allows for an explanation of why the latter has undergone a series of substantive transformations even as the nominal form of an older sovereignty principle has been preserved and generalized.

No blood for oil?

Retort's principal concerns, however, lie elsewhere. Their objective is to address the limitations of the slogans and analyses offered by today's anti-war movement. A focus on the Middle East logically follows. The notion that some combination of Oil, Israel and Islam defines the specificity of the region and the US relation to it is not uncommon, and much of *Afflicted Powers* is an attempt to disentangle and weigh the various elements of this series. In a wider context, of course, what distinguishes this zone is its partial insulation from post–Cold War trends that have everywhere else resulted in neoliberal structural adjustment and corresponding regime changes. To date, its old guard of family rulers and police states has without exception held on to power. In terms of its intended regional effect, the invasion of Iraq was supposed to be a step towards abolishing this anomaly—suddenly less tolerable

9   *AP*, p. 81.

after the attentats of 9/11—with a dramatic nation-building experiment. Victory over the Baath regime was intended to send a powerful signal to the Arab elites of the need for a modest dose of *perestroika*, and to the Arab masses of American invincibility and Israel's status as an untouchable beachhead of the new regional order. But this course of action was also meant to have a global demonstration effect as the first clear test of the legitimacy of preventive war and regime change as a strategic-legal norm of the New American Century. This should be near the centre of any account of what Retort call 'the contradictions of military neoliberalism under conditions of spectacle'.[10]

Oil is a focus of much of the commentary on the origins of this war. For the anti-war movement, indeed, it has seemed an overwhelmingly obvious explanation of it, from start to finish. And how can its significance be denied, given that the organizers of this enterprise and their well-wishers in the strategic community often met such charges with an unruffled 'so what?' Yes, they said, we need to pry the oilfields out of the hands of Saddam and his henchmen so they can't wreak more destruction. Such candour was no doubt unsettling for those who assumed that the sordid truth had to lie deeper below the surface. Indeed, those who seek to explain the invasion and occupation of Iraq in terms of oil interests are presented with an embarrassment of riches: the unprecedented ties of both the first- and second-in-command to the petro-industrial complex; a fire sale of crony capitalist development contracts; hostile takeovers of French and Russian agreements by Anglo-American super-majors; installation of a pliable swing producer to diminish dependency on the House of Saud; oil leverage over other capitalist centres; and the clinching of the status of petrol as a dollar-denominated store of value.

What is the position of *Afflicted Powers* on all this? Retort argue that while the future of capitalism still depends on the control of

---

10   *AP*, p. 15.

a few strategic resources, the No Blood for Oil argument fails to penetrate the enigmatic core of fossil fuel capitalism, falling back on populist stereotypes of scams and lobbies. Their purpose is not to deny the abundant evidence for the existence of the latter, but to provide an account of the wider context in which the profits of the American oil industry could possess a significance for US policy in the region far beyond what the share of this sector in the national economy would suggest they should have. For the first question that must be asked when constructing a more plausible explanation of the role of oil interests in the calculation of US policy, is how American super-majors could ever be powerful enough to drive up the price of crude when they do not control supply, and higher prices must be borne not just by consumers but by all other firms—an aggregate incomparably larger than Big Oil.

Is there any way to explain why one economic sector might exercise an influence on American policy in the Middle East vastly disproportionate to its actual size, yet cannot exercise this power to achieve any sustainable 'price leadership'? *Afflicted Powers* makes a commendable effort to do precisely this by developing an alternative to what can be regarded as the most sophisticated attempt to present oil—not just as an industry, but as a strategic use-value whose supply is bound up with the future of the capitalist system—as the main motivation for regime change in Iraq. According to this view, the invasion's principal aim was to secure the reserves of Iraq in anticipation of a coming peak—the so-called Hubbert's Peak—in world oil production, after which a rapid depletion of regional fields will set in. Underlying the claim is a Malthusian anticipation of imminent scarcity. What the various End of Oil prophecies that have circulated since the seventies ignore, however, is the periodic recurrence of the opposite danger—glut and falling prices. Such interpretations also fail to address the ongoing investment in hitherto inaccessible fields from Alberta to the Bight of Benin. These developments, Retort argue, must postpone the moment of peak production into a future too distant for markets and regimes to compute. In any event, they point out that natural gas is the future of the industry and its geography lies largely outside the Middle East.

Weapons and wells

Malthusian assumptions, moreover, cannot explain the half-century pattern of a very gradual long-term rise in the price of oil, with fluctuations cutting against the trend in response to real, anticipated and imagined political turbulence. In Retort's view, the determinants of these fluctuations and their distributional consequences are the real story that needs to be uncovered and theorized. *Afflicted Powers* offers an overview of the history of empires, regional state formation and the scramble to control and manipulate the most lucrative nodal points in the extraction and distribution of petroleum, in order to frame a new understanding of these determinants and consequences. The story begins in the early years of the last century, with a semi-colonial patchwork of weak dynastic entities propped up as cover for massive concessions to Western oil consortiums. Iraq was forged as an artefact of such oil politics. The League of Nations Mandate to Britain required it to perform cosmetic nation-building tasks and share the loot with French and American oil companies. A client monarchy and rigged elections provided the requisite façade of semi-statehood. By the 1930s the Big Three controlled 70 per cent of world oil output, and American investment in the region's fields was increasing rapidly.

In a second phase, nationalist regimes began to take over these semi-colonial concessions and extra-territorial corporate fiefdoms, a development associated with the names of Mossadegh in Iran and Qasim in Iraq. American and European oil companies were relegated to the sphere of distribution, where they by and large remain to this day. us administrations learned to live with this new state of affairs as the price of oil smoothly adjusted to the growth of demand in Western economies. Despite the formation of OPEC in the early sixties, technological development steadily brought down its real price over this entire period. The Yom Kippur War of 1973 led to a brief second wave of Arab nationalism resulting in an oil embargo against the US. While the ensuing price spike stoked inflation in the world economy, most of these surpluses ended up being recycled by low absorbers (the Gulf dynasties with little interest in using oil revenues to build up national power) back into US banks, and by both high and low absorbers into the profit margins of weapons manufacturers around the world. The balancing act that took shape in the eighties between Western economic growth, oil company profits, and high absorbers (states like Iran and Iraq) was more or less satisfactory to all the major parties. When periodic breakdown occurred, the US intervened decisively to hold the centre—an elusive equilibrium price—against potential turbulence. The geopolitical determinants of price movements in this period were the Iranian Revolution and its containment, the Iraqi invasion of Kuwait and the Gulf War, the establishment and decay of the sanctions regime and, more speculatively, storms on the horizon in Saudi Arabia. But by the end of the nineties regional tensions seemed to be declining, and this, combined with the deflation of the stock-market bubble in the US, led to glut and plummeting prices for the super-majors.

Such was one of the contexts, Retort contends, in which a high-risk regime change in Iraq—one of the pipedreams of right-wing strategic planners in the nineties—began to seem an attractive prospect for many inside the industry, as well as for policy circles who tend to identify its interests with those of the US *tout court*. Before the grim realities of the occupation set in, there was much bold talk in Washington about American proconsuls imposing a neoliberal revolution from above, with the privatization of Iraq's nationalized oil assets first on the agenda. The oil industries of the 'developing world' had been tenaciously resistant to privatization, but with an Iraqi client installed in OPEC, optimists foresaw the beginning of the liquidation of these last holdouts of statism. Neo-conservative ideologues announced that this was the first step in a wider structural adjustment to the norms and even the way of life of the new American century.

The lesson of Retort's narrative seems to be that while Big Oil is central to the explanation of the invasion and occupation of Iraq, the No Blood for Oil argument is a misunderstanding of the force field of world demand, war and speculation in which fluctuations in the price level of this commodity turn out to abound in geopolitical subtleties. The alternative offered by *Afflicted Powers* develops out of various qualifications to the thesis proposed by two Israeli scholars that links the political economy of oil to that of the weapons trade—a connection that these writers, focusing on the way OPEC oil revenues created the market for a massive expansion of the private arms industry in the US, call the Weapondollar–Petrodollar Coalition.[11] After the sixties, so this argument runs, the US shifted from the provision of weapons to clients in the form of aid to the promotion of a private arms trade; since then the OPEC share of world market demand for arms has risen from 9 to 36 per cent. For the Retort collective, however, this is only one segment of a larger circuit connecting oil to engineering, construction, financial services and hedge funds. This vast regional and offshore vortex draws into it bountiful underworld streams of laundered and drug money, consisting, they suggest, of 'trillions of dollars' of speculative hot money, although they concede that such estimates are little more than guesses. In this combustible field, the objective of US planners is to ensure, against all hazards, that it is their priorities that supervene on the logic of supply and demand. Nitzan and Bichler go so far as to claim that, by ratcheting up regional instability, American interventions have had the intended effect of staving off collapsing petrol prices, and enriching the beneficiaries

---

11   See Jonathan Nitzan and Shimshon Bichler, *The Global Political Economy of Israel*, London: Pluto Press, 2002.

of oil price inflation. For the authors of *Afflicted Powers*, this is to simplify a far more opaque picture. But although they write as if—after criticizing and qualifying the alternatives—they are going to provide a more adequate account, they ultimately fail to do so. Perhaps, however, this very failure to reconstruct the geo-economic constellation they scan into a causal pattern is a way of bringing home an earlier claim that the contemporary conjunction of capitalism, war and the spectacle is dissolving the intelligible field of strategies.

Images of Israel

In their genealogy of the current disaster in the Middle East, Retort address a directly related case in which the norms of realist statecraft have also seemingly broken down. Why has American support for Israel shot up in a period in which the Zionist state has become a major liability in terms both of its regional strategic interests and its hegemonic credibility? It is easy to forget that this most special of all special relationships came into existence in stages. Although Washington had initially been cool to Israel's debut as a regional power, by the late fifties the rising fortunes of radical Arab nationalism brought about a reassessment of Israel's role as a deterrent against potential threats to American oil interests. The US stake in a Jewish bulwark in the region grew steadily after the IDF overwhelmed Arab armies in 1967. Israel—alongside Pahlavi Iran—was rapidly fortified as a sub-imperial guardian holding the balance against the Soviet-equipped Arab armies of Egypt, Syria and Iraq. From the early eighties onwards, however, the fit between Israeli and US objectives in the region began to loosen. Yet Washington's commitment to Jerusalem has become increasingly unconditional.

The explanation of this anomaly offered by *Afflicted Powers* nimbly side-steps what is often thought to be the most obvious explanation: the influence of the Israeli lobby, strengthened by an emerging alliance with the Christian right, within the United States. Without wholly denying it, Retort claim that this development needs to be situated in the logic of the media sphere. For in their eyes it is less Israel itself, than Israel transfigured by the magic of the spectacle into an ideological totem of American identity, that has become the tail wagging the dog. The problem here is just what constitutes the *pays idéel* of Zionism in this imaginary. Retort argue that while 'modern states are often slower to fall prey to a set of spectacular illusions and compulsions than the other sectors of societies they govern',[12] once fixated on a mythological image of their identity, they often become incapable of pulling back to a colder assessment of their interests. While suggestive, their account remains itself captive to the TV screens whose effects they seek to lay bare, as if the only perspective on the ideological dimensions of this conflict is from the couch. The ideological mould of US–Israeli relations cannot be completely reduced to the surface images of beleaguered citizens and brave soldiers confronting terrorists, and the occasional bad apples in the midst of so much everyday heroism. There is more to the ideological development that determines this imagery than that.

For the moral authority that the US claims for itself—over and above its role in promoting markets and democracy—has increasingly come to rest on its identity as the modern defender of the Jewish people. Any perusal of the journals that educated Americans read demonstrates the centrality of this historical mission in the contemporary imaginary of the country. Putting aside the truth of the claim, its expansion as a discourse has been striking. Figuring retrospectively as a rationale for America's battle against the Third Reich, from the seventies onwards it became a powerful thrust in the propaganda war against the USSR, while at the same time underscoring the need to batten down Arab nationalism, as an emblem of all the dangers surging within the Third World. More recently, if there has been some decline (not much) in the popularity of the Jewish state elsewhere in the West, this has if anything enhanced its attractiveness for those Americans

12 *AP*, p. 122.

who don't think much of foreigners anyhow. Within the country, of course, the topic of Israel has long become a criterion for dividing legitimate from illegitimate voices in the great American political conversation.

In the view of *Afflicted Powers*, Israel's time in the sun of the spectacle is coming to an end. Older images of Israel as a pioneering progressive beachhead of the West, it contends, have given way over the last twenty years to the now familiar scenery of a colonial disaster zone. This claim reads more like—rather desperate?—self-reassurance than a sober description of the prevailing image of the 'only democracy in the Middle East' and the bedrock public support it commands, in Europe as much as in the United States. But even if—all diplomatic evidence to the contrary, from Paris through Karachi to Beijing—its international legitimacy were devalued, what would this imply for the future political trajectory of Zionism? Here Retort neglect to contemplate what might be a disturbing corollary of their more general thesis on war and the spectacle. For Israel is perhaps the only state in the world that closely approximates to their conception of a military capitalism. It is also a land where not a few continue to believe that another regional war might provide them with the main chance, messianically conceived.

A revolutionary Islam?

Reflections on the history of radical Islam round out Retort's portrait of the colonial battlefields of the world system. Remarking that while the anti-war Left has emphasized the role of oil in the political economy of Empire, it has neglected to address the nature of its most conspicuous antagonist; they maintain that an adequate response to the geopolitical moment that begins with 9/11 requires a gauge of the stakes of the battle between America and jihad. While some have seen in 'the War on Terror' merely a pretext for pushing through a second installment of the Reagan Revolution, *Afflicted Powers* argues that the new Islamic vanguards have, in fact, shaken Empire in the realm of image power, provoking it to reckless overreach. Given Retort's intellectual debt to Guy Debord, this might at first seem like a startling claim. For Debord did not take terrorism very seriously at all, and his judgment of its effects was wholly deflationary: 'This perfect democracy fabricates its own inconceivable enemy, terrorism. *It wants, actually, to be judged by its enemies rather than by its results.*'[13] This verdict has more than a semblance of plausibility. Compare it to the claim made by *Afflicted Powers*, that Islamic fundamentalism is 'something like a mass movement with a nearly unlimited pool of potential operatives'. Islamists, in the eyes of Retort, have 'a political project that is global in reach and ambition, anti-imperialist and . . . revolutionary in practice'.[14]

But here too fixation on the televisual screen of the social world can be deceptive, as the distinction between reality and appearance is, in this case, belied by the very phenomenon itself. Do militant Islamic cells form an elusive mobile network, ready to strike at any moment the bourses and theme parks of the Abode of War? Or are they a tiny fringe, stranded on the edges of a sea that is everywhere drying up? Looking at their numbers and prospects for coming to state power, it seems clear—at least until Iraq changed the picture—that the latter is much closer to the mark. But it is in the very nature of this war that a bombing anywhere in the world seems to verify, on the screens that both Westerners and Muslims watch, the existence of a vast, many-headed foe. Yet in this age of the so-called multitude, what is striking is the fellah-like passivity of the Arab masses, even as they daily watch, enraged, images of the battlefields of Palestine and Iraq. The Arab street has so far remained impotent. Whether more people than ever are watching Al Jazeera or are in chat rooms does not change the fact that they, like their counterparts in the West, are spectators in this mother of all asymmetrical wars.

---

13 Guy Debord, *Comments on the Society of the Spectacle*, London: Verso, 1990, p. 24.
14 *AP*, pp. 137–8.

Counter-modernities

Afflicted Powers offers an account of the history of Islamic
fundamentalism that culminates in provocative reflections on the
problem of a radical political subjectivity today. Fundamentalism
began as a current within a wider modernizing movement seeking
to revitalize the Islamic world in the era of colonialism. Retort's
identification of Islamic fundamentalism with modernity—more
precisely counter-modernity—is based on their interpretation
of the significance of Sayyid Qutb, the intellectual fountainhead
of revolutionary Islamic politics. The radicalism of this figure is
indeed remarkable, his œuvre distinguished by a severe rejection
of scriptural exegesis in favour of an Islamic identity theory
garnished with references to sundry texts from the annals of
political Romanticism. Although Retort point out that Qutb's
influence cut across the Sunni–Shia divide, and was a significant
ingredient in the cocktail of ideas that flowed into the political
theologies of the Iranian revolution, it is the Sunni sector of the
Islamist phenomenon that informs their generalizations, which
demand that we reconsider the meaning of modernity in light of
the ongoing war of the spectacle between America and its Islamic
nemesis. Here their argument takes an unexpected turn. For little
in the preceding discussion prepares the reader for the ensuing
claim: namely, that modernity is always stalked by its radical
brother, a counter-modern vanguard that Retort polemically trace
from Lenin to Bin Laden. Fifteen years after the former's statues
were toppled, *Afflicted Powers* asks the improbable question: 'why
does Leninism never die?'[15] For an answer, it turns to Nietzsche's
reflections on the persistence of the ascetic ideal.

There are two obvious objections, however, to this injunction
to understand Al-Qaeda in the light of *What is to be Done?* Firstly,
anarchism is far more a part of the history of 'terrorism' than

---

15   *AP*, p. 172.

Leninism, a fact that should have prompted more circumspection. Secondly, the claim that the 'ideal makes more converts, not less, as modernity lives on', seems to cross the line separating paradox from absurdity.[16] The point could be put more reasonably, perhaps, as follows. World-historically speaking, Bolshevism presented itself as the concrete negation of bourgeois society, an assessment that was shared by its adversary. Those who seek to fill the void left behind by the departure of this tradition will be drawn inexorably to a comparable form of ascesis. The militant figure envisaged by Qutb in his *Signposts Along the Road* bears more than a passing resemblance to an unacknowledged Russian model:

> How to initiate the revival of Islam? A vanguard must set out with this determination and then keep going, marching through the vast ocean of jahiliya [the state of ignorance preceding and surrounding Islam] which encompasses the entire world . . . The Muslims in this vanguard must know the landmarks and the signposts on the road to this goal . . . they ought to be aware of their position vis-à-vis this jahiliya which has struck its stakes throughout the earth.[17]

Compare this with the spirit and details of the following passage from *What Is to Be Done?*:

> We are marching in a compact group along a precipitous and difficult path, firmly holding each other by the hand. We are surrounded on all sides by enemies, and we have to advance almost constantly under their fire. We have combined, by a freely adopted decision, for the purpose of fighting the enemy, and not of retreating into the neighbouring marsh, the inhabitants of which, from the very outset, have reproached us with

16   *AP*, p. 184.
17   Sayyid Qutb, *Ma'alim fil-Tariq* [Signposts Along the Road] (1964), as cited in *AP*, p. 132.

having separated ourselves into an exclusive group and with having chosen the path of struggle instead of the path of conciliation.[18]

The historical meaning of this affinity—if that is what it is—cannot be deciphered without a more discriminating account of the contemporary landscape. For one of the distinguishing features of this is surely the neutralization of whatever was signified by the term Leninism. It is true that some of the affects of the Cold War animate the horror of the postmodern West before the figure of the suicide bomber, whose deed, it is thought, is akin to pronouncements of nihilism from the time of *The Possessed*. For while killing people from afar is at least understandable, killing oneself for a cause has ceased to be. In suggesting that the strength of this militant ideal stems from an understandable aesthetic horror before the spiritual wastelands of the Last Man, set against the backdrop of a planet of slums, do the writers of Retort reveal the nerve centre of their own opposition to military neoliberalism in the age of the spectacle? Such a deduction would be implausible, given their critical conception of such radical subjectivity as a form of revolutionary romanticism. They imply that there is an easy slide from this stance to Bolshevism, or now radical Islam. Accordingly the task of the day is to articulate 'a non-nostalgic . . . non-fundamental, non-apocalyptic critique of the modern'.[19]

But it is not easy to know how to interpret this commendable sentiment when we are told that 'we have rarely been closer to hell on earth.'[20] The valences of Retort's prose pass from starkly aphoristic depictions of a world at war to a surprisingly bland indictment of the spectacle, taxing commodity aesthetics and consumerism with 'suppressing social energies'. The radical political negativity of *Afflicted Powers* is at odds with this muffled *Kulturkritik*. Alain Badiou offers a more judicious formulation of the problem when he writes: 'there is

---

18   Vladimir Ilich Lenin, *What Is to Be Done?*, Peking: Foreign Language Press, 1975, p. 10.
19   *AP*, p. 185.
20   *AP*, p. 175.

currently a widespread search for a new militant figure—even if it takes the form of denying its possibility—called upon to succeed the one installed by Lenin and the Bolsheviks at the beginning of the century, which can be said to be that of the party militant.'[21] This succinctly captures the relationship between the conditions of radical subjectivity and its activation in new forms of collective organization. But certainly, such a way of conceiving the contemporary historical situation will not appear convincing to those who want to banish this legacy from the 'movement of movements'. The title of *Afflicted Powers* is an allusion to deliberations among the defeated rebels of *Paradise Lost*. The identification of the radical position with the overthrown Satan and his lieutenants is a motif of the experience of defeat from Milton to Bakunin. But Retort side-step the question of who really are the defeated that can experience and think through the depths of this position today. The attempt to put the names Seattle, Genoa and Chiapas into this slot rings hollow. The career of Guy Debord was a failed attempt to articulate a politics adequate to the austere severity of his diagnosis of the time. But his is a legacy that deserves its own *What is to be Done?*

The permeation of the spectacular

Afflicted Powers appeals throughout, not uncritically, to Debord's category of the spectacle. In its telling, the attacks of 9/11 were a highly effective blow to the American imperium at the level where it has become most vulnerable—the spectacular. But although the book has many acute or tantalizing things to say about the workings of the spectacle today, these are never brought into full focus. Explanations of the current scene in terms of primitive accumulation and of the spectacle are juxtaposed more than integrated, leaving the obvious theoretical tensions between the two unresolved. Yet Debord's conceptualization has wide

21   Alain Badiou, *Saint Paul: The Foundation of Universalism*, Stanford: Stanford University Press, 2003, p. 2.

implications for the field of contemporary politics, national and international.

One of the more striking indices of the contemporary power of the spectacle—the symbiosis of competing market and media forces that drives the machinery of contemporary public opinion—has been the emergence of the contemporary equivalents of great men at the helm of business and state. The spectacle typically credits these figures—a president, a finance minister, most of all a central banker—with magical powers to preserve and create values, despite all evidence to the contrary, only to deflate their reputations not long afterwards. Just as an entrepreneur passes from CEO of the month one year and into jail the next, in the aftermath of 9/11 the simulacrum of public opinion has conferred statesman-like qualities on certain leaders, as if to goad them on to disaster. The strategic direction of state power in the geopolitical arena is becoming increasingly subject to the performance criteria of a televisual construction of social reality. The flitting screens of this pseudo-world have become the more or less exclusive focal points of the experience of social reality, and not just within the most ill-informed strata of American consumers. The logic of teleprompt governance has made significant inroads into the previously more hard-headed worlds of business and foreign affairs.

Meanwhile the lifeworld is colonized by an unstoppable barrage of polls, talking heads, panics and cloying human interest dramas, in which the experience of history collapses into an eternal present.[22] For Debord the impact of this new mode of social domination is to precipitate 'a general shift from having to appearing—all "having" must now derive its immediate prestige and its ultimate purpose from appearances'.[23] The spectacle, in this view, sets into motion a struggle for mastery

22   *AP*, p. 21.
23   Guy Debord, *Society of the Spectacle*, Detroit: Black & Red, 1970, Chapter 1, p. xvii.

in the realm of the image. What is the specificity of this domain as a strategic field? 'Just as the logic of the commodity reigns over the capitalists' competing ambitions, or the logic of war always dominates the frequent modifications of weaponry, so the harsh logic of the spectacle controls the abundant diversity of media extravagances.'[24] The sequence of commodity–weapon–spectacle appears in this passage as the integrated moments of a new social logic of domination. But Debord also considered the possibility that the waning of any collective experience of history might have punishing consequences for the stage managers of this new order themselves. The spectacular mediation of the political sphere has resulted in the partial de-realization of what once could be called 'objective' strategic interests. 'Once the running of the state involves a permanent and massive shortage of historical knowledge, the state can no longer be led strategically.'[25]

But while the mediatization of politics has been effective in subjecting public opinion to the verdicts of the market, it has simultaneously erected barriers to the enterprise of empire-building. Contemporary enthusiasts for imperial Rome or Britain lament the sensitivities of a population that cannot stomach a few thousand American casualties for such a good cause. A major, probably irreversible, sociological transformation of baby-boom capitalism is at work here. The plebeians refuse to die in wars, the rich refuse to pay for them. The spectacle has resulted not only in weak citizenship at the bottom, but also faulty intelligence at the top. With an eye on the mounting chaos in occupied Iraq, it is not difficult to conclude that the Republican administration's attempt at grand strategy is now heading for the shoals. 'The dimension of spectacle has never before interfered so palpably, so insistently, with the business of keeping one's satrapies in order.'[26]

---

24 Debord, *Comments on the Society of the Spectacle*, p. 7.
25 Ibid., p. 20.
26 *AP*, p. 37.

War and capitalism

Afflicted Powers treats the United States and the contemporary universe of capital as if, politically speaking, they were one. No other state, save Israel, is accorded significant attention. How plausible an assumption is this, even for polemical purposes? Historically, the relationship between geopolitical rivalry and the global pattern of capitalist development raises a number of extremely difficult theoretical problems. For the experience of successive eras appears to differ fundamentally. In one period, structural adjustment and integration into the world market promoted a relaxation of international tensions in the core; in another, they led to a vertiginous escalation of great power rivalries; while through both, colonial conquest and tribute generated many a heart of darkness on the non-capitalist peripheries of this expansionary civilization. Is there any general relationship between war and capitalism at all, or can there only be theories of specific conjunctures? Even if the latter is more likely, it remains true that it is the evolution of capitalism alone that provides a long-term developmental account of the successive socio-economic transformations that determine the relative wealth of nations, and the field of selection in which different strategies of state formation, including ones based on the attempted suppression of capitalism, come to be tested.

Capitalism arises out of an 'original' separation of the means of coercion from the social relations of production and exchange, which alters the relationship between the internal and external fields of the state apparatus, as war and diplomacy cease to be a continuation by other means of the predatory extraction of surpluses from subject peasants and townsmen. Retort's claim that 'war is modernity incarnate' fails to capture the consequences of this both categorical and real separation of the political from the economic and its materialization in a new relationship between the internal and outer fields of the political. Although the emergence of a specialized, outwardly directed apparatus of statecraft is a development that long precedes the advent of capitalism, the formation of the modern capitalist state generates a novel structural problem for such war machines. Since war and diplomacy are no longer aligned to a logic of appropriating surpluses through conquest and tribute, the pay-off for the enormously costly business of amassing geopolitical power not infrequently becomes objectively indeterminable as a means of achieving security, or any other aim.

'Anarchy' as defined by the realist school of international relations means that if even one state chooses to pursue its aims with force, all others will be compelled to do likewise. But the escalation of hostilities within this emergent field can result in an unpredictable transformation of the goals and strategic interests of each state, radically altering the way they might otherwise have articulated these. Machiavelli noted this, observing that some states are open to such modification in the process of escalation, while others try to neutralize it 'constitutionally'.[27] Famously, in the first half of the twentieth century, the test of total mobilization for war led to a transformation of certain states so radical that the classical bourgeois structure of state–society relations mutated into a fundamentally different one, that no one had planned or even anticipated. To varying degrees, all the principal antagonists of these wars of planetary re-division underwent such changes, the Nazi regime furnishing the most explosive and ultimately self-destructive example of this flight forward. The geopolitical field in which states are exposed to this dialectical transformation of their interests is to be distinguished, of course, from those more neutralized regions and dimensions of the inter-state system where the dynamics of competitive mobilization and counter-mobilization are kept within bounds. But there is no sharp dividing-line separating the most acutely rivalrous from the somewhat more

27 Niccolo Machiavelli, *Discourses on Livy*, Chicago: University of Chicago Press, 1996, pp. 135–38.

pacified zones of the inter-state system, where rulers are in some measure insulated from the harsh and volatile criterion of relative power—i.e. winner–loser strategic situations. The key question concerns the historic relationship between the more open, dynamic and dangerous field of inter-state competition and the long-term pattern of capitalist development. In particular: does this point to the conclusion that the Great Game must eventually come to an end?

For the combined and uneven development of capitalism within the matrix of an older inter-state order has had a fundamentally different impact on the internal and external fields of what Weber called the territorial monopoly of violence. The contrast is essentially this. If the domestic organization of public power has been subject to the ongoing imperative of creating a socially acceptable environment for capital accumulation, the alignment of statecraft to the pursuit of external conditions for accumulation has been a far less systematic process, one typically over-determined by episodic compulsions of inter-state competition for highly variable security goals.[28] The distinct performance criteria at work in its domestic, as opposed to geopolitical, fields of operation constitutes a duality at the heart of the modern capitalist state that is inherently difficult to manage—particularly if the state in question is a 'Great Power' striving for a place in the sun. For the pattern of state formation that began in the nineteenth century in response to the discipline of emerging market norms led to a comprehensive internal domestication of political violence, but did not bring about a comparable reorganization of the relations between states of the sort envisaged by Kant on the eve of this great transformation. While the vectors of world capitalism seem to point to the eventual withering away of a rivalrous pluriverse of sovereign powers—since head-to-head war in its core regions threatens the very existence of the system—globally speaking, this trend has manifested itself only erratically.

---

28   Michael Mann, *States, War and Capitalism: Studies in Political Sociology*, Oxford : Basil Blackwell, 1988, p. 152.

An unstable intermezzo

The event structure of the geopolitical field is highly sensitive to unforeseen contingencies, unlike the more insulated and institutionalized domestic environment. Are there then uniform compulsions structuring this field, that dictate a power and security imperative across the whole system? If so, they cannot be simply a matter of external constraints on generically conceived political structures, for such dictates need to be internalized 'constitutionally' by the individual states in question. As Weber recognized, Great Powers must actively posit them, on pain of risking their status as such. Today, however, to the degree that the bare existence and most essential objectives of such states are no longer directly threatened by rival powers, the question is how far such compulsions have ceased to operate.

Some major states still struggle to raise their international power ranking, even if this entails disruption of the status quo, although the number of these has steadily declined from the era of Ranke. Germany and especially Japan, the biggest economies in the world after the US, have more or less dropped out of the ring, a situation that would have been unimaginable in an older era of warring states. While there is presently a drift towards higher levels of tension at the summit of the international power hierarchy, to all appearances the inter-state system is now, structurally speaking, in an unstable half-way condition between resilient vestiges of an older power logic, and a *de facto* multilateralization of military violence that belies the appearance of antithetical sovereign interests at the top. There are no theories that explain in general terms what advantages accrue to major states in the current world market environment from possessing more military power than their peers and competitors; or why their arsenals are strategically directed at other major powers (China and Russia) when the use of most of these instruments was long ago made obsolete by their sheer destructiveness, except in the event of a remote last resort.

According to Stephen Biddle, this state of affairs—in effect for nearly a half century—has not fundamentally transformed the built-in strategic orientations of the most powerful states:

> Major war is also the primary planning yardstick for most world and regional powers. For most of the post–Cold War era, the US military was sized and structured to win two, nearly simultaneous major regional conflicts; the Bush administration has modified this standard to winning one while holding the line in another, but the standard is still set in major war terms.[29]

What kind of wars are the most powerful states actually capable of winning, and what kind of wars are their existing arsenals designed to wage? No advanced capitalist state even has a contingency plan for assaulting another one (although this is wrongly generalized into the claim that 'liberal-democracies' have never fought one another), and the only conceivable wars that the US and its main allies could possibly fight and win are against weak states with little popular support. If the evolution of military arsenals among the major states has nevertheless moved only fitfully in the direction of altering the targets of their force structures and weapon systems, this is principally due to the unique, mixed position of the Chinese and Russian states—high in the international power hierarchy, yet outside the liberal-capitalist core. Exacerbating this state of affairs, war machines built up during a century of Great Power conflicts have proved extremely difficult to redesign for other aims. Under conditions in which the inherited means continue to structure aims, the relationship between 'objective' power measurements and their actual deployment as instruments of strategy becomes opaque. 'Logically unsound unitary notions of military capability that mask crucial tradeoffs' may be the stock in trade of IR

---

29   Stephen Biddle, *Military Power: Explaining Victory and Defeat in Modern Battle*, Princeton: Princeton University Press, 2004, p. 8.

theories.[30] But if in the era of Great Power wars the validity of these notions was periodically subject to the harsh trial of head-to-head encounters between force structures and weapon systems, current measurements of capability lack the structuring logic of this decisive means of settlement. What role does military power play in determining a state's position within international ranking systems; why and to what extent is it still a decisive dimension of state power? The inability of existing theories even to pose these problems speaks to a deeper crisis of the classical categories of geopolitical rationality.

Epistemic shifts

Carl Schmitt's *Concept of the Political* was an attempt to probe the multiplying anomalies generated by these political categories and distinctions, in a context in which the boundaries, legal prerogatives and *raison d'être* of the state had been thrown into serious question. He argued that theories centred on the figure of the sovereign state were ill equipped to grasp the volatile links between interpenetrating systems that were emerging out of the de-standardization of the older international dispensation. But this is true of all theories and not just IR realism. Marxists, for example, have always more or less accepted the Hegelian conception of the state as the embodied national synthesis of antagonistic group and individual interests. But this canonical conception of the state confronts problems when there is no longer a plurality of actively competing states, all of whom can and must see each other as a certain magnitude of power in a cold calculus of war and diplomacy. The historic geopolitical field had its specific schemas that structured 'the widespread perception that economic strength is a necessary precondition for military strength; that economic and military power is fungible; that economic decline leads to military

---

30   Ibid., p. 4.

weakness; and that economic policies merit co-equal treatment with political and military considerations in national strategy making'.[31] While such equations continue to inform debates over the defence budget, trade and account deficits and long-term threat assessments, it is increasingly difficult for anyone to determine to what extent and why they remain valid.

The crisis and protracted demise of an older geopolitical field in which traditional categories remained operative, and capitalist states had to maintain themselves, unfolded over the first half of the twentieth century through catastrophic wars. It eventually resulted in the delegitimation of war as the ultimate settlement of inter-state conflict. But while this expressed the exigencies of suppressing outright wars between powerful capitalist states, and later—through far less stable arrangements—between such states and the Communist bloc, outside this zone the consequences of this development were much more problematic. For what has replaced the concept of 'war' as a legitimate instrument of settlement between nominally equal sovereign states is an essentially asymmetrical, discriminatory framework of legal disputes between states of vastly unequal status. For the few remaining fully sovereign states, the use of military force is afforded cover by the 'international community', while illegitimate 'rogue' states are subject to invasive, destabilizing qualifications of their nominal sovereignty in the form of sanctions, international supervision of their weapons programmes, no-fly zones and regime change.

Whether any of these methods constitute a state of war or not has become a rather arbitrary, indeed superfluous determination. A long-term epistemic shift seems to be occurring which is blurring older distinctions between war and peace, belligerents and neutrals, and soldiers and non-combatants, and the resulting international disorder is reflected in the increasingly contentious and arbitrary application of these terms. In effect, what scenarios of conflict

---

31   Ibid., p. 14.

qualify as 'war' for the purposes of any systematic investigation of its relationship to the interests of states, social classes and even whole social formations? Radical political philosophies today often make extreme claims about the role of violence—'war' in a vastly expanded sense—in the constitution of society. But the suggestion that war is the constitutive power of modern politics—discernible in both *Afflicted Powers* and *Multitude*—amounts to little more than a slack metaphorics, detracting attention from a sober assessment of the capacities and limits of military power in the present conjuncture. What too does 'anti-war' mean, when the meaning of war, and the labelling of violence, has become a matter of such intensely politicized—or alternatively, legalistic—semantics: how many of those who protested hostilities against Iraq welcomed them against Yugoslavia?

Constituents of the present

Such general considerations open up some windows, at least, on the specificity of the present. The structural crisis in the relations between capitalism and geopolitics has created a historical situation too fluid to capture in the form of a compelling totalization. But this does not mean it is impossible to pick out salient novelties of the contemporary scene. To begin with, the subtraction of the Soviet Union from the international system at the turn of the nineties has created a power vacuum around American planning in which the ordinary calculus of the risks or gains of war is to a considerable extent diluted or suspended. This slackening has been amplified by the widening gap in power projection capacities between the US and all other states, stemming from the technologies of the 'revolution in military affairs'. The first Gulf War was the initial laboratory of the new satellite-guided, laser-precision warfare, whose successes exceeded even the most optimistic Pentagon forecasts. Iraq, it is hard to remember, had previously been thought to possess the fourth most powerful army in the world. Having dispelled any post-Vietnam doubts about

American military prowess, strategic planners could now set their sights on bigger targets than the small fry of the 1980s. In fact, the Balkan Wars of the next decade provided the opportunity for the testing and integration of still newer weapon systems, appearing to accelerate the obsolescence of the armaments of all other states. Yet it is not at all clear, looking back over the last fifteen years, to what extent the RMA has transformed the balance of power between more substantial states, or made traditional modes of military organization obsolete. For Pentagon enthusiasts of the new art of war, however, the temptation to assume both as settled facts has been great.

At roughly the same time, the *raison d'être* of all Western arsenals was put 'objectively' into question. After the end of the Cold War and the undisputed victory of liberal-democratic capitalism, what was all this military power now for? Under the Clinton administration, armed force was assumed to be a means to accomplish a civilizing mission of liberal–democratic pacification in an external state environment that was softening. The notion that nation-states are being superseded is vastly exaggerated. But to varying degrees, and at varying speeds, many states are indeed ceasing to act as a coherent concentration of the interests of nationally defined elites, as these former social cores are transformed into a 'cosmopolitan' layer whose fortunes lose any organic connection with the viability of their respective local economies, and so *ipso facto* with the well-being of a large percentage of their own populations. By contrast, the old geopolitical game of balancing was, in part, motivated by elites whose power and prestige depended on performing at least decently in this arena. After the Second World War, strata of this kind were either uprooted or emasculated in the defeated countries, yielding to successor formations single-mindedly committed to growth and stability, and so more than willing to entrust their protection to American statecraft. More broadly, since the end of the Cold War the link between domestic hegemony and vigilant nation-state building has become ever looser, as oligarchs, the wealthy and even aspiring middle classes all struggle to get their money and children out of their own countries and into the leading one. This accounts for some of the contemporary tendency to bandwagon behind us demands, although this is arguably now giving way to a new and unstable stalemate.

The reasons for such incipient chaos are clear. America's twentieth-century ascent to world power took off when it emerged as a creditor state over the ruined and indebted belligerents of the First World War. us surpluses were the main levers with which Washington pried open and restructured rival economies in the capitalist cores of Europe and Asia, from the Versailles Treaty to the Marshall Plan. Since the seventies, however, this has evolved into a very different relation to the rest of the world, as the us has become a debtor country on a steadily increasing scale. The foundations of American power have fundamentally altered. us current account deficits have mounted to unsustainable levels, in a global setting where the normal balancing mechanisms and signals of the world economy—bond yields and interest rates—have virtually ceased to function.[32] A quarter-century of boom and bubble economics has created a context in which long-term strategic planning has lost its objective foundations in long-term economic trends, in more than one respect.

In part, this is because the increasingly speculative nature of the booms and busts of the last decades has generated radical changes in the way that risk and value are assessed—methods of assessment that have begun to spill over from the world of markets into geopolitical planning. In systems theory this would be described as the de-differentiation of sub-systems. Current imperial enterprises are, *inter alia*, the expression of an erosion of the barriers insulating military and diplomatic strategizing from the mentalities of high-risk financial operations. The autonomy of strategic intelligence in the American state is in danger from a new direction: a generation

---

32 'Traffic lights on the blink? Capital markets are hindering, not helping, global economic adjustment', *Economist*, 18 August 2005.

of planners-cum-business leaders raised in a market environment
that amply rewards hostile takeovers, downsizing, outsourcing
and the arts of cooking the books. The performance standards for
determining whether any of this works and for whom are presently
in dispute. An observation by the American Secretary of Defense
encapsulates this moment in history: 'we lack metrics to know
whether we are winning or losing the war.'[33]

Reckoning

Great Powers, according to Michael Mann, repeat whatever they
think secured them their last victory. The Cold War, for thinkers
of the American right, was won when leaders were elected who had
the courage to break out of détente, pursue the arms race to final
victory and unleash the free market with massive tax cuts, without
flinching before escalating account and budget deficits. Only five
or so years before, as they tell it, America was still reeling from its
humiliation in Indochina, on the defensive from Afghanistan to
Central America and gripped by domestic malaise and self-doubt.
The Reagan Revolution is held to be the great turnaround of modern
American history, creating a politico-ideological environment
that can be repeated today, given the appropriate triggers. The
unsustainability of this flight forward is only just beginning to be
registered by American policy elites. A painful reckoning is in store
for those who have grown accustomed to low-casualty victories, and
to thinking of deficits and debts as magnitudes that can be managed
by grandstanding and wishful thinking.

It would be a mistake, however, to think this need presage any
dramatic reversal of rank-ordering in the international system. The
genre of history that tells the story of the ascent of Germany or
the US to world power, or of the eclipse of the British Empire, no

---

33 Cited in Alan Krueger and David Laitin, ' "Misunderstimating"
Terrorism', *Foreign Affairs*, vol. 83, no. 5 (2004), p. 13.

longer plausibly represents the vicissitudes of national destiny. For in the past thirty years of capitalist restructuring, the rise and fall of powers has become the tale of a decade—often a mere half of a decade—in the sun. Among such episodes are the rise of Japan through the seventies, followed by an American resurgence under Reagan, subsequently undercut by an unstoppable Japanese expansion, followed by a decade of Japanese stagnation; or, at the other end of the world, the re-emergence of Germany as once more a unitary state, and Great Power in the making, only to be diagnosed a few years later as the sick man of Europe. What too of the European Union as a new comet in world politics, suddenly deflected from its course by a couple of plebiscites? But the *pièce de résistance* of this genre must surely be the abrupt deflation of grand strategies for a new American century. Each of these turning points was greeted with great fanfare and trepidation, with the publication of books and articles replete with modern and ancient precedents. We are now told that it is China's turn at the leading edge of world history. Judging by the track record of this increasingly flimsy narrative of the rise and fall of Great Powers, this is no doubt a sign that it too is poised for a fall.

So we return, amidst a muddled post-classical landscape of failed states, regime change, humanitarian interventions and WMD interdiction, to the main question that stalks *Afflicted Powers*, and to which it eludes an answer. Why did US leaders ditch the status quo with its manageable levels of risk, held in check by various installations and outposts of the American Empire, and court a potentially catastrophic blowback in Iraq? If indeed the intertwining financial and strategic formulae of American hegemony have evolved to the point where they depend—in ways that are not fully understood by its leaders—upon such gambles, then they are not long for this world. Looming over the horizon, moreover, is another question that no analyst so far seems very interested in broaching. What would the impact of a sharp world-economic downturn be on the entire geopolitical field? This is the great unknown of the current conjuncture.

5

The Role of Force in History

How should Western military interventions of the past decade be situated within the millennial epic of human civilization? The theme itself, in all its hoary grandeur, might bring to mind lectures on civic virtue and occidental destiny from Harvard or the Hoover Institute. But Azar Gat's *War in Human Civilization* has little in common with these best-selling tributes to exemplary republics and military orders.[1] Instead of a few glosses on famous battles, Gat—a specialist in Security Studies at Tel Aviv University and a major in the IDF Reserve—has attempted nothing less than a survey of the entire history of organized violence, from the hunter-gatherer origins of humanity to the current security predicaments of liberal democracies. *War in Human Civilization* sets out to resolve questions that have long been at the centre of controversies in anthropology and historical sociology. What is war? Has armed strife been endemic to all known forms of human society? Did violent group conflict take place amongst pre-historic hunter-gatherers, did it begin with the onset of agriculture, or take off after the formation of the first states? What role has war played

---

1   Azar Gat, *War in Human Civilization*, Oxford: Oxford University Press, 2007; henceforward WHC. I borrow from Frederick Engels the title of his spirited riposte to military-technicist accounts of the unification of Germany. See Engels, 'The Role of Force in History' [1887–88], *Marx/Engels Collected Works*, vol. 26, pp. 453–510. This chapter originally appeared in *New Left Review* 2: 47, September–October 2007.

in different forms of society, from the earliest city-states to the present day?

A work that succeeded in answering any one of these would arguably be a scholarly landmark. Gat has made a heroic attempt to deal with them all in the form of an evolutionary epic which begins with our hominid ancestors and ends with a few modest suggestions on how the West should respond to the threat of terrorism. The hunter-gatherer state of nature, the first village settlements, the rise of agriculture, the foundation of the earliest states, barbarian frontiers, empire building, the early modern European Miracle, the transition to capitalism, all culminating in a monumental account of the rise and fall of mass-mobilization warfare in the West— the episodes in this chronicle of civilization have a topical weight that is independent of the theory which seeks to subsume them. Whatever the limits of the latter, the work exhibits a pleasantly old-fashioned historical literacy that will hopefully prompt those with other conceptions of human development to consider enterprises on a comparable scale.

For in Gat's view, this entire macro-historical sequence is to be read as an unfolding expression of our inexorable, biological propensity to survive and expand. What he offers is a panorama of the civilizing process in the nineteenth-century tradition of social evolutionism. While the original grand narratives of this ilk have largely disappeared from the mainstream—how many today have read a single page of Herbert Spencer, Ludwig Gumplowicz or Karl Kautsky?—Gat's undertaking must be seen in terms of a much broader project to restore this once vastly influential school of thought. Socio-biology is currently experiencing an ascendancy reminiscent of its glory days in the Belle Époque. While biological essentialism in its overtly racist form has fewer adherents than a century ago, ongoing advances in human genetics seem destined to spawn a form of neo-social darwinism better adapted to contemporary values, and with good prospects for becoming, once again, a dominant ideology.

This adaptability of evolutionary theory to prevailing conditions has manifested itself in the changing significance of history itself. The first generation of social evolutionists emerged in a Europe saturated with historicism; in the current ideological context, the problem of change over the *longue durée* can be handled more casually, by banishing old-fashioned anxieties surrounding the specificity of different times and peoples. As a result, the many recent attempts to offer an evolutionary account of the direction of history, in terms of the interplay of evolved propensities to conflict and cooperation, lack the characteristic breadth and occasional depth of the classics of this tradition. The virtuoso scholarship and intellectual range of Gat's earlier works on the history of military thought, however, would seem to raise the hope that his latest contribution might change this state of affairs at a stroke. In three books (1989, 1992, 1998), reissued in 2001 in a single volume entitled *A History of Military Thought: From the Enlightenment to the Cold War*, Gat produced a formidable work of intellectual history that deserves consideration in its own right—a striking precursor to *War in Human Civilization*. It effectively captures the main episodes of three centuries of writing on military affairs, in a narrative of the rise and fall of Clausewitzian hegemony and the subsequent formulation of the containment doctrine.[2]

Theories of battle

The first volume of the series, the outcome of his doctoral thesis under Michael Howard and published when Gat was still in his twenties, traced 'the quest for a general theory of war' from Machiavelli to Clausewitz.[3] Gat argued that the classical military theory revived during the Renaissance initially focused almost

---

2   Azar Gat, *A History of Military Thought: From the Enlightenment to the Cold War*, Oxford: Oxford University Press, 2001; henceforward HMT.

3   Azar Gat, *The Origins of Military Thought: From the Enlightenment to Clausewitz*, Oxford: Oxford University Press, 1989.

exclusively on the glories of past forms: Xenophon's account of the combat formation of the Spartan phalanx; Polybius on the Roman legion. In Gat's judgment, the early-modern classical spirit was oblivious to the historical contexts of war. He seconds Clausewitz's dismissal of Machiavelli's supposedly 'ahistorical' approach, in failing to register the impact of firearms: 'The art of war of the ancients attracted him too much, not only its spirit, but also in all of its forms.'[4] The Enlightenment brought an enthusiasm for mechanical precision to the ideal of martial excellence: map-making and statistics would bring artillery and infantry manoeuvres into accord with the principles of geometry. The stunning mid-century victories of Prussian arms under Frederick the Great during the 1740–48 War of the Austrian Succession occasioned an outpouring of technical literature of this kind.

It is Clausewitz—the central figure of the first volume—who is given the honour of having formulated the most radical criticism of this ahistorical approach, writing in the shadow of the Prussian defeat and his own capture and imprisonment by the French in 1806. From 1792, the Revolution's desperate defensive mobilizations had overturned the old-regime textbooks, as the great emergency *levées* of the Terror created enormous makeshift armies that were forced to improvise new line formations, firing sequences, and velocities of manoeuvre. Thermidorean juntas of generals and civilian fixers would appropriate the earlier successes of popular improvisation, and the Emperor's campaigns be made the subject of a literature that would haunt European military planning up until the grinding deadlocks of the First World War. Gat's meticulous reconstruction situates Clausewitz's intellectual development firmly within the context of German idealism and historicism, a climate of ideas that allowed him to grasp the relationship between particular ages and their unique modes of warfare.

---

4   Letter to Fichte, 11 Jan 1809, cited in *HMT*, p. 8.

Gat follows Howard in his approach to the long-standing disputes over the apparent contradiction between Clausewitz's summary of the aim of war as 'definitive victory' and his renowned proposition that 'war is but a continuation of policy with other means'—from which it would follow that war could not be exclusively defined in terms of 'absolute' hostilities, and that limited war should be regarded not as an adulteration, but as a legitimate form in its own right. Gat demonstrates that in 1827, with the first six books of On War already completed, Clausewitz concluded that 'the test of experience' suggested that there were two types of war—and furthermore: 'There is no denying that a great majority of wars and campaigns are more a state of observation than a struggle for life and death.'[5] Clausewitz's ambivalence could be seen as a prefiguration of the conflicting tendencies at work in the statecraft of the upcoming century: would the further development of bourgeois civil society find expression in a new geopolitics of 'limited' warfare—or alternately, in a return to the 'absolute' hostilities of the Napoleonic Sturm und Drang?

Inventing deterrence

The long nineteenth century covered in the second volume of the trilogy is described as an 'age of epigoni' for military thought, overshadowed by the titans of the previous age.[6] Adopting a narrative framework that could have come from the pages of Lukács's The Destruction of Reason, Gat maintains that, after the defeats of 1848, liberal cosmopolitanism rapidly lost ground in respectable circles to an aggressively imperialist social Darwinism (here treated with cool scholarly neutrality). It was the First World War that brought about the final discrediting of 'Clausewitzian' doctrines of offensive war, as belligerent armies

---

5   HMT, p. 215.
6   Gat, The Development of Military Thought: The Nineteenth Century, Oxford: Oxford University Press, 1992.

came to a standstill behind barbed trenches on the Western Front from September 1914 until the German Spring Offensive of March 1918. Gat neglects Gramsci's reflections on the larger historical consequences of this stalemate, although no other thinker he considers remotely approximated the Sardinian's comprehension of the decline of offensive strategy in both the military and political fields of post-war Western Europe. Reflecting on the failures of revolutionaries in the West to follow the Bolshevik road to power, Gramsci concluded that this stemmed from a historical divergence of military-political conditions on the two fronts. On the Western front, sudden revolutionary breakthroughs had become exceedingly unlikely:

> The same thing happens in the art of politics as happens in military art: war of movement increasingly becomes war of position, and it can be said that the State will win a war in so far as it prepares for it minutely and technically in peacetime. The massive structures of the modern democracies, both as state organizations, and as complexes of associations in civil society, constitute for the art of politics as it were the 'trenches' and the permanent fortifications of the front in the war of position: they render merely 'partial' the element of movement which before used to be the 'whole' of the war.[7]

The final volume of *The History of Military Thought* offers a lively portrait of the geopolitical, economic and intellectual landscape in the age of fully mechanized war, culminating in reconsiderations of the work of the British Mosleyite J. F. C. Fuller and his erstwhile disciple, the military journalist and historian B. H. Liddell Hart.[8] A phantasmagoric vitalism infused Fuller's vision of a military overcoming of the industrialized slaughter of the trenches; his

7   Antonio Gramsci, *Selections from the Prison Notebooks*, London: International Publishers, 1971, p. 235.
8   Azar Gat, *Fascist and Liberal Visions of War: Fuller, Liddell Hart, Douhet and Other Modernists*, Oxford: Oxford University Press, 1998.

Tanks in the Great War foresaw a sweeping mechanization of armies led by vanguards of highly mobile tank squads, in a new age of specialized military elites. Ideas such as these were more avidly embraced in Weimar and Nazi-era Germany than on the home front, but could inspire all those who dreamt of cleaner, more focused battles. Liberals as well as fascists were determined to prevent the repetition of a world war that would seal the fate of the West. Gat's final chapters narrate the passage of Liddell Hart from disciple of the fascist Fuller to unofficial strategist of a liberal imperialism now wavering before the mounting threat of the Third Reich.[9] Liddell Hart's formulation of a limited-war doctrine in the 1930s drew heavily—to the point of plagiarism—on the writings of his former mentor Fuller. The British Empire was in danger, its Great Power pre-eminence fading fast. It was now clear that blockades of world-market sources of raw materials would not stop a continental power capable of constructing its own economic *Grossraumordnung*: the home country itself was now vulnerable to submarine blockade. In this security context, the value of overseas colonies vis-à-vis the costs of maintaining them began to decline. Such was the historical setting in which Liddell Hart developed his vision for an endangered empire; this was no blinkered defence of a tottering status quo, however, but a grand strategy that looked beyond the horizon of war to secure the conditions of a prosperous, stable peace. Already in the mid-1920s, underscoring his long-standing dispute with Clausewitz, Liddell Hart had maintained that:

> The *destruction* of the enemy's armed forces is but a means—and not
> necessarily an inevitable or infallible one—to the attainment of our goal
> ... All *acts*, such as defeat in the field, propaganda, blockade, diplomacy,

9   Gat suggests that his own account of Liddell Hart's career rebuts John Mearsheimer's devastating portrait of the man, but offers very little by way of character rehabilitation. John Mearsheimer, *Liddell Hart and the Weight of History*, Ithaca: Cornell University Press, 1988.

or attack on the centres of government and population, are seen to be but means to that end.[10]

But what was this end? It is on this point that Gat identifies the enduring significance of Liddell Hart's thought for the security predicaments of Western liberal imperialism, then and now. These demand a flexible combination of military, financial and ethical pressure; above all, the mainsprings of the economy must be left intact. The strategic flexibility of liberal imperialism could not be understood by 'the Clausewitzians'; but, Gat argues, 'As Liddell Hart grasped, a fundamental fact about Britain's political position in the 1930s was that, while already being a satisfied imperial power, she had progressively become a consumerist, liberal-democratic society with no interest in major wars unless the status quo was seriously threatened.'[11]

Liddell Hart's reputation plummeted with the initial successes of the *Blitzkriegen*; but Gat charitably suggests that, unlike the proverbial generals, he was always one war ahead. By 1947, in the *Foreign Affairs* article that signalled the start of the Cold War, the essentials of Liddell Hart's conception of deterrence had become an intellectual cornerstone of Western statecraft; a fact that Kennan himself later acknowledged.[12] Concluding his trilogy, Gat remarks that, though Liddell Hart's theories have been dismissed as advocating 'wars without the spilling of blood', at the turn of the twenty-first century the unwillingness of the West to accept the sacrifice of life in war has become 'an overwhelming social imperative'. Even in Israel, though 'the nation in arms is still there', smaller forces of professionals will increasingly be preferred to the masses of reservists, 'both for the

---

10   Liddell Hart, *Paris, or the Future of War*, London: Kegan Paul, 1925; cited in *HMT*, p. 677.
11   *HMT*, p. 753.
12   See the article by 'X' in *Foreign Affairs* 25, 1947; reprinted in George Kennan, *American Diplomacy, 1900–1950*, Chicago: New American History, 1951.

capital-intensive, high-tech battlefield and for the lowly "policing" of hostile populations'. For the West,

> When force is applied, it is usually along the lines first mooted during the 1930s and championed by Liddell Hart. The favoured techniques include economic sanctions; the provision of money and hardware to strengthen local forces against adversaries; blockade; naval and aerial actions; limited, 'surgical' operations by highly mobile and technologically superior striking forces . . . These methods have had a mixed and often disappointing record . . . Still, given the nature of modern Western societies, of their foreign affairs, strategic requirements, and cultural sensibilities, this way of war-making appears to be their norm, as much as all-out war was for their predecessors.[13]

Thus Gat's *History of Military Thought* draws to a close. A reader might be disappointed to discover that, after this 800-page *tour de force* from the age of Machiavelli to the aftermath of the Berlin Wall, no more searching conclusions on the present conjuncture are put forward. But such a strangely blank concluding passage could be symptomatic of deeper obstacles to thinking about the role that war is to play in a world dominated by liberal-capitalist states. In 2001, when Gat's collected trilogy was published, it may have seemed as if America's soaring fortunes and undisputed might was bringing an end to the age of sovereign states, ushering in the liberal millennium of elections, money and humanitarian police operations. A mere half decade later, the outlook seems far more turbulent.

Persistent hostilities

How, then, should we define the current geopolitical order? It could be described as an unstable half-way condition in which entrenched vestiges of an older power logic have for the moment

[handwritten marginalia: all the benefits of a liberal democracy]

---

13   *HMT*, pp. 827–8.

forestalled a long-standing trend towards the neutralization of sovereign rivalry at the top level of the inter-state system. Does this persistence of hostilities stem from the resistance of anachronistic regimes and movements to liberal-market expansion? Realists would answer in the negative, insisting that the inter-state order itself will continue to organize national interests antagonistically, regardless of such constitutional and ideological differences. Does American hegemony safeguard the collective interests and long-term stability of the dominant players within the world-system? The contrary claim—that it has become obsolescent, even destabilizing, since the end of the Cold War—is gaining credence, yet alternative hegemonies are still purely speculative. What explains the persistence of Western capitalism's enormous military arsenals (indeed, the likelihood of their further development and expansion) in an era in which serious threats to liberal democracy and free-market imperialism have more or less disappeared? It is now simply out of the question that they might be used against comparably equipped states like Russia or China, and yet Islamists and other assorted rogue elements seem too inconsequential a threat to justify the maintenance of such formidable war machines.

Gat's latest work, *War in Human Civilization*, compresses all the major geopolitical problems of the present conjuncture into the question: 'Under what conditions, if at all, can war be eliminated, and is it declining at present?'—and seeks an answer in the natural history of our species.[14] It is as if, at the liberal-democratic End of History, archaic vestiges of geopolitical strife could only be explained by an irrepressible, genetic fate. Gat once again demonstrates his skill in deploying a vast quantity of anthropological, archaeological and historical material, although the qualities of intellectual independence and elegant composition that distinguished *A History of Military Thought* are less evident in this latest volume. *War in*

---

14 *WHC*, p. ix.

Human Civilization has an old axe to grind—namely, that human beings are innately aggressive—and a more repetitive structure, in which this point is driven home repeatedly.

Gat begins by examining the evidence for violent intra-species conflict during the two million or so years of the *Homo* genus—the '99.5 per cent of biological history' in which small hunter-gatherer bands roamed the planet, preceding settled development. The debate on warfare during this period has been polarized, in his view, between Hobbesians, for whom men are naturally violent, and Rousseauians, who believe that, in their pristine condition, primitive human beings were peaceful, and only became violent when exposed to guns, liquor and missionaries. Siding with the Hobbesians, Gat sets out the case for aggression as an 'innate but optional tactic' for survival during humankind's long evolutionary process.[15] He is keen to point out that there is 'no normative implication' in the mechanism of 'blind natural selection' that privileges those best qualified to survive and reproduce. Intra-specific fighting takes place in nature 'because the decisive factor in the evolutionary contest is individuals' efforts to pass on their *own* genes', rather than those of strangers.[16] Males can opt to engage in aggression in order to win or take as many mates as they can, so as to increase the number of their descendants; and females seek to select the most vigorous male providers to protect the far smaller number of their offspring they can raise. A greater propensity for aggression, on the one hand, and for child rearing, on the other, are what chiefly distinguish men and women, in this view. While violent males are obviously more likely to die off—and often at

---

15   The hominid line is estimated to have diverged from that of chimpanzees some 7 million years ago, while the *Homo* genus emerges with *Homo erectus* around 2 million years ago; archaic varieties of *Homo sapiens* had evolved by 500,000 years ago, and *Homo sapiens sapiens* by around 100,000 years ago. Gat sees the exquisite cave paintings of the Upper Paleolithic (15,000–35,000 years ago) as evidence of 'a mind that is indistinguishable from ours in its capacity': *WHC*, p. 5.

16   *WHC*, pp. 144, 43.

such rates as to make their tactics rather questionable in terms of survival and reproduction—for most of our history as a species, the potential rewards for aggression have been sufficiently high that some have risked it, while others, perhaps less violence-prone, were forced to follow suit in order to stay in the game. The females mostly opted for, or were taken by, the brave.

It is not only through offspring, however, that genes are passed on, but also through close kin: siblings share 50 per cent of the same genetic material, cousins around 12.5 per cent. In evolutionary terms, it therefore makes sense to sacrifice oneself to save more than two siblings, eight cousins, thirty-two second cousins, etc. This evolutionary 'logic of kinship', Gat argues, extends far beyond the clan or tribe. Societies are alliances between kin groups, and stand or fall to the degree to which they enhance the prospects for the survival and reproduction of their individual members. Yet in a sense, all the members of these circumstantially bonded groups remain at war with one another. The words of a traditional Arab proverb express the semblance of necessity that this view acquires under conditions of scarcity, whether natural or man-made: 'I against my brother; I and my brother against my cousin; I and my brother and my cousin against the world.'[17] All viable political communities, in Gat's opinion, including modern nations, have an ethno-biological core, even when this is surrounded by a shifting penumbra of metics. Historical evolution is the result of the ongoing recombination of these core alliances, whose constituents are under pressure to adopt practices that maximize their fitness in the given environment, with or without their existing allies.

As an 'innate but optional' tactic, however, aggression is a highly variable element of our inherited behavioural make-up. Its triggers—the 'proximate mechanisms' of desire—have been subject to a rather weak selective pressure. Unlike hunger and, apparently, lust, aggression 'turns on and off' in anticipation of

---

17   *whc*, pp. 45–6.

potential rewards. The 'on' switch may be activated by the thrill of the fight, 'the competitive exercise of spiritual and physical faculties, and even cruelty, blood lust and killing ecstasy'. On the 'off' side, aggression may be suppressed by 'fear, spiritual and physical fatigue, compassion, abhorrence of violence, revulsion at bloodshed'.[18] Indeed, there may be circumstances in which the rewards of fighting are so outweighed by the penalties that it switches off for long periods of time and even for whole societies. According to Gat, male aggression can be more or less sublimated into peaceable forms of competition, 'even though the evolutionary aim'—the fight for food or sexual conquest—'remains unconscious'. If so, it would seem difficult to determine the relationship between so changeable a propensity and the actual level of violence in any society, measured in fatalities. The claim that these behaviourally modified antagonists pursue the evolutionary aims of survival and reproduction, albeit unconsciously, makes little sense as an account of human behaviour. Indeed, as human society emerges into the historical era, Gat switches ends for means. Now:

> Rather than the evolutionary ends themselves, it is the proximate mechanisms, those behaviours that carry emotional gratifications and which originally evolved as a means to attain somatic and reproductive ends, that motivate human behaviour. Where radically new conditions sever the original link between a proximate mechanism and its original evolutionary end, it is [the former] that people are tied to by powerful emotional stimuli.[19]

One problem with Gat's approach is that it cannot explain, but only note *post facto*, the varying propensities to conflict that characterize the different communities he proceeds to examine. Another is the failure of *War in Human Civilization* to define what exactly 'war' is, as opposed to aggression more generally. Following Franz

---

18   *WHC*, p. 39.
19   *WHC*, p. 47.

Boas, Gat suggests that differentiations between 'blood feud', 'warfare' and 'homicide' are 'largely arbitrary, reflecting our view as members of more or less orderly societies'.[20] Northwest American Indians, he claims, would not have bothered with such distinctions; nor, perhaps, with those between a bird and a plane. Yet if 'war' is simply the struggle for existence, pitting members of the same species against one another, then, of course, all life forms always will be 'at war'. But there would then be little point in asking more specific questions regarding when and under what conditions human beings began to fight wars, and continue to do so. If warfare is conflated with the entire gamut of conflict within a single species—and why limit it to the intra-specific?—not only would the focus on human arms be lost, so too would the topic of 'civilization' fade out into a general field of competitive selection, whose ultimate belligerents are merely selfish genes.

From nature to culture

A further, more insuperable problem arises when Gat seeks to extend his explanatory theory beyond the stage of 'human evolution in nature' to include the totality of social development over the last ten thousand years. For the more ambitious burden of his argument is that evolutionary theory can provide an adequate account of how qualitative changes from one form of society to another have taken place, from the Neolithic era onwards. Having covered two million years of human evolution in its first 145 pages, *War in Human Civilization* is obliged to wrench its Darwinian framework away from any scientific basis in its efforts to provide, over the course of the next 500 pages, a neo-evolutionary explanation for the emergence of agriculture, the origins and development of the state, the transition to capitalism and the denouement of liberal democracy. Gat accepts that:

---

20   *WHC*, p. 47.

once humans had evolved [sic] agriculture, they set in train a continuous
chain of developments that have taken them further and further away
from their evolutionary natural way of life as hunter-gatherers . . .
Original, evolution-shaped, innate human wants, desires, and proximate
behavioural and emotional mechanisms now expressed themselves within
radically altered, 'artificial' conditions, which were very different from
those in which they had evolved.[21]

But Gat never clearly defines the terms of the 'cultural evolution' that
will now succeed the biological as his theoretical framework. At one
point this is simply a case of 'analogies': both deal with the 'recursive
reproduction of replicating forms—biological or cultural—the
occasional variations of which are at least to some degree subject to
all sorts of selective pressures'. Elsewhere, 'biological and cultural
evolution represent a continuum', segueing into each other.[22]
Structures such as states or chiefdoms are simply claimed to 'evolve'.

Gat's account is vague, to say the least, about the units upon
which evolutionary selection mechanisms operate. It oscillates
between population-fitness criteria, according to which a society
is merely the sum of its kin groups, and the claim that various,
vaguely individuated practices are themselves the units upon
which evolutionary selection operates. But this argument conflates
the random nature of genetic mutation with the conscious level
at which individuated practices are adopted from a range of
alternatives. It could be argued that neo-darwinians are actually
Lamarckians in their blithe acceptance of this conflation of blind
mutations and intentional innovations. The theory of natural
selection, as it is understood today, posits a discontinuity between
the mechanism that generates random genetic changes and the
mechanism of their reproduction through differential survival
rates and sexual selection. It should be obvious that no comparable

21 *WHC*, p. 145.
22 *WHC*, p. 150.

discontinuity exists between the conditions of origination and those of dissemination at the level of human praxis. Most socio-biological arguments attempt to discount the significance of this difference by pointing to patterns of development roughly analogous to natural selection which take shape in social contexts of scarcity and competition. These assume that the only possible forms of 'second nature' are ones that mimic the natural compulsions of survival and expansion. But as Marx observed, this category-conflation between nature and culture becomes historical reality in the form of quasi-natural compulsions that govern the various modes of our cultural second nature.

With the development of agriculture, and of more complex social forms, the cultural-historical emerges from the natural and, Gat suggests, 'the link between ends and adaptive behavioural means' is severed. Yet nature re-emerges, if in an increasingly opaque fashion. For the thymotic drive persists even in contexts where violence only indirectly boosts subsistence, now focused around sundry intangible goals that take on a life of their own, at odds with the compulsions of security and breeding. From Plato to Kojève, it has often been argued that an indifference to life in this mode is what opens up the horizons to alternatives. Gat certainly attempts to account for the emergence of the distinction between nature and culture. But the corrosive implications of acknowledging this distinction on his whole account are never acknowledged. A second nature of cultural goals might drift away from the exigencies of security and reproduction. Weakly selected, male aggression could turn off permanently, unless the main, second-nature objectives remained in some manner connected to the prime directive of survival. Gat's concept of 'war', however, is loose enough to fit any number of alternate scenarios, and can more or less be stretched to cover the harsh struggle to subsist and reproduce, even where this does not give rise to violent conflict. Hobbes conceived of the natural state of hostilities in which everyone is exposed to violent death as a condition that could be brought to an end. Gat conceives of it more elastically, as a permanent environment in which humans interact, more or less violently.

Savages and scholars

If Gat's work is in part a polemic against misguided Rousseauians, he might do well to recall the warning of the *Discourse on the Origin of Inequality*: 'It is no light undertaking to separate what is original from what is artificial in the present state of man.'[23] Without a doubt, the topic of the distinction between 'nature' and 'culture' is alive today; the issue is whether the neo-evolutionary framework can explain it, and whether the ethnographic and historical cases that Gat discusses confirm that theory, or reveal its limitations.

The evolution of *Homo sapiens* is arguably the right place to begin an inquiry into the problem that Rousseau raised, and thus to delineate the specific forms of human society in which conflict and violence could be plausibly described as 'war', in the sense of a phenomenon that has a history. The study of the hunter-gatherer form of society opens up an empirical approach to these interrelated problems: to the extent that we can speak of human states of nature, it would be here. Since the 1960s, anthropologists working on the subject of primitive warfare have indeed largely been divided into 'Hobbesian' and 'Rousseauian' schools. Lawrence Keeley, a doyen of the first group, argues that a generation of scholars refused to accept the considerable ethnographic and archaeological evidence for violent conflict amongst contemporary and pre-historical hunter-gatherers, and even amongst more stratified bands and tribes. Their key move was 'to save the Rousseauian notion of the Noble Savage, not by making him peaceful (as this was contrary to fact), but by arguing that tribesmen conducted a more stylized, less horrible form of warfare than their civilized counterparts

---

23 Jean-Jacques Rousseau, *Discourse on the Origin of Inequality*, Indianapolis and Cambridge: Hackett Publishing Company, 1992, p. 34.

waged'.[24] Primitive war was seen as a staged ritual, involving shouting, brandishing and, *in extremis*, an occasional casualty. Ethnographers found in this ceremonial strife a humanity absent from the violent world of twentieth-century civilization.

But in focusing on these 'nothing fights'—as they were contemptuously called by one Highland New Guinean people— anthropologists were averting their eyes from more sanguinary hunter-gatherer tactics, including the frequent resort to surprise offensives resulting in staggering casualty rates; Gat repeats Keeley's claim that the death toll from such raids exceeded the highest rates of twentieth-century industrial warfare.[25] For Keeley, these scholars were whitewashing the violence of the hunter-gatherer past. The ethnographic evidence on the handful of peoples who were truly conflict-avoidant was of little consequence, in his view. Remnant primitive populations were not representative of those who had hunted and foraged before the expansion of agriculture pushed them into the desolate zones they now occupied. If these impoverished refugee communities were less prone to battle it was only because they had little choice.

But even here there was little true peace. Comparative anthropological research on incidents of violence amongst remnant pre-state peoples—a broad category that embraces not just Stone Age hunter-gatherers but tribal horticulturalists and pastoralists as well—reveals a disconcerting pattern of brutality in disputes over women, sorcery and trespass. *War in Human Civilization* describes at some length the first-hand account of William Buckley, an escaped convict who for thirty-two years lived amongst aboriginals. This was Australia before the white man had overrun it. After returning to settler civilization in 1838,

---

24   Lawrence Keeley, *War Before Civilization*, New York and Oxford: Oxford University Press, 1995, p. 9.
25   The more than questionable assumption behind Keeley's statistics is that four dead out of a population of forty eight is somehow comparable to five million dead out of a population of sixty million.

Buckley provided a not unsympathetic account of a people highly prone to violent bickering over marital abductions, rape and broken promises, remarking of the women: 'these dear creatures were at the bottom of every mischief.'[26] For Gat, tales of Stone Age Australians and Tasmanians at the dawn of contact give us a privileged glimpse into a once universal human condition: a pre-historical world of feuding, lynching, head hunting and small-scale genocides. He dismisses the claim that these micro-wars can be attributed to bouts of material scarcity. The Eskimo and Indian tribes of the 2,500-mile Pacific Northwest Coastline, a region teeming with fish, game and fowl, waged ocean canoe expeditions against villages hundreds of miles away. These subjects of Franz Boas's heroic fieldwork seem to resemble the hunter-gatherer communities who once occupied the most bountiful subsistence niches on earth, yet whose encampments are replete with evidence of exorbitant butchery. Why did human beings ever quit this violent Golden Age, so congenial to their nature?

Pristine origination

While *War in Human Civilization* unfolds a grand narrative of evolutionary advances towards ever-higher levels of social complexity, I will argue that its theory of demographic competition and existential conflict cannot account for some important local transitions to agriculture, nor for the origins of the first 'pristine' states. His neo-evolutionism can neither explain cases of the 'contingent' emergence of new logics of domestication, exploitation and authority, nor address the evidence for the long pacification of hostilities that preceded these changes.

The book's account of an evolutionary sequence of rising levels of cooperation and strategic aggression, from *Homo erectus* to *Homo sapiens*, implicitly relies on claims for the increasingly significant

26 *WHC*, p. 70.

role of hunting and meat-eating in setting this trend: bands of migrant African hunters were equipped to bring down not just the most formidable beasts, but each other as well. It seems a strange lacuna then that *War in Human Civilization* barely mentions the late Pleistocene extinctions of Eurasian megafauna, brought about by climate change and over-hunting; such drastic discontinuities in the conditions of survival and reproduction have a tendency to drop out of Gat's story. Big-game hunting went into sharp decline following the end of the last Ice Age; in the Levant, the final disappearance of the largest animals was followed by a protracted decimation of once-bountiful gazelle herds. The consequences of this massive regional change in the subsistence environment are spelled out by Keith Otterbein: 'The first people to domesticate plants did not have war, and they did not have war because they had ceased to be hunters of big game.'[27]

Yet the decline of hunting did not lead to a demographic crisis, for the same climate changes brought about a great expansion of wild-cereal habitats. In this context, the population densities of sedentary foragers increased between 11000 BC and 9000 BC, the material basis for the rise of pre-Neolithic Natufian culture in the region. Keeley himself writes of this new order of human things: 'Not only is there no indication of an increase of warfare in this period, there are no indications of warfare at all.'[28] This withering away of the warrior-hunter lifestyle cannot be brought into focus in Gat's account, although the behavioural consequences of the sudden shift from carnivore to herbivore with regards to aggression and gender relations should be obvious. Ancient forms of hominid male bonding must have dissolved with the demise of hunting. If Rousseau got the chronology wrong, he was right in thinking that these pre-state foragers were initially loosely attached and peaceable. He also

27   Keith Otterbein, *How War Began*, Texas: Texas A&M University Press, 2004, p. 13.
28   Keeley, *War Before Civilization*, p. 120.

recognized that such large-scale changes resulted in fundamental transformations in our nature, and not just its expressions.

In fact, the entire *Discourse on the Origin of Inequality* is organized around a problem which Gat neglects: how to explain the emergence of a practice that no one individual or group could have intentionally implemented, because no one had ever done it before; and because its successful adoption requires an alignment of human beings with each other and with an always opaque environment that lies beyond the scope of their conscious coordination. The problems involved in changing a whole mode of life can be minimized in retrospect, especially when the change leads to material gains for later, vastly larger generations. But an explanation of the emergence of a new order out of antecedent conditions, and the observation that, after its emergence, it increased population and fitness, are two different things.

It is at this point that such evolutionary theories fail as accounts of historical change. Even if one accepted the analogy they posit between natural and cultural-historical evolution, their more fundamental limitation is their inability to account for qualitative transformations—'mutations'—within the latter domain. Not only do these theories conflate the category of random genetic inputs with that of intentional innovation, they are also unable to distinguish the latter—the conscious adoption of new practices— from the structures that determine their conditions of possibility: the practical and conceptual parameters of a world. These modes of second nature are not causal in the manner of blind nature, but nor are they the product of subjective agency. Within these worlds, a 'dialectic' emerges between partial structure and thwarted agency, which overlaps with, but is not identical to, the discontinuity between blind natural change and conscious intentional action. The concrete corollary of this claim would be that qualitative historical change is almost never the result of intentional adoption of new practices by individuals seeking to maximize their pre-given interests. We know, in any event, that hunter-gatherers who came into contact with agriculture often chose not to adopt it, as its blessings are indeed mixed. The long Neolithic era of subsistence agriculture and husbandry brought about millennia of explosive demographic growth, yet over 80 per cent of its population consisted of toiling, sick and malnourished peasants. This was the heavy price humans paid for a modest increase in food security.

Arms and seeds

Different modes of material life have specific rules of reproduction to which both groups and individuals will conform, in the absence of any known, feasible alternatives. Although foragers are keen observers of plant life, it is nearly inconceivable that anyone could have intentionally invented the arcane practices of crop domestication. Attentive to this Rousseauian problem of origins, Jared Diamond has suggested that foragers unwittingly fertilized seeds in the manured spittoons of their initially makeshift camps and villages. In the Fertile Crescent, such unplanned selections of mutant wheat and barley strains that did not scatter their grains to the winds resulted in the emergence of the first genetically modified crops. Thereafter, these and other wild species took thousands of years of human selection to become domesticated, during which time the burgeoning gardens of these proto-peasants would have been highly vulnerable to violent disruption that could liquidate these fragile sources of livelihood, and force cultivators into niches better suited for defence than grain. As a consequence, for thousands of years, in various places on earth, there was peace. By about 8000 BC, systematic crop cultivation had been established in the Fertile Crescent, followed by animal husbandry a thousand years later. In Egypt, local hunter-gatherers added crops to their diet of wild plants and animals, and then gradually phased out the wild foods.[29] Otterbein suggests that the slower decline of hunting and foraging

29   Jared Diamond, *Guns, Germs, and Steel*, New York: W. W. Norton, 1997, p. 102.

along the Nile kept alive violent conflicts, and thus delayed the emergence of agriculture, which came later as an imported practice from Mesopotamia.

In Gat's neo-evolutionary story, the uniform pressure of demographic growth and technological innovation seamlessly tip the advantage from hunting and gathering towards agriculture. The evidence for a dramatic change in the species environment at the onset of human, animal and crop domestication in this key region is ignored, in favour of a narrative of continuous, violent evolution: 'Everything we know ethnographically about historical horticulturalists suggests that the lives of their pre-historical predecessors were insecure and fraught with violent death.'[30]

While conceding 'the inherent ambiguities of the archaeological markers of warfare in pre- or proto-state environments', Gat goes on to make a lengthy case for the pervasiveness of war in the early Neolithic Fertile Crescent. Even before the small game hunters and foragers of this zone assumed an agricultural mode of life, super-villages were forming at Abu Hureyra, Catal-Huyuk and Jericho; from around the ninth millennium BC onwards, these people were living behind fortified walls. In Jericho the walls grew to immense heights as countless generations of builders and successive waves of newcomers made their contributions of mud and stone. For Gat, this is solid evidence for a state of hostilities. Renowned for the much later episode of their destruction narrated in the Book of Joshua, the walls have occasioned long-standing controversy. In Otterbein's judgment, 'the walls of pre-biblical Jericho are almost a litmus test indicating whether a scholar is a hawk or a dove.'[31] On the crucial first millennia of the Neolithic transition, scholarly opinion is overwhelmingly dovish: there was no similar large settlement in the entire area, and in fact, no archaeological evidence of warfare until the old settlement was conquered for the first time in 7000 BC. According to Ofer-Bar Yusef, the walls of Jericho were

30 *WHC*, p. 173.
31 Otterbein, *How War Began*, p. 33.

for flood control and mud flows. Nor is there any evidence for fortifications in other zones of endogenous plant domestication—the Nile, Yellow River, Indus Valley, Mesoamerica, highland Peru and West Africa—until much later. Gat, undeterred, claims that 'fortifications can serve as a mark of violent conflict only in a positive manner.'[32]

War did, of course, eventually erupt after the millennia of pacification that accompanied the original phase of endogenous plant domestication—and it did so before the advent of the first states. But this raises another problem for Gat's narrative: it is arguably precisely because violent conflict did return in regions such as the Levant, where plants and animals were first domesticated, that states, properly speaking, did not emerge. Just as a long peace preceded and accompanied the Neolithic transition, so too a relative peace appears to have prevailed in the lower Tigris–Euphrates basin before, and for thousands of years after, the spread of domesticated plants into this region around 5700 BC. Yet it was in this setting that pristine state formation took place. Confirming this picture, Michael Mann notes that the proximity of later Sumerian cities—within sight of one another—strongly suggests the absence of warfare at their foundation.[33]

But if pristine domestication was, arguably, incompatible with war, agriculture as such was not. From the original centres of plant domestication, farming spread in waves to cover most of the earth's cultivable surface. The population take-off in the wake of these initially separate histories of agriculture was immense, the world population shooting up from 5 million to approximately 100 million after only 5,000 years of expanding tillage; peoples who had not originally developed agriculture in their own habitats could now adopt the package from others. In Eurasia, this demographic explosion often involved the forceful displacement or absorption

32   *WHC*, p. 175.
33   Michael Mann, *The Sources of Social Power*, vol. 1, Cambridge: Cambridge University Press, 1986.

of aboriginals, clashes between different groups of agriculturalists, and constant strife between them and the pastoralists who swarmed on their peripheries.

[handwritten: many states grew from of sustenance stability and security]

Origins of the state

State-based civilization arose in many, though not all, of the original zones of plant domestication. Gat's neo-evolutionary narrative circumvents the hurdles of pristine state formation by diminishing the distinctions between tribal–clan polities, early states, and the secondary states that came after and in emulation of them. All such polities, in Gat's view, arose spontaneously out of demographic expansion and wars of pastoralists and agriculturalists. In the vortex of 'evolutionary development', any number of initial conditions could spark the sequence that led from villages and tribes via centralized chiefdoms to petty states, and thence to larger ones. According to this view, the state is not a distinct form of political organization, but merely a later phase in a process that leads organically to higher levels of complexity and centralization, conditions permitting. Just as *War in Human Civilization* provides no definition of war as distinct from violent conflict in general, it also offers no definition of the state, to distinguish it qualitatively from tribes and chiefdoms. Neither war nor state could be a distinct phenomenon within its evolutionary paradigm: 'State emergence from stratified/chiefly tribal society—with all the related marks of the state period—kept occurring in different and variably connected regions of the world almost up to the present.'[34]

[handwritten margin note: "weak state is weak state, is weak war"]

For Gat, the tribe-to-state spiral would begin when a charismatic warlord attracted enough armed followers to allow him to break free of his dependence on a tribal assembly or council of elders. He would then distribute the booty of war to maintain his companions, with a view to generating ever greater resources for himself and

---

34 *WHC*, p. 232.

[handwritten: liberal drives realism even in early state; seems unlikely in proto-state period]

his men. As his retinue expanded, the distribution of rewards would become increasingly unequal. This process of redistribution scrambled the old kin networks by subsuming the clans of the conquered as well as their clients and dependents, constituting the ethnic core of a new people. But if this was the basic script for the origins of centralized chiefdoms, did such communities then go on to become states? The Book of Kings describes Saul's creation of a fragile state from a tribal confederation, but the primitive Israelites were, at this point, surrounded by hostile cities and empires whose sophisticated institutions could be adopted wholesale. Without this context, such polities invariably failed to cross the threshold to establish sovereign extractive control over a territory and its inhabitants. Gat offers many examples of purported tribe-to-state escalations from Asia, Africa, the Pacific islands and the Celto-Germanic periphery of the Roman empire. But he acknowledges, after discussing Tacitus's account of Maroboduus's rise from confederate chieftain to monarch, that this was not a path to statehood: 'These echoes of early kingship in the Germanic realm help to demonstrate how frail and susceptible to disintegration the early state structure tended to be.'[35]

Was conquest the immediate catalyst of pristine state formation, or did the latter require the prior establishment of pacified relations of surplus extraction? Gat claims that there is no need to dichotomize between *Innen-* and *Aussenpolitik* in explaining the emergence of the very first states, arguably because he does recognize that these pose a special problem. If pristine state formation was the outcome of a general evolutionary logic that unfolded wherever conditions permitted, there would, of course, be no need to distinguish the first states from the secondary states that were formed from conquering or emulating them. Gat argues that these distinctions should not be too sharply drawn, since after the advent of the first states, new states were often established by conquest. But gliding over the question of

---

35   *WHC*, p. 244.

origins makes it impossible to register the *unnaturalness* of territorial statehood—the radical break it entailed from the forms of community that preceded it, or, for that matter, to determine the role played by force in its inception. Otterbein's comprehensive comparative study of these beginnings suggests rather that the arrival of warfare in a region of peaceful agriculturalists could prevent the development of the state, 'just as a west-to-east-blowing El Niño wind rips off the top of a developing hurricane'.[36] While early state formation was not pacific, the emerging ruling bloc arguably required freedom from external threats to break the old social contract. At this point another—always problematic—distinction, between war and forms of coercion directed at subjects who are not enemies, would have to be made.

In *The Sources of Social Power* Michael Mann formulated the core problems surrounding the ancient origins of state-based civilization. Firstly: 'How did some acquire permanent power over the material life chances of others, giving them the capacity to acquire property that potentially denied subsistence to others?' And secondly: 'How did social authority become permanently lodged in centralized, monopolistic coercive powers in territorially defined states?'[37] In addressing these problems, Mann's Weberian historical sociology reformulates the enigma addressed in Rousseau's *Discourse*: how was consent to this inequality secured, or rather how was the lack of consent overridden? Mann points out that whereas the transition to agriculture and the emergence of rank societies occurred independently and in many places, the autochthonous transition to state creation based on the appropriation of surplus was very rare, as it required the formation of a quasi-public authority that was very difficult to achieve, and often even to conceive: 'Movement towards rank and political authority was endemic but reversible. Beyond that nothing was

---

36 Otterbein, *How War Began*, p. 96.
37 Mann, *The Sources of Social Power*, vol. 1, p. 49.

sustainable.'[38] If nascent society was a cage, he suggests, its doors were left unlocked, for its members could still revolt or flee. What then were the specific circumstances in which human beings were caged, permitting concentrations of power to cross the critical threshold without triggering an exodus? For Mann, it is only in naturally fertilized alluvial fields—river valleys, lakesides and deltas subject to flooding and silting—that human beings chose not to flee the cage but to cleave to their diminishing shares, even as others began to live off their life chances.

Further, and possibly no less decisive, precipitants and adhesives of statehood are ignored in Gat's account. In its relentless emphasis on agonistics, *War in Human Civilization* barely mentions the role of writing in the consolidation of the new public order, and the unprecedented organizational possibilities that this development opened up, in introducing abstract classifications and context-independent communication. In this story of the sword and the plough, the book plays little role. But with the possible exception of the Inca realm, writing was, in fact, indispensable in crystallizing the authority of nascent states in every zone of their pristine emergence, even though thereafter it often rapidly disseminated into the stateless peripheries of these civilizations. Perhaps Gat downplays the role of writing to avoid turning the focus away from armed and virile men towards the more ascetic lives of scribes and priests, men who have contributed so little to the procreation of the race. The spiritual authority of those 'who have subjects and do not govern them' by arms is rendered inexplicable.[39]

A symptomatic curiosity of *War in Human Civilization* is its exclusion of the dimension of meaning—and hence of legitimacy—from its account of human history. Ideas and ideals, Gat avers, are important in 'identity formation', but their meanings are little

38   Ibid., p. 67.
39   Niccolo Machiavelli, *The Prince*, Chicago: University of Chicago Press, 1998, Chap. xi, p. 135.

[handwritten margin note, top: and yet the ideas become more complicated and manifest themselves into the lives of beings that still have relatively unchanging needs]

. more than 'necessary illusions', and have little independent role beyond reinforcing the logics of rule. As the story moves further away from its hominid beginnings, culture is cut adrift from the biological state of nature, and Gat's evolutionary theory debouches into a slack power jargon that maintains only the semblance of a continuity between them: 'Forms of power flow and translate into each other, or to put it in a less reified manner, possessors of power move to expand and guard it, among other things by gaining hold and tightening their grip on the various levers of power.'[40] Such passages accord with the common sense of both the Foucauldian and the more positivist wings of contemporary scholarship; tautological notions of power are found in both. What, though, are the consequences for this story of humankind? In a work of such universal ambition, Gat bypasses the Weberian theme of world religions. Yet even if religions never alleviated, as opposed to simply interpreting, human suffering, their conspicuous presence as organizations and systems of meaning in the superstructures of civilization drastically limits the plausibility of Gat's reduction of society to military-power logics.

[handwritten margin note, right side: Culture makes our world and our ways of acting on it for control of ideological motivation the fear of culture + the unknown]

Hordes at the gate

Gat's narrative skips the earliest, temple-based polities of Sumer, going directly to the martial era of kingship that began in the early third millennium, when the city states of Sumer were conquered by pastoral marcher lords such as Sargon of Akkad, 'whose fathers had lived in tents'. He draws liberally on Diamond's *Guns, Germs, and Steel* in tracking the origins and consequences of this emerging bifurcation between farmer and pastoralist within Neolithic societies. In southwest Asia, the niche terrain between fertile and arid lands was occupied by peoples practising a mix of rudimentary husbandry and scratch farming—like the later shepherds, brigands

---

40   *WHC*, p. 234.

and fugitives on the fringes of Canaan, the *habiru* or Hebrews. It is in the subsequent dialectic between Eurasian agrarian civilizations and the pastoral, and later nomadic, hosts who hovered on their borders, that military innovations came to play a determining role. In their intercourse with agrarian civilizations, pastoralists were often the innovators. Horse domestication and the wheel first arose on the great steppe—4,000 miles broad, 1,000 miles deep—stretching from the Ukraine to Mongolia. The later breeding of a larger equid made possible the introduction of horseback cavalry by 900 BC in Western Eurasia, reaching China five centuries later during the period of the warring states.

Gat's story of the role of force in history now begins to assume a specifically military logic, in which Eurasian states and empires rise and fall as the pendulum of military superiority swings back and forth between horse and infantry, from ninth-century BC Assyria to the Swiss pike phalanx of the fifteenth century. Here the author's own military judgments come into play. Although Gat hedges his claims to such an extent that it is difficult to determine whether he thinks cavalry was ever the superior military branch west of the steppe, his considered opinion seems to be that it was only on vast, flat and sparsely populated terrains that mounted warriors had a decisive advantage over infantry formations.

The medieval ascendancy of feudal knights was thus a historical anomaly that had already come to an end by the late Middle Ages, as the flower of French chivalry was cut down by the English longbow and Swiss pike. The phalanx formation of archaic Greece inaugurated the pre-eminence of infantry in the pattern of Western war from Sumer to the Roman Republic. In Gat's view, the phalanx was the military expression of civic modes and orders that are distinctive to the West. Close-quarter shock infantry tactics were standard throughout most of its history, distinguishing it from the East where soldiers avoided frontal combat. Even Europe's later forms of heavy cavalry inclined toward close-quarter shock battle, as distinct from the light-cavalry missile tactics of the Near and Far East. But such opposed modes were adapted not just to the different peoples and authority structures of these two zones of Eurasia, but more directly to the geographical terrains that underlay these divergences. As a result, Eastern expansion hit its limit on the opposite coast of the Aegean, and later Kiev, while Western expansion, before the eighteenth century, came to an end just east of the Levant, roughly where Parthian cavalry archers scored their victory over Crassus's legions in 53 BC. Where the Islamic conquerors of Spain and Sicily or the Ottoman overlords of the Balkans fit into this account is not clear.

Rise of the West

The penultimate theme of *War in Human Civilization* is the opposition of East and West, more specifically the causes of Europe's later overwhelming ascendancy. Among the various accounts of European exceptionalism, from Machiavelli to Weber, Gat opts for Montesquieu's geographical determinism. The fact that Western Europe was not exposed to a vast pastoralist steppe frontier—in contrast to the Middle East, China and Northern India—was what set its history down a different path. Geography conspired to prevent the formation of a continental empire after the collapse of the Pax Romana. On the western fringes of Eurasia, geopolitical systems of warring states were the norm. But the European soil itself, and the form of cultivation to which it gave rise, reinforced this regional aversion to imperial despotism; the dispersed, dry farming of Western Europe was less labour intensive and more individualistic than the irrigation crop regimes of East and South Asia whose peasants tended, as a result, to be more servile than their rugged occidental counterparts.

However speculative such reflections, by the eighteenth century the pre-industrial European great powers were, by most accounts, militarily superior to the empires ruled from the Sublime Porte, the Forbidden City and Red Fort. Had centuries of competition in the European multi-state zone boosted late Absolutist military capacity beyond the formidable levels attained by the contemporary gun-power empires of the Near and Far East? Surprisingly, Gat dismisses the claim that the European Miracle can be explained by an early-modern 'revolution in military affairs'— though this is where one would expect his argument to lead. It was not, he maintains, military formations and the art of war but rather the size of the exploitable resource base that ultimately determined the outcome of inter-societal conflict. So can Europe's later ascendancy be explained in terms of an early-modern fiscal breakthrough? After all, so many centuries of incessant warfare between rival European polities would have likely deepened their fiscal grip, allowing them to extract a greater tribute from their subjects than was possible for Ottoman, Manchu and Mughal rulers. But Gat also rejects this claim for a pre-industrial tributary superiority of European states. Adam Smith's observation that no more than one per cent of an entire population could ever be supported as fully professional soldiers, held true for ancients and moderns, East and West alike. European absolutism's occasional lurches beyond this limit ended in bankruptcies.

Instead, Gat at this point shifts the emphasis from arms to commerce, as the factor that ultimately separated the West from the rest. It is not at all clear what has happened to our 'innate' behavioural propensities, long since unmentioned. Having dropped the genetics of aggression earlier on in the story of civilization, military force itself wanes in importance and begins to share the lead role with the spirit of commerce, before being superseded by it. In this, as in other respects, Gat follows in the footsteps of Herbert Spencer.

The great transition

But what distinguished this European-centred colonial and trading system from the vast and sophisticated commercial worlds of contemporary South and East Asia? Gat lamely proffers that Asian merchants had fewer reasons for long-distance sea voyages, as if the fact that its raw materials and markets were farther from home could explain Europe's transition to capitalism. In fact, for thousands of years, commercialization throughout Eurasia had expanded and contracted in line with Malthusian population cycles, the aggregate expression of age-old logics of peasant subsistence and reproduction. From remote antiquity, the existence of urban concentrations of rulers and their retainers living off surpluses appropriated in the form of corvée, rent and taxes invariably stimulated the formation of vast trading networks and merchant hierarchies, but left intact and indeed reinforced the agrarian stagnation at the base. The surpluses fuelling commercialization were skimmed and racked from subsistence cultivators. Even if the Euro-Atlantic colonial and trading system was a more developed version of this age-old symbiosis of merchant capital and coercion, it is not at all clear how further advances along the same lines could have dissolved the great entrenched reefs of peasant subsistence communities that relied on their own plots to achieve a modicum of food security.

Capitalism could be described as a wholly novel dynamic of economic development that overcomes the aggregate Malthusian consequences of peasant survivalism by *enforcing* market dependency on all those who have to make a living, compelling them to compete, specialize and innovate; the consequence of which is the incessant growth of productivity and income. Over time, this leads to a steep reduction in the number of people required to produce food, from the post-Neolithic norm of 80 or 90 per cent to the single digits of today's rich capitalisms. The transcendence of the zero-sum logic of coercive extraction of surpluses from peasants living off nature's meagre bounty is a major turning point in the narrative. The precondition and consequence of this great transformation is the elimination of coercion from the process of systematically reaping the fruits of other people's labour: 'It would only be with modernity—at the very same time that the ability to generate force grew exponentially, in line with growing productivity—that the tie between force and wealth acquisition would begin to unravel.'[41] But Gat belongs to the overwhelming majority of contemporary scholars who do not recognize the problem of how this 'tie' actually unravelled. The economic superiority of capitalism makes it seem natural to assume that when legal and political barriers to trade fall, the spontaneous order of economic development takes off. This is Adam Smith's story of how commercial-civil society emerged when feudal lords, covetous of luxury goods from afar, shed their wasteful retinues and economized on estate management to raise money for these baubles. Enterprising merchants then hired redundant retainers and ex-peasants, and the great, virtuous cycle of bartering and trucking began in earnest.

For Gat there was no essential disagreement between Adam Smith and Karl Marx on the origins of this unprecedented social condition, an order of things that seems to relegate all other modes of life to stages of pre-history. Like Smith, 'Marx maintained that the capitalist market economy differed from earlier forms of social organization in that . . . its extraction mechanism was predominantly economic, rather than based on the direct use or threat of violence.'[42] But as Robert Brenner's classic essay on the agrarian origins of capitalism makes clear, the breakdown of exploitation through force—the feudal protection racket—did not by itself clear the way for economic development, for this happened throughout continental Western Europe in the fourteenth and fifteenth centuries, and the result was a more or less legally free peasantry that seized the opportunity to continue in its traditional mode of subsistence reproduction, only now less burdened by arbitrary exactions.[43]

---

41   *WHC*, p. 442.
42   *WHC*, p. 492.
43   Robert Brenner, 'The Origins of Capitalist Development: A Critique of Neo-Smithian Marxism', *New Left Review* 1: 104, July–August 1977.

As Marx once observed, the more natural market society seems to be, the more difficult it becomes to recognize the problem of a transition to capitalism. In this respect Gat does not exceed the assumptions of his contemporaries, who often seem to regard it as nature's default mode of production. But as with the origin of the state, the advent of capitalism cannot be explained by the elimination of sundry obstacles to a pre-existing spontaneous course of development. In his comparative history of late-medieval and early-modern property regimes, Brenner argued that in England alone this ancient Malthusian deadlock was broken by an anomalous, unintended outcome of class struggles between lord and peasant that opened up the path to the primitive accumulation of capital. Feudal forms of coercion sustaining lordly incomes collapsed, without tenants being able to secure the legal control of their plots that would have allowed them to pursue food security in the old way. A mutant system arose, depriving both landlord and tenant of non-market access to the means of their subsistence, compelling them to compete, specialize and innovate. How it thereafter spread from early modern England raises a whole series of other controversies. But like the origins of agriculture and the state, the advent of capitalism is a development that cannot be explained by a transhistorical, evolutionary logic of subsistence and reproduction leading to ever-higher levels of 'complexity'.[44]

Empire of liberty

War in Human Civilization proceeds to consider the fate of military conflict in the age of world capitalism that began, by most accounts, in the nineteenth century. Thomas Paine's crisp judgment on this historical situation anticipated the conclusion of

---

44   Nor, of course, have modern revolutionary projects of social change conformed to the distinction between purposive action within a mode of production, on the one hand, and transitions between them which are not merely unintended, but processes 'without a subject', on the other.

liberals from Constant to Bentham: 'If commerce were permitted to act to the universal extent it is capable, it would extirpate the system of war.'[45] Classical liberalism emerged in the context of a long suspension of inter-state hostilities that set in after Waterloo. The wars of the Revolution and Empire had inadvertently realized Adam Smith's criticism of the old regime of mercantilist war by destroying it, eventually turning the Atlantic into the *mare nostrum* of British-centred world capitalism. The number of wars among the Great Powers decreased dramatically after 1815. Gat sets out to resolve two profound questions concerning the epochal trendline that began with the structural unravelling of 'the tie between force and wealth acquisition'. Firstly, what was the geopolitical logic of the first era of world market capitalism, in terms of manpower mobilization and arms races? Secondly, why did the pacification trend of the nineteenth century break down in the twentieth?

With the onset of industrialization, modern states became better able to tap the wealth of nations, despite the separation of public from private spheres. The explosive growth of productivity notwithstanding, Gat shows that a simultaneous increase in manpower costs kept the peacetime limit of armed men removed from production at around the classic one per cent. But in times of war, a wholly unprecedented nine per cent of the male population could be called to arms. This burgeoning military capacity remained for the most part latent over the course of the century, but the American Civil War was an ominous indicator of things to come. The second industrial revolution was forming the administrative and economic conditions for the next century's lurches into total mobilization. What were the geopolitical catalysts that activated this potential? According to Gat, each industrial revolution, from the first to the latest, revolutionized weapon systems, compelling states to make costly adjustments to traditional force structures and politically controversial changes

---

45   Cited in *WHC*, p. 510.

of strategic orientation. J. F. C. Fuller, the Mosleyite theorist of tank warfare whose work played such a salient role in Gat's earlier *History of Military Thought*, argued that the rate of technological innovation had reached a point where the best-armed forces of the present generation would be crushed in open battle with a well-equipped opponent from the next. Massive land grabs by white settler states and colonies to one side, it is arguable that military predation was ceasing to be an effective means to increase national wealth during this period. Nonetheless, for the European Great Powers, the penalty for falling behind in arms races that continued even through periods of peace could be a catastrophic surprise when the test of force finally came.

Gat accepts Lenin's conclusion that decades of free-trade capitalism mutated into a pattern of inter-imperialist rivalries over monopolistic spheres of influence. What are his judgments on the ideologically defined contending powers that arose from the carnage of industrial civilization's First World War— Communism, Fascism and liberal democracy? Gat demonstrates an admirable impartiality in considering the alternatives, and rejects claims that the victory of the latter was fore-ordained. Communism failed because it could only leap forward once, on the back of collectivized peasants. Gat suggests that fascist forms of state capitalism might have been more viable—as economically efficient as the liberal variant of capitalism, but more committed to maximizing population fitness and growth. On Gat's account, there are good reasons to think that fascism was a viable regime choice for capitalist societies confronting economic collapse, extreme security threats and population decline.

Why then did the liberal-democratic camp so decisively prevail in the struggle for world power? This is the subject of a vast political science in the us, much of it self-congratulatory. Gat exhibits a cool disregard for the pieties of this wall-to-wall consensus. The contingencies surrounding American entry into both world wars do not conform to the logic of an inevitable liberal victory. Just as in 1914, liberal states were allied with Tsarist autocracy, without which they would have had no chance, so too in the Second World War the outcome was sealed by a contingent alliance of the Anglo-Saxon states with the Soviet Union. Gat argues that the tendency of democracies to ally with one another only became a significant geopolitical factor during the Cold War. In his view, the endlessly repeated assertion that democracies do not go to war with one another withstands sceptical scrutiny only by improbable qualifications. One might add that if the thesis regarding liberal democracies and war is limited to the post-1945 era, the significance of this is diminished by the fact that nuclear weapons eventually neutralized all inter-state conflict in the industrialized core: after all, during the Cold War, there were no frontal collisions between the Communist and liberal-democratic states either. In any case, before, during and after the Cold War, liberal democracies ruthlessly pursued realist strategies: 'the hard record seems to support no particular peaceful inclination on the part of liberal democracies.'[46]

Both leaders and followers in the West today have much to congratulate themselves on. But the lax cultural climate of capitalist democracies, the bounteous harvest of victory over Fascism and then Communism, contains its own dangers in Gat's estimation. Affluence has resulted in an increasing aversion to hardship and discipline, as the farmers and factory workers of yesteryear give way to the flabbier, more voluble type of today's service workforce. Declining birth rates, ageing populations and the steady erosion of patriarchy have pacified once testosterone-driven societies. The conclusion of *War in Human Civilization* seems to be that the most advanced phase of civilization has superseded the evolutionary rationale for war: 'imprudent vehemence . . . appears to have all but disappeared in the affluent, consumer-hedonistic, liberal-democratic societies that developed after the Second World War.'[47] The

46   *WHC*, p. 572.
47   *WHC*, p. 600.

decline of bellicosity has posed a challenge to the guardian power of Western capitalism, and American leaders need to develop a new Way of War consonant with contemporary social characteristics. Gat has suggested that the example of Liddell Hart, pioneer of a flexible strategic orientation for the inter-war British Empire, might be a beacon today for its American counterpart, historically susceptible to oscillations between isolationism and over-extension. The doctrines of containment—armed co-existence, client-state imperialism, sanctions regimes, propaganda—are the elements of an unsurpassed hegemonic formula for post-militaristic empires.

Future wars

There have been three periods of pacification in the core of advanced societies since the beginning of the nineteenth century: between 1815 and 1854, between 1871 and 1914, and from 1945 to the present. What does the future hold? Gat seems to dismiss the idea that terrorists could inflict much damage on Western societies, or destabilize them through provoking disproportionate retaliation. In the grand scheme of things, Islamists seem to be of little consequence: 'They represent no alternative model for the future and pose no military threat to the developed liberal-democratic world, as did the fascist powers, which were among the world's strongest and most advanced societies.'[48] The attacks of 9/11 might almost be dismissed—after all, adjusting for population, the fatalities caused by these spectacular attacks amounted to the equivalent of only forty Israeli dead, not much for a people inured to such events. But with little regard for consistency, Gat then expresses his views on this 'unprecedented horror' in more familiar tones: 'The 9/11 mega-terror attacks constitute a landmark in history and in the development of large-scale human deadly violence', etc.[49]

---

48   *WHC*, p. 644.
49   *WHC*, p. 637.

Sound bites such as these seem jarringly out of place in a work that prides itself on being—and mostly is—tough-minded and impartial. To give them a semblance of weight, Gat presents the usual scenario of terrorists with WMDs, but can only adduce the infamous Aum Shinrikyo cult of Japan. Consistency demands a further nuancing of his theoretical framework, suggesting a form of combined and uneven neo-social evolutionary development: while male aggression may have been neutralized in the ambience of liberal-democratic affluence, its triggers are elsewhere to be found in abundance, and in the Orient there exists a religion uniquely suited to activate them. Before such 'super-empowered angry men', deterrence will be difficult; but the main point, from a Western perspective, is not to be provoked into destabilizing campaigns.

The storm clouds over the old cradles of civilization indicate a wider strategic problem that Western states have confronted since the end of the Second World War, and which is unlikely to go away even if a more prudent policy of deterrence is adopted. Why have liberal states, victorious over both Fascism and Communism, so often failed to prevail in asymmetric conflicts on the underdeveloped peripheries of the world system? Decolonization itself was the first, but largely manageable expression of this problem. Although European colonial expansion annexed vast territories and populations to the modern capitalist core, in Gat's view, much of what was conquered was of little economic or strategic significance to it, and so was easy to give up. His depiction of the relationship of the US to the remainder that did have value is admirably clear:

> Countries that successfully underwent industrialization, such as those
> of East Asia, were absorbed into the capitalist global economy (even
> though usually developing behind protectionist walls), while being
> shielded by western military power; and countries that possessed critical
> raw materials, most notably the oil-producing Persian Gulf States, were

similarly shielded, while their domestic stability was fostered by the techniques of informal imperialism.[50]

One of the main geopolitical problems confronting the US-centred world-system is the lack of viable military options should one of these more crucial clients defect, for in Gat's view it is unlikely that today's Western populations would have the stomach to pacify rebellions with crushing force, even in the half-light of embedded coverage. While the great arsenals of civilization can no longer be used against one another without risk of mutual destruction, recent developments confirm a longer-term trend exposing the limits of the direct use of military force against irregular, asymmetrical resistance. The so-called Revolution in Military Affairs created a mirage that led US policy makers into thinking that they could reverse the legacy of decolonization, in a heartland of twentieth-century nationalism. Gat expresses some conventional scepticism regarding the wisdom of US attempts to 'export democracy' to troublesome clients and failed states, situated within the context of a long career of humanitarian enterprises: 'Wilson and his successors discovered in failed efforts to establish democracy through intervention, including military intervention—in Mexico, the Dominican Republic, Haiti, Nicaragua, Costa Rica and Guatemala—democracy is neither desired by all, nor unconditionally sustainable.'[51]

Since it is hard to believe that such formulations can be attributed to naivety on Gat's part, one must assume that they are the considered views of a policy intellectual with his finger on the pulse of a liberal American and European establishment, rattled by 'unilateralism' but confident that, come what may, it is always others who are responsible for the violence and squalor that thwarts the spread of civilization.[52] In the concluding reflections of

---

50   *WHC*, p. 561.
51   *WHC*, p. 652.
52   The author belongs to a generation of Israelis who, after Oslo, have come to accept the hard facts of life.

War in Human Civilization, Gat suggests that after a brief period of post–Cold War pacification, a time of troubles may be ahead. The possibility of a world-economic downturn or even collapse cannot be ruled out. The rapidly sinking fortunes of neoliberalism might encourage states and movements to break away from the world market and build autonomous economic regions. In a recent article in *Foreign Affairs*, Gat suggests that if these scenarios materialize it will become clearer that the main geopolitical threat to the West is neither Salafist terrorism nor the Islamic Republic of Iran, but the authoritarian capitalism of rising China and sinking Russia.[53] In any event, the great arsenals of the West are in no danger of becoming obsolete anytime soon. How effective they will be in promoting *la mission civilisatrice* on the various battlefields of this planet of slums is another matter.

Post-nature?

Gat's neo-social darwinist chronicle finally ends, like his earlier intellectual history, on the featureless terrain of journalism and policy studies. The author's apparent aversion to historical forecast confines him to the very near future. For this epic of the blind course of nature must falter and retreat before the onset of biotechnological civilization—or, alternatively, barbarism. Of course, even as such transformations invalidate the last arguments for genetic determinism, those who experience this further plasticization of nature may cling to reified notions of it all the more emphatically. The danger is that the contemporary mismeasure of man, unlike its racist nineteenth- and twentieth-century predecessors, looks to an actual techno-scientific understanding and control of the codes of life. As a result, it is conceivable that the ideological naturalization of capitalism might begin to crystallize into a real one. In this

---

53   Azar Gat, 'The Return of Authoritarian Great Powers', *Foreign Affairs*, July–August 2007.

context, other traditions of thought will prove to be more useful for thinking about the alternatives to what the 'spontaneous' evolution of society holds in store for us. What are the futures of inequality, community, procreation and violence in this latest phase of second nature? These are questions for a latterday Rousseau.

II

Reflections on Politics

6

The National Imagination

Eric Hobsbawm, in his final chapter of a survey on the history of nationalism, claimed that the nation-state had embarked on a declining curve of historical viability, and that the beginnings of its fossilization would clear the way for deeper explorations into its origins, impact and possible futures.[1] Not long afterwards, this judgment appeared to be refuted by the resurgence of national causes in the former Communist world. Hobsbawm, however, had suitably qualified his prediction so as to take into account the outbreak and intensification of national conflicts in such contexts. His claim that the nation-state was no longer a 'vector' of historical development meant only that the trend lines in the most dynamic zones of the world system had begun to push beyond familiar national dimensions.

Although Hobsbawm alluded to Hegel, the notion of capitalism bypassing the nation-state is, of course, one of the central themes of classical Marxism. The latter held that economic laws of motion would come into conflict with the constricting frame of the national market by way of either free trade or imperialism, or some combination of the two. But the historical vision of the *Communist Manifesto* is undoubtedly more complex. The prediction that all that is solid—national cultures included—will melt into air is

1   E. J. Hobsbawm, *Nations and Nationalism Since 1780*, Cambridge: Cambridge University Press, 1990. This chapter originally appeared in *New Left Review* 1: 211, May–June 1995.

balanced by another: that the expansion of capitalist civilization will promote the formation of territorially bounded, modern bourgeois states. Although these two themes jostle with each other in the pages of the *Manifesto*, Marx as well as later Marxists, believing that proletarian revolutions were imminent, stressed the first theme over the second, for therein dialectically lay the possibility that the widening cosmopolitan scope of the market would throw up working classes of proportionate scale. Yet the transnationalization of the productive forces that capitalism is now setting into motion is historically unprecedented. Confounding established expectations, its main thrusts seem to undermine the very bases of successful class struggle in advanced industrial societies, and it is difficult to foresee the conditions under which the organized working classes will rise up again 'stronger, firmer, mightier'.

The Site of Struggle

According to Marx, the modern class struggle passes through a series of historical stages beginning with riots and the breaking of machinery, and ending in nationwide civil wars. As a preliminary condition for the successful conduct of the class struggle, the unregulated competition of all against all must be suppressed within the ranks of labour. Historically, this was accomplished by dint of struggles and negotiations that took place throughout the state, aimed at regulating capital's purchase of labour-power. In Marx's theory, then, the state is not just the functional weapon of the possessing classes; it is also the unrecognized site and point of concentration of the struggle against those classes, ratifying the results of that struggle. Far from opening the gates to more expansive working-class organization, the eclipse of the state deepens labour's functional subordination to capital and threatens to dissolve the site and boundaries of sustainable collective action against it.

This development is difficult to understand from within the framework of Marxism—and not only because of the strain thus placed on its theory of the state. The graver challenge is to the 'anthropological' basis of its very conception of history. For Marx, the irresistible scalar expansion of world capitalism could only temporarily leap beyond the dimensions of sustainable collective action against it. Capitalism's laws of motion, even as they continually pulverized the cultural and material basis of all limited forms of membership, would supposedly, and incessantly, recreate the bases of class solidarity at ever more cosmopolitan levels. No single Marxist idea has been more discredited than this one, inasmuch as even the semblance of such a dialectic has been overthrown.

Régis Debray has argued that the principal victories of the Left in the twentieth century emerged out of an unacknowledged liaison with the nation, and that the future of the Left depends on its ability to reinvent a national politics for the twenty-first century.[2] Behind this strategic assessment stands the claim that the well-spring of political action resides in the pathos of national membership, for it is only in the form of a 'people' that the masses erupt into political life and make history. In this view, nations are like the 'fused groups' of Sartrean philosophy—in a political sense, existentially more decisive than class as communities of fate. The problem with Marxism, according to Debray, is that its central concerns do not enable it to grasp the enigmatic subjectivity which such collectivities assume.

As a characterization of Marx's writings, this is perhaps only half true; the *Grundrisse*, in fact, contains many rich insights into the material foundations of the pre-capitalist peasant community. In his intriguing sketches of what for him were the four basic types of agrarian civilization in Eurasia—Oriental, Slavic, Mediterranean and Germanic—Marx argued that the distinctive communal

---

2   Régis Debray, 'Marxism and the National Question', *New Left Review* 1: 105, September–October 1977, p. 33.

organization of entitlement, cooperation and exploitation formed the primordial social relationship of these pre-capitalist societies. Capitalism is premised on the epochal suspension and negation of the communal organization of direct producers in their relation to nature, to one another and to their appropriators. Released from the semi-natural, communal provision of peasant subsistence, whole regions of the earth are plunged into an inescapable market dependence, setting into motion the ceaseless, wave-like expansion of the productive forces.

In this view, the structure of modern society arises out of the anarchic interplay of market forces, out of the counter-finalities of alienated labour. In the *Philosophy of Right*, Hegel argued that the modern sovereign state, though based on this condition of radical alienation, transcended it by imparting to peoples organized into political communities a higher level of ethical life, historical personality and collective agency. Marx, in his famous critique of this work, retorted that the political community constituted by the modern state was merely an 'imagined community', powerless because unreal. In his essay 'On the Jewish Question', he depicted the public identity of the 'completed bourgeois state' as post-Christian. However, if stripped of all cultural and historical particularity, as he argued such a state must be to achieve its final form, one must ask in what sense it could be considered national. Indeed, in conventional terms, the completed bourgeois state would seem to be post-nationalist as well as post-Christian. The undetermined national dimension in this conception of the modern state is internal to all subsequent Marxist theory. Debray's criticism in this sense holds true: while Marxists spent enormous amounts of time theorizing the bourgeois state, they left unresolved the question of what it means for a state to be a nation-state. The political or economic concepts of, for instance, civil society or modes of production are not commensurable with the anthropological practice of naming communities: terms like 'Chinese capitalism' are semantically unstable, if necessary, conjunctions. The enigmatic and under-theorized juxtaposition here of a reference to a bounded community defined by language, territory or descent with a reference to an abstract social process indifferent to such boundaries brings to light the difficulties that Marxism had in formulating an effective critique of such communities of fate.

Hegel, like Marx, had little sympathy for Romanticism, with its celebration of venerable and invented customs. The emphasis in Hegel, as in Marx, is mostly on the state, but the state's relationship to the culturally defined collectivity to which it gives form is maintained as a problem and a source of tension, not extinguished as was the case in the essay 'On the Jewish Question'. 'Nations' in Hegel's theory express the phase structure of human history, each successive phase an embodiment of Reason in the customary, or what Hegel called the ethical, life of a people. Thus was there a Chinese, an Indian, a Persian, a Greek, a Roman and finally a German nation. 'Nation' here is broadly synonymous with civilization, a largely non-ethnic and only vaguely geographic category. In fact, Hegel's 'German nation' is simply a synonym for the most advanced forms of modern civilization: representative government, rule of law, civil society, the modern bourgeois family and individualism—not Germanhood in any ethnic sense. This German nation came into its own, not when disparate Germanic peoples got their own state (an objective that Hegel himself opposed after the dissolution of the Holy Roman Empire), but rather when post-revolutionary Europe finally settled into the architectonics of the modern state. The diversity of peoples with respect to customs, institutions and beliefs is aligned to a higher rationality, but the connection between the low ethnographic fact and the lofty self-determination of Reason remains unresolved: What is specifically 'German' about the German nation? In Hegel's theory of development, the ethnically distinctive character of the nation is left as an opaque anthropological reminder.

An early text, *The Positivity of the Christian Religion*, expresses this problem with clarity and drama. Hegel here defines the nation more conventionally, as a community of customs, memory and fate, with 'its own imagery, its gods, angels, devils or saints who live in the nation's traditions, whose stories and deeds the nurse tells her charges and so wins them over by impressing their imagination', as well as its own 'ancient heroes' whose valor and exploits are widely commemorated.[3] But he then proceeds to argue that 'real' history is not the story of such communities: world-historical progress brings with it massive erasures in the fabric of ethnic life, creating new peoples to accomplish new tasks. For Hegel, the greatest transformation in history prior to the French Revolution was the rise, and the Reformation, of Christianity. Those Germanic tribes drawn into the orbit of that Christian revolution were forever sundered from their shadowy and shapeless ethnic pasts:

> Christianity has emptied Valhalla, felled the sacred groves, extirpated the national imagery as shameful superstition, as a devilish poison and instead given us the imagery of a nation whose climate, laws, culture and interests are strange to us, whose history has no connection to our own. A David or Solomon lives in our popular imagination but our country's heroes slumber in learned history books.[4]

For the early Hegel, such hybridization was lamentable, yet possibly reversible; later he saw it as necessary and irreversible. The progressive nations in Hegel's schema have no real ethnic memories and no ethnic lineage. They appear as the episodic subjects of a harsh, discontinuous history of freedom.

These notations on Hegel and Marx are meant to expose some of the tensions and displacements of emphasis involved in this interface of two images of the nation: as a general type of modern state or society and, in any given case, as a particular community

---

3   In Shlomo Avineri, *Hegel's Theory of the Modern State*, Cambridge: Cambridge University Press, 1974, p. 21.
4   Ibid., p. 20.

of fate whose outlines have been shaped by a history of language, settlement and politico-religious renewal. The point of opening a discussion of nationhood with Hegel and Marx is that there exists, in both their theories of world history, a gap between a story of generic modes and orders and an underdetermined ethnography of peoples. This gap reveals itself during attempts to grasp the dominant form of modern political community: the nation-state. The lacuna indicated here is not specific to Marxism per se, as it in fact raises some of the central unresolved problems of classical social theory: 1) In the context of a modernity defined by agonistic individualism and impersonal forms of social power, can agency be exercised by large-scale collectivities? 2) To what extent does socio-political change depend on the existence of such problematic collective subjects? 3) What is the more politically consequential form of modern collective subjectivity—nation or class?

Anderson and imagination

Benedict Anderson's small book *Imagined Communities* is distinctive in the contemporary literature on nationalism in the centrality it accorded to the issues just cited. Composed during the unexpected and disappointing aftermath of the victory of national liberation forces in Indochina—the downward spiral of Cambodian genocide, Vietnamese intervention and Sino-Vietnamese war—and published in 1983, it reflected on the significance of these events in a manner approaching the clairvoyant. At the time of the book's publication, the Soviet bloc seemed glacially stable, yet Anderson foresaw a coming collapse along national lines. Viewing the Indochinese tragedy as a culmination of two decades of hostility between 'actually existing socialisms', he noted that the belligerents had been making ever fewer references to socialist ideology and ever more references to 'sacred national interests'. The outbreak of national disputes between regimes still officially committed to the dogmas of internationalism underlined the need, in his view, for a fundamental re-evaluation of the whole problematic within which the Left had conceptualized the problem.[5]

In this spirit, Anderson proposes that nationalism should perhaps be seen not as an ideology like 'liberalism' but rather as the modern counterpart to kinship. But this initial suggestion to see the nation as an invented kinship structure is then overtaken by a more conceptually developed equating of the nation with an elective religious community. Obviously, presenting the nation as an imagined kinship form evokes associations quite different from identifying it with a world religion. The abrupt transition from one to the other reveals an ambivalence concerning the politics of nations and nationalism. Very simply put, is modern nationhood exclusive like kinship, or inclusive like the religious fellowship described in Galatians 3, in which there would be 'neither Jew nor Greek . . . neither slave nor free man . . . neither male nor female'?

Arguing the latter for most of the book, Anderson holds that nationalism, apparently like religion in this respect, is neither an 'ideology', in the sense of a doctrine, nor a form of 'false consciousness'. Both national community and religious community are grounded in a convocation with anonymous others: 'All communities larger than primordial villages of face-to-face contact . . . are imagined. Communities are to be distinguished, not by their falsity/genuineness, but by the style in which they are imagined.'[6] Here Anderson is claiming that social identity is a structured and shared symbolic projection and that, moreover, such organized outpourings of the imagination are impervious to being debunked by the enlightened mind.

Modern liberalism and socialism, it is implied, have failed to offer rich, compelling solutions to the arguably ineradicable problem of our finitude—the existential challenges of suffering,

5   Benedict Anderson, *Imagined Communities: Reflections on the Origin and Spread of Nationalism*, rev. ed., London: Verso, 1991 [1983]; henceforward *IC*.
6   *IC*, p. 6.

sickness and death. For Anderson, the enduring achievement of the great world religions was their ability to address the longing for solutions to these brute contingencies of existence within the framework of the narrative rituals that punctuate the life cycle. Although intensely local in its manifestations, Christianity, like Islam, could be experienced more broadly by the multitudes who journeyed to its sacred centres, participating in the geographies of pilgrimage and consuming the narratives of faith. A thin stratum of Latin literati imparted a semblance of uniformity to these narratives and representations through which the medieval world experienced itself. In a largely illiterate, dialect-divided agrarian civilization, Latin language uniformity gave the Church an authority, an institutional cohesion, that transcended and attenuated the jurisdictions of secular powers.

Anderson sees the origins of the modern nation in the early modern expansion of vernacular literacy that fomented the demise of this pan-European ecclesiastical order. Protestantism used vernacular texts to devastating effect in its pamphlet war against the Church and its allies, activating communities that had taken shape beneath the Latin-literate ruling stratum. Anderson argues that although neither Luther nor Calvin propounded national causes, in a sense the medium became the message. Literate civil societies were shaped and more sharply differentiated from one another as the mass-production techniques of early modern 'print-capitalism' standardized the norms and increased the density of social intercourse within particular vernacular languages.

But how do such cultural formations come to be imagined as 'nations' in Anderson's sense? That is to say, how do they appropriate the experience of the sacred attributed to world religions and give it civic and territorial shape? A recurring theme in the book is Marxism's failure to address 'the sacred', understood as a longing for immortality through membership in an imperishable collectivity. As in Durkheim, Anderson conceives the sacred as an anthropological constant of social life; the novelty of modernity lies in the fact that the national form it assumes is essentially secular. While the sacred and the secular might seem antithetical, for Anderson they intersect in the symbolic artefacts of the nation-state, such as the Tomb of the Unknown Soldier. This strange civic deity is the object of a communion reminiscent of an ancestor cult, but here intimacy is crossed with the anonymity of modern society.

This linking of an anonymous modernity and the sacral reverses Max Weber's verdict on modernity; instead of an iron cage, the arrival of the modern social order gives rise to a collective re-enchantment specific to it. Introducing the term 'imagined community', Anderson attempts to resolve the theoretical tension between two conflicting images of the nation: modern society is an abstract social system that is nonetheless experienced as a transcendent community of fate. Anderson's print-capitalism thus becomes a force that shatters old idols only to incessantly invent new ones. This is not simply Weber stood on his head; it is a departure from the Marx of the *Manifesto* as well. Instead of capitalism, the great profaner of all that is sacred, there is print-capitalism, the matrix and crucible of the secular reconstitution of the sacred.

How convincing is this attempted inversion of classical social theories of modernity? Accounts of modernity organized around science, bureaucracy or capitalism have had difficulty explaining why, over the past century, great multitudes have often shown themselves willing to endure enormous hardship and even death to acquire and maintain a homeland. The sacrifices required of citizens on many occasions during these epic struggles revealed an immense capacity for collectivization dormant within structurally atomized bourgeois societies. But it is precisely here, at the point of ultimate sacrifice, that the identification of the national with the sacred becomes questionable. A robust national identity deals in high stakes yet offers, at best, a monument to the soldier's heroic death. Unlike prophets, nationalists do not actually promise immortality. The modern national identity seems to offer far less consolation than does religion, and it is not entirely clear how in Anderson's argument the one could ever fill the void left by the decline of the other. But if we move away from this association of nation with elective religious community, and back to its original identification with forms of kinship, then another—albeit less 'progressive'—solution to this modern problem of the mobilization of sacrifice becomes apparent. For if there is an anthropologically invariant desire to overcome death through communal bonding, then arguably not only have the ties of kinship played this role more universally than have the salvation religions, but they have often done so without regard to any otherworldly rewards. The blood connection has unparalleled intensity, immediacy and naturalness: atheists, nationalists and Christians in equal numbers rush to save their children from burning houses. Even the most universalist of modern constitutions makes allowance for the mythic ethnic core of society, which must always be defended in the face of existential threats.

Only quite late in the book, however, does Anderson return to this equation between kinship and the imagined affinities within the nation:

> While it is true that in the last two decades the idea of the family-as-articulated-power-structure has been much written about, such a conception is certainly foreign to the overwhelming bulk of mankind. Rather, the family has been traditionally conceived as the domain of disinterested love and solidarity. So too, if historians, diplomats, politicians, and social scientists are quite at ease with the idea of 'national interest', for most ordinary people of whatever class the whole point of the nation is that it is interestless. Just for that reason, it can ask for sacrifices.[7]

While representations of the nation depend heavily on familial and fraternal motifs, the figure of the nation as an imagined kinship

---

7   *IC*, p. 131.

structure, as suggested earlier, is in fact not compatible with Anderson's focus on elective religious community. It is important to remember that, despite the melancholic tone of its introduction, the book has an almost uniformly positive view of nationalism, maintaining that its fundamental norm is fraternity, not hatred of and invidious comparison with the enemy. But the narrowing affinities of kinship seem too dependent on ethnic mythologies to serve as a ground for so generous a conception of the nation. The analogy to world religion better conveys an image of the nation that is open, even cosmopolitan, in its horizons. Pointing to the affinities between religious conversion and political naturalization, Anderson suggests that both are premised on conceptions of membership that supersede the raw fatalities of birth, kinship, and race. Ironically, this rather positive equation takes its terms from Lord Acton's famous polemic against nationalism. Shaken by the Risorgimento, Acton argued that modern nationalism represented a reversion to the unethical premises of the ancient world, in which 'merely natural' bonds of kinship and ethnic descent provided the basis for political association, whereas 'Christianity rejoices at the mixture of races'. For Anderson, by contrast, it is modern nations that rejoice in a sort of imagined mixture of races.

This depiction of nationalism is certainly foreign to many on the liberal Left, who see its exemplification in fascism and, more generally, the politics of ethnic cleansing. Disputing such associations, Anderson offers some moving lines from nationalist poetry and anthems to demonstrate that 'it is astonishing how insignificant the element of hatred is in these expressions of national feeling'.[8] The sharp distinction he draws between nationalism and fascism relies not simply on this charitable hermeneutic of the themes of patriotic fraternity, but also on his careful selection of case studies, drawn heavily from the eighteenth- and nineteenth-century Creole revolts in the Americas, with their constitutions

---

8   *IC*, p. 129.

and high republican ideals. The principle, if not the practice, of this Creole republicanism constitutes for him the paradigmatic form of nationhood. These insurgent, idealistic elites struggled to lead societies which, despite their great ethnic and racial diversity and division, came to be imagined as national communities—and they invented broad and inclusive genealogies to match these aspirations:

> The son of an Italian immigrant to New York will find ancestors in the Pilgrim Fathers . . . Spanish-speaking mestizo Mexicans trace their ancestries, not to Castilian conquistadors, but to half-obliterated Aztecs, Mayans, Toltecs and Zapotecs . . . San Martin's edict baptizing Quechua-speaking Indians as 'Peruvians'—a movement that has affinities with religious conversion—is exemplary. For it shows that from the start the nation was conceived in language, not in blood . . .[9]

Anderson stresses language because it defines membership in ways fundamentally connected to his specific conception of the nation. Language is intimate and natural, and thus, in the minds of an overwhelmingly monoglot humanity, deeply associated with the essence of oneself. The quasi-naturalness of these cultural formations sustains the idea of the nation as an eternal collective. Few of us conceive of even a distant future in which our own language is not spoken; many have difficulty imagining a past in which our language did not exist. And yet, despite its intimate association with self and being, language defines a form of collective membership which, unlike race, can be acquired:

> If every language is acquirable, its acquisition requires a real portion of a person's life: each new conquest is measured against shortening days. What limits one's access to other languages is not their imperviousness but one's own mortality. Hence a certain privacy to all languages . . .

---

9   *IC*, pp. 133, 140.

> Seen as both a *historical* fatality and as a community imagined through
> language, the nation presents itself as simultaneously open and closed.[10]

But there are, of course, several ways in which nations are not
'conceived in language'. Throughout the world the boundaries of
nation-states and the boundaries of linguistic distributions rarely
overlap—many nations share the same language; many states
are officially multilingual; in some states the official language
is no one's mother tongue. If the first possibility raises no
insurmountable difficulties for Anderson's claim, the second and
particularly the third suggest that language is only one dimension
of the 'nationality principle'. More problematically, these different
possible configurations raise the question as to whether there are
any cultural attributes that uniformly demarcate nationhood.

Notwithstanding such boundary problems, Anderson's
argument remains compelling. The conception of the modern
nation as an imagined community offers some advantages over any
attempt to subsume it under the concept of 'ideology'; the vaguely
Hegelian claim that nationalism is therefore likely to be with us
for some time, despite cosmopolitan protests and reveries, is also
plausible. And, like Hegel, Anderson maintains that reconciling
oneself to this situation has its advantages, as a world of nations is
not the worst of all possible worlds. A note of improbable optimism,
in fact, lies behind the formulation that 'nations are conceived in
language not in blood'.

The nation in arms

Anderson's focus on language involves an attempt to uncover
something deeper than citizenship. For him, mere membership in
a political community does not generate an imagined collectivity, a
'people'. While individuals might obey a Leviathan, no one would

---

10   *IC*, pp. 135, 133.

willingly—or, indeed, be obligated to—die for it, as Hobbes himself acknowledged. By contrast, a nation can legitimately issue the call to arms, which, if successful, evokes a collective identification that overrides and subsumes the tug of competing 'partial' memberships—class, family, town, workplace.

The problem for Anderson's thesis is that the cultural affinities shaped by print-capitalism do not in themselves seem sufficiently resonant to generate the colossal sacrifices that peoples are at times willing to make for their nation. It is difficult to see how a civil society conducting its quotidian affairs in a vernacular could inspire the same pathos as a religion whose mandate encompasses issues far weightier than mere life on this earth. If societies are imagined in sacred idioms, then vernacular sociability seems to offer much less in this regard than does religion. Anderson attempts to address the problem by claiming that the social organization of language in the modern world (schools, newspapers, novels) gives rise to a belief in the antiquity and imperishability of the nation. Yet such a belief could hardly be the basis of a compulsion to make sacrifices for that nation. To believe that French will be spoken in the twenty-fifth century is not the same as declaring, 'France is eternal.' Only the latter evokes a project, a struggle and a call to arms, and all this has arguably little to do with language.

The reason that the political nature of nationality warrants greater emphasis is not because the state is more important than language or culture in determining which groups are nations and which are not. Rather, the centrality of the state is posed by the very question which organizes Anderson's whole problematic: not what the nation is, but why people are willing to die for the one they consider theirs. Absent the possibility of sacrifice, it is doubtful whether the nation could evoke the affective peaks of collective belonging that Anderson attributes to the national imagination.

'Collective sacrifice', 'fatality', 'Tomb of the Unknown Soldier'—this is the language and imagery of war. But Anderson addresses the relationship of war to the pathos of national identity only fitfully, no doubt discomfited by its implications.[11] The state is not absent from Anderson's treatment of the 'cultural roots of the nation'; on the contrary, he presents a lengthy discussion of the role of absolutist state formation in shaping the cultural grids of what would later become nations. But here the rule of the state is strictly analogous to that of print-capitalism. The proto-bureaucracies of early modern Europe were simply an alternate path to the vernacular sociability which elsewhere emerged out of the Reformation and the market. The state, then, stirs the national imagination merely by giving territorial shape to a language of public life. But it is doubtful that either this strangely pacific process of state formation or the cultural affinities produced by print-capitalism would be capable of generating 'sacred' idioms of collectivity.

Max Weber, always attuned to the role of force in history, offered a few penetrating reflections on the relationship between national culture and the burdens of *Machtpolitik*:

> The political community is one of those communities whose action includes, at least under normal circumstances, coercion through jeopardy of life and freedom of movement. The individual is expected ultimately to face death in the group interest. This gives to the political community its particular pathos and raises its enduring emotional foundations. The community of political destiny, i.e. above all of common political struggle of life and death, has given rise to groups with joint memories which have often had a deeper impact than the ties of merely cultural, linguistic, or ethnic community. It is this 'community of memories' which constitutes the ultimately decisive element of national consciousness.[12]

---

11 His examples on this point are revealing. As indicated earlier, he draws very heavily on anti-colonial and national liberation struggles in which it is claimed that fraternal love of one's country trumps hatred of the colonizing people and their culture, as the source of national solidarity. But if this is true (and Frantz Fanon, for one, thought that even in these cases the record was mixed), can the same be said of war between states? The introductory reflections on the bewilderingly abrupt passage in the Indochinese theatre from anti-imperialist struggle to inter-state conflagration suggest that powerful hatreds and powerful loves are not so easily separated.

12 Max Weber, *Economy and Society*, p. 903.

For Weber, as for Hegel, the modern state possesses a historical purpose, or project, because it organizes a community into a sovereign polity ready for war. It is during war that the nation is imagined as a community that embodies an ultimate value. Ironically, after offering a positive portrayal of nationalism as the great political passion of the modern age, Anderson concedes that in fact war has always been the decisive test of this form of imagined community:

> The great wars of this century are extraordinary not so much in the unprecedented scale on which they permitted people to kill, as in the colossal numbers persuaded to lay down their lives . . . The idea of the ultimate sacrifice comes only with the idea of purity, through fatality . . . Dying for one's country, which usually one does not choose, assumes a political grandeur which dying for the Labour Party, the American Medical Association, or perhaps even Amnesty International cannot rival, for these are all bodies one can join and leave at easy will.[13]

Two implications in this passage cut against the general tenor of Anderson's idea of the nation. The first is that instead of the civic baptism of peasants into Frenchmen, or Quechuas into Peruvians, its conditions of possibility are located in the perpetuation of a sort of state of nature between nations. The second is that the most tenacious solidarities of recent centuries did not arise spontaneously from the social organization of vernacular language, but rather through the risks of membership in a political 'community of life and death'.[14] Thus, imagined nationhood, with its sacral affinities to religion, is not some

---

13   *IC*, p. 132.
14   Does the rise of the far Right signal a reversal of these developments? The striking thing here is the degree to which older national animosities have effectively disappeared from within its ranks, replaced now by a common hatred of the non-European immigrant. But regarding this hatred of the culture of foreigners, not 'redeemed' by love of one's compatriots—is it nationalism?

phenomenological constant of modern social life. It speaks in the voice of Fate most pointedly in times of war, when it acquires a monopoly on the precise meaning of patriotic behaviour. The nation then ceases to be an informal, contestable or taken-for-granted frame of reference, becoming instead a precise, univocal and resolutely imagined identity.

In contemporary Western Europe, after fifty years of a thorough pacification of inter-state relations, it is difficult to imagine the nation in sacred terms; other zones of the world system have moved more erratically down the same path. What had once been Great Powers were stripped by post-war agreements of their colonial empires, institutionally distinctive constitutions and full geopolitical sovereignty. Even as certain of those agreements now come undone, their institutional legacy is probably irreversible—the neutralization of any danger of war in this theatre has closed off the sources of the great political enchantments of the previous period. It is not just 'globalization' that has put a question mark over the future of the nation-state; in addition, after such an unprecedentedly long peace, the social and cultural atmosphere is unable to sustain themes of high drama in the political sphere. In a Europe where 'coercion through jeopardy of life and freedom of movement' is a fate reserved only for the immigrant worker, new social and cultural divisions have come to replace national ones.

But for Anderson, the vector of historical development does not bring a kinder and gentler world. Assertions of collective 'identity' are attempts to neutralize the encroachments of an advancing social universe of capital. As the patterns of contemporary cultural and economic life relentlessly frustrate the desire and need to live in communities, these become 'imagined' only in the negative sense, that is, disconnected from any sense of historical reality and the possibility of social transformation. Ethnic pastiche evokes an ersatz sense of belonging:

Consider the well-known photograph of the lonely Peloponnesian *Gastarbeiter* sitting in his dingy room in, say, Frankfurt. The solitary decoration on his wall is a resplendent Lufthansa travel poster of the Parthenon, which invites him, in German, to take a 'sun-drenched holiday' in Greece. He may well never have seen the Parthenon, but framed by Lufthansa the poster confirms for him and for any visitor a Greek identity that perhaps only Frankfurt has encouraged him to assume.[15]

I began by pointing out that the legacies of Hegel and Marx lacked a concrete conception of a people, a political anthropology. It might be thought that this criticism would lose its force when such communities of fate become inoperative, when nationalisms become increasingly 'spectral'. Unfortunately, to paraphrase Marx, such spectres weigh too heavily. If modern society had settled into a form in which archaic imaginings of communal freedom had finally been neutralized, there would of course be no need to revisit the national question. But perhaps the social question, too, could no longer be posed.

Anderson challenges those who would too hastily conclude that the by-passing of the nation-state sets the stage for the long-awaited 'open society'—liberal, tolerant, multicultural. He suggests that there are in fact limits to how open society can be: beyond those limits, solidarity falters. Anderson begins *Imagined Communities* by contrasting cosmopolitan ideologies such as liberalism and socialism with the elementary forms of social community. But these ideologies have always tacitly relied on an image of society as an ultimately finite association. The successes, failures and compromises of both traditions stem in large measure from the fact that these communities are imagined as nations in the modern world, and that the only versions of these creeds which have any measure of practical success are those which have tailored their

---

15   Benedict Anderson, 'Exodus', *Critical Inquiry* 20: 2, 1994, p. 322.

message to the limited sympathies of nations. Is it true that the masses have erupted onto the stage of history only in the form of nations? The Russian Revolution was perhaps the exception: not just 'the Revolution against Capital', to use Gramsci's phrase, but a revolution also against the order of nations—that other, once equally formidable limit to the revolutionary will. But retrospectively, in the opening years of the twenty-first century, that great rebellion appears more than ever to have been a unique event. Anderson's book is a reminder that future awakenings of the wretched of the earth may yet put into question the present verdicts on the nation-state.

7

The Oracle of Post-Democracy

Sheldon Wolin's magisterial study of Tocqueville is the culmination of a remarkable body of work on the history of political thought, the harvest of four decades of engaged reflection. *Politics and Vision*, published at the close of the Eisenhower era in 1960, was the landmark that defined this enterprise.[1] In it, Wolin surveyed almost the entire history of political philosophy with the aim of probing the role its canonical texts had played in framing—or alternatively constricting—interpretations of what was at stake in civil wars, from the age of the classical polis to the heyday of Bolshevism. In the exhausted aftermath of these immense struggles, he argued, contemporary thought confronted a quite new situation: the near complete eclipse of the political, as a multifarious tradition of civic discourse, by a new order—the pseudo-consensual management of mass society. The main texts of the classical syllabus addressed only fitfully, if at all, the perils of this erasure of politics. It was now imperative to read them against the grain in order to bring the unprecedented problems of apathetic democracies—which he later more aptly dubbed post-democracies—into sharper focus.

In *Between Two Worlds*, Wolin brings this line of interrogation to bear on Alexis de Tocqueville. The form of his book is, as

1   This article first appeared in *New Left Review* 2: 13, January–February 2002, and is a review of Sheldon Wolin, *Tocqueville Between Two Worlds: The Making of a Political and Theoretical Life*, Princeton: Princeton University Press, 2001.

he explains, unusual. It is not a straightforward textual study, nor a conventional intellectual biography. If its central focus is the two volumes of *Democracy in America*, Wolin also pays careful attention to Tocqueville's penal writings, co-authored with his friend Beaumont, and considers his memoirs of the 1848 Revolution. He treats *The Old Regime and the French Revolution* much more cursorily, and omits altogether Tocqueville's involvement—a central concern under the July Monarchy—with the French conquest of Algeria. Biographically, Wolin sketches in the principal phases of Tocqueville's career, without exploring the intellectual influences on him in any detail, or tackling the existential conundrum of Tocqueville's tortured relations with Christian doctrine. What *Between Two Worlds* offers instead is an arresting critique of Tocqueville's theoretical trajectory, illuminated against the backdrop of his public career.

The iconoclastic charge of the book can be measured against the current apotheosis of the deputy from Valognes. Historically, Tocqueville has always enjoyed a well-deserved reputation as an important thinker. In 1835 the first volume of *Democracy in America* was already a best-seller. But his standing underwent a spectacular elevation with the neo-conservative reaction to the political turbulence of the sixties. The French and American versions of this creed found in Tocqueville the perfect theorist of a converging anti-radical agenda: as an enemy of both revolutionary virtue and emancipated consumerism, he could steel rattled establishment nerves in both Paris and New York. In France the former Communist François Furet, overturning the hegemony of Marxist historiography of the French Revolution—the *nouveaux philosophes* soon followed—hailed Tocqueville as a sober demystifier of the dangerous mythologies of the revolutionary imagination, a veritable prophet of the Gulag. Here the key text, obviously, was *The Old Regime*. Neo-conservatives in the US, meanwhile, turned to Tocqueville as the sagacious defender of America's historically moderate democracy: in their view, student rallies, ghetto riots and the sexual revolution were all the result of a fatal relaxation in the mores of affluent capitalism—a predicament that Tocqueville had apparently foretold. No one had seen more clearly the essential role of religion in stabilizing any democracy. Daniel Bell's call for a 'return of the sacred'—the need for a compensatory reenchantment of market society—looked back to the acquisitive, sober, church-going world portrayed in *Democracy in America*. The two rediscoveries fitted naturally together, since the French drive to eliminate Jacobin and Marxist residues that had led to misplaced sympathies for the USSR during the Cold War required rehabilitation of the US as the desirable alternative instead. Furet was eventually fêted in Chicago as much as in Paris.

Today, the cult of Tocqueville stretches far and wide, and its expressions have never been so extravagant. '*Democracy in America* is at once the best book ever written about democracy and the best book ever written on America,' declares the distinguished (conservative) constitutionalist Harvey Mansfield, introducing a new edition of the classic. 'I am hard put to come up with a better book on democracy or a better book on America,' nods the leading (liberal) historian Gordon Wood (*New York Review of Books*, 17 May 2001). Wolin's study is a salutary check to such effusions. An admiring demystification of a now almost sacrosanct figure, *Between Two Worlds* offers an account of Tocqueville's remarkable vision of modernity immune to the vagaries of fashion. For, from any standpoint, Tocqueville has two irrepressible claims to actuality: he was the first and greatest theorist of a politico-intellectual condition in which democracy is the only legitimate form of government; relatedly, he was an often uncannily acute forecaster of the world-historical significance of American expansion. The stature of *Democracy in America* rests upon these two considerable achievements.

Wolin begins by comparing Tocqueville to other theorists of modernity. The fundamental contention between Marx and Tocqueville hinges on whether the central social dynamic of modernity is best understood in terms of capitalism or democracy. There are two reasons, he suggests, to turn to Tocqueville. Firstly, Marx never integrated America into his account of the world-historical future of capitalism, an omission that compromises all of his prognoses. Secondly, he argues that Marx, despite his profound grasp of capitalism, cannot help us theorize the specific historical problem Tocqueville confronted: the precarious status of the political as a zone in which the order of human things is in contention. Marx worked on the assumption that the development of productive forces could eventually lead to the supersession of the rule over human beings by the administration of things. By itself his account of class struggles unfolding in and between modes of production cannot register a predicament in which the political as the possibility of transformative collective agency has been foreclosed, prior to the abolition of private property and the state, because it does not see politics as an intrinsically valuable form of existence, whose autonomy is in need of safeguarding.

In their own way, both Marx and Tocqueville were theorists of the world-historical transition to middle-class society, as well as commentators on the same political landmarks of the period from 1789 to 1851. For Marx, the French bourgeoisie was a class whose revolutionary political career was exhausted in the heroic paroxysms of Jacobinism, fated to descend thereafter into the prosaic world of private enterprise, philistine careerism and *bien-pensant* piety. The possibility of bourgeois-revolutionary agency depended on lofty, ultimately ephemeral, illusions of restoring ancient republican civic virtue. Marx essentially agreed with Benjamin Constant that it was a grandiose historical delusion to believe that ancient citizenship, as a way of life based on the primacy of the political, could be superimposed on the privatized realm of bourgeois civil society—the material foundation of modernity.

For Wolin, Tocqueville's significance lies in his departure from this early liberal-Marxist consensus. He did not accept its verdict on the fate of the citizen in the bourgeois world. The most pressing historical problem according to Tocqueville was the political education of the European bourgeoisie in the era of transition to democracy. His journey to the United States in 1831 convinced him that it was indeed possible for the middle classes to govern a great state, a still contentious proposition in Orleanist France. But in contrast to Guizot or even John Stuart Mill—a kindred spirit across the Channel—he did not see parliaments as the political training grounds of a new middle-class elite. Despite his later career as a deputy he never became an enthusiast for representative government.

What could Europeans learn from America about government by the people? Tocqueville's admiring observations on the town-hall assemblies of New England never develop into any coherent account about what democracy means on a more extensive national plane. The Union in the Jacksonian era was still very much a confederation of semi-sovereign states and Tocqueville's reflections on American democratic politics move from local to state assemblies. But he did not consider the overarching federal framework holding together these settler states as a specifically democratic arrangement. It is not clear, then, at what level European states could become democratic in partial imitation of the Americans. Added to these constitutional peculiarities of the New World were Tocqueville's disparaging Old World judgments on the ability of commoners to handle affairs of state far above the local level. The result is that it is often difficult to determine what Tocqueville meant by popular government, and on what plane he was appraising its results and prospects.

In fact, his whole conception of democracy is entangled in a fundamental antinomy. Attempting to report what he saw in America to his French contemporaries, he could never decide whether he meant by it participatory government on a local level, or its near antithesis—an atomized social condition under a modern centralized state, the decisive legacy of the French Revolution, in his view. Tocqueville did not, then, construct any systematic theory of democracy—let alone modernity—so much as compile an album of striking portraits and forecasts. (Wolin claims that this was a novel mode of theorizing, though his case arguably relies too heavily on the Greek etymology of the word *theoria*: to see, to journey, to know.) On the whole, when Tocqueville considered democracy in general, contemporary France loomed large, and New England slipped into the background. In many ways, as a ramified embodiment of the principle of equality, Tocqueville's conception of democracy resembles Weber's equally amorphous understanding of rationalization: an isomorphic standardization of the social totality—administration, law, economy, culture, finally even family life. The equality that democracy establishes is a condition in which all social relations come to be based on the uniform status of individuals under the law.

Tocqueville's resignation to this equality, which set him apart from all other aristocratic thinkers of his generation, was always qualified by deep misgivings about the ultimate consequences of this process. Where would it end: in an orderly scramble for wealth and mediocre happiness—bourgeois democracy—or in a more ominous scenario? 'Does one think that after having destroyed feudalism and vanquished kings, democracy will recoil before the bourgeoisie and the rich?' he asked in the introduction to *Democracy in America*. Liberty, by contrast, attracted his unqualified devotion as the ultimate political value, whose worth could never be estimated in terms of its costs and benefits. But the liberty Tocqueville praised was neither ancient nor distinctively modern. Rather it was feudal in origin, rooted in the status autonomy of the lords, clergy and burghers of a bygone era. This fragile legacy of particularistic liberties was under siege, he thought, from the levelling passions of the emancipated common man, working in tandem with the centralizing drive of modern administration that absolutism had set into motion. Even in an America which still abounded in local liberties, he discerned the deadly traces of this inexorable progress of equality, and feared what it would bring. 'The entire book that you are going to read was written under the pressure of a sort of religious terror in the author's soul, produced by the sight of this irresistible revolution that for so many centuries has marched over all obstacles, and that one sees still advancing today amid the ruins it has made.' But Providence itself had doomed aristocracy to extinction. Tocqueville realized that his terror was not ultimately justifiable on Christian grounds. Unlike a previous generation of counter-revolutionaries—Bonald, De Maistre—he insisted that Christianity upheld the spiritual equality of all before God; and unlike Nietzsche, he could not bring himself to abandon it for that reason.

Tocqueville's tempered admiration for American democracy thus stemmed in part from the Protestant piety he encountered amongst Americans of all walks of life. Indeed one of the principal lessons that the United States held for contemporary Frenchmen was that democracy could be a stable, because god-fearing society. But despite Tocqueville's avowed hostility to the reckless scepticism flaunted in Enlightenment salons, he found the cultural legacy it had created in France more congenial than the morally upright, tediously businesslike credo to which most Americans seemed to subscribe. How then could this America of the Farmer's Almanac exemplify in his mind the awesome dynamic of the democratic revolution? The answer lies in the way the variegated materials of *Democracy in America*—idealized accounts of town-hall government, descriptions of an ornate and fragile federalism, anecdotal character portraits of Americans—come to assume epic proportions, as the material transformation of a vast continent by an anonymous multitude of ordinary people armed with hatchets, newspapers and bibles. Emerging from non-stop waves of settlement were those monotonous landscapes that to this day form the *Lebenswelt* of much of America. Marx had a basically positive view of this ceaseless expansion of the boundaries of Yankee society, excusing its present primitivism on the grounds that it was still too busy transforming the natural world to have the time to develop a more advanced superstructure of political consciousness. Although Marx's classical taste would have been repelled by the gushing strophes of Whitman's *Leaves of Grass*, he would have recognized the poet's vision of a Promethean modernity as his own:

> We primeval forests felling,
> We the rivers stemming, vexing we and piercing deep the mines within,
> We the surface broad surveying, we the virgin soil upheaving,
> Pioneers! O pioneers!

By contrast, the spectacle of this vast secular revolution left Tocqueville cold; he anticipates Baudrillard's vision of an America of strip malls, highways and billboards:

> Some believe that the new societies are going to change their appearance daily but my fear is that they will end by being too unalterably fixed in the same institutions, prejudices, *mœurs*, that mankind will halt and remain within self-imposed limits; that the mind will yield and fold endlessly in and on itself without producing any new idea; that mankind will exhaust itself in trivial, lonely and sterile activities, and that for all its perpetual movement, humanity will cease to advance.

By this account the closure of the American mind antedates the era of political correctness by at least a century and a half. Tocqueville's American admirers have understandably always been discomfited by his claim that there was no country in the world where there was less intellectual independence and freedom of discussion than in the United States. His gaze as he contemplated oncoming American centuries was often less than serene, as if he saw something extremely disturbing on the horizon. Wolin's portrait vividly recaptures his mood as he looked to the future: tense, foreboding, living in anticipation of a spiritually catastrophic defeat. In that sense, he can be read—so Wolin suggests—as an unreconciled critic of the foreclosure of political alternatives in the neutralizing ambience of consumer capitalism. It is often difficult to separate this admirable intransigence from its patrician background—intellectual independence came with an old family house in the country from which one could contemplate the big political picture with detachment. But Tocqueville's *hauteur* never became programmatic: if the decline of his class tempted this scion of an ancient Norman family to indulge in quixotic reminiscences of feudalism, he was too much of a realist to put much stock in them. On his travels in America, no hazy sentimentality for a bygone past was extended to the slave-owning planters of the antebellum South. Tocqueville roundly condemned slavery as an outrage, and later worked to abolish it, albeit gradually, in the French Antilles.

But if his rejection of slavery speaks to contemporary sensibilities, his attitude towards the pauper and prisoner of his time resonates with the meaner instincts of today's not-so-silent majorities. Every inmate of a penitentiary should be condemned to solitary confinement. The correct response to the emerging social question was a vigilant gendarmerie and more Christian philanthropy. John Stuart Mill's cautious hopes for a rapprochement between liberalism and socialism form a striking contrast to Tocqueville's far more strained attempts to reconcile democracy to the invaluable political heirlooms of the old regime. Wolin does not mince words about the intellectual burden of this side of his work. Tocqueville always wrote as if he were one of the last of the Mohicans, but for all his despair he successfully conveyed to future elites a supple teaching in the art of containing revolutions. Indeed, Wolin goes so far as to claim that the effect of much of Tocqueville's writing was to incorporate democracy 'into an obliquely counter-revolutionary project'. Thwarted in his time, Tocqueville prevails today. But his victory is accompanied by the total rout of the vision he most cherished—a high politics for a democratic age.

Part of the reason for this outcome, Wolin argues, lies in
a void within Tocqueville's thought itself. Missing from his
account of democracy—as either local self-government, or a
uniform atomized society—is any conception of democracy as
a constituent power capable of making and remaking political
orders, that is to say, democracy as actual popular sovereignty.
This theoretical neutralization of democracy was the direct
expression of an abiding scepticism about the political capacity
of faceless multitudes. Yet the terrifying debut of the sans-culotte
onto the political stage was an event of the recent past. Why then
did he insist on denying the possibility of its repetition, rather than
simply sounding the alarm bell of reaction? Perhaps because there
was a side to him that was imaginatively closer to the experience
of the First Republic than any Legitimist's son should have been.
He was capable of surprising confessions. Faced with the prospect
of a society in retreat from politics, Tocqueville could write with
inflammatory passion: 'I would have preferred a revolutionary
condition a thousand times more than our present misery . . .
Will we never again [*nota bene*] see a fresh breeze of true political
passions . . . of violent passions, hard though sometimes cruel, yet
grand, disinterested, fruitful, those passions which are the soul of
the only parties that I understand and to which I would gladly give
my name, my fortune and my life?'

At such moments, Wolin remarks, 'Tocqueville's prose is
passionate and intense as he seizes the possibility that within
modernity itself, and despite the powerful attraction towards
private concerns and pleasures, politics might be restored as the
defining centre of social life and essential to the development of
human possibilities.' But he goes on to note that these moving
sentiments were ultimately dependent on an aestheticized vision
of a high politics cleansed of the violent rancour that conflicts
over essential interests will always generate. Politics from below
was another matter—especially if passionate, hard or cruel. For
all his laments over the decline of the political, Tocqueville was

consistently hostile to any attempt to expand it beyond carefully delineated boundaries. Faced with attempts amongst workers to establish associations to further their interests, he lost much of his characteristic sang-froid.

The insurrection of the Parisian proletariat in the June Days of 1848 was a litmus test of his attachment to democratic principles: under pressure of the crisis, all of his previously sublimated reactionary impulses erupted to the surface in an unabashed authoritarian decisionism. His diagnosis of the constitutional predicament of the Party of Order is a striking anticipation of Carl Schmitt's partisan mode of legal interpretation. Tocqueville, if anything, exceeded him in sheer bluntness. 'Socialism was at the gates', he recalled, so it was more urgent 'to put a powerful chief at the head of the republic than to organize a republican constitution.' Indeed, in the events leading up to the Eighteenth Brumaire of Louis Napoleon, Tocqueville played a part not unlike that of his Rhenish admirer prior to the Nazi seizure of power. In his memoirs, Tocqueville stressed the esteem in which the budding dictator held him: 'I believe that of all his ministers, and perhaps of all of the men who did not want to take part in his conspiracy against the republic, I was the most advanced in his good graces, who saw him closest, and was best able to judge him.' Tocqueville both helped to invest the Presidency of the infant second Republic with vast powers under its new constitution, and then counselled Louis Napoleon to violate the same constitution and seek a second term. Later he was bitterly disillusioned by the outcome. Reflecting on such parallels, Schmitt had good reason to express a nostalgic identification with Tocqueville, after the Third Reich had gone the way of the Second Empire.

In his brief tenure as French Foreign Minister in 1849, Tocqueville helped to lay down guidelines for the subsequent diplomacy of Napoleon III: rhetorical support for liberty, material support for its enemies. In Rome this meant the gallows for those who, in the name of liberty, took up arms against the Pope. He was quite prepared to envisage sacking and devastating the city to put down Garibaldi's Republic—if that were necessary, he said, 'I have no hesitation'. Although his retrospective assessment of the politics of the second French Republic was not so far from Marx's—'low tragedy performed by provincial actors'—he could never bring himself to see the role he had played in setting up the stage on which a mediocre swindler managed to prevail over all the political celebrities of the parliamentary *juste milieu*. In surveying this chapter of his career, Wolin spares Tocqueville from the savage ridicule of Marx—or for that matter Flaubert. In the pallor and inanity of his performance, Tocqueville not infrequently appears to step from the pages of *The Sentimental Education*.

In the midst of the complacency and exhaustion that engulfed France in the aftermath of the establishment of the Second Empire, Tocqueville returned to musing about the servility of modern democracy, willing to vote in a parvenu master rather than respect the distinction of old families. But in *The Old Regime and the French Revolution* this familiar refrain is frequently interrupted by a premonition that Europe might be entering an era, not of popular apathy, but of permanent revolutions—not slow social homogenization, but violent upheavals and transvaluations, with the propagation of a new world religion promising a complete transformation of the human condition. Such a vision of the future lent an ominous grandeur to the Revolution that had inaugurated the democratic era. 'This was something quite unprecedented: a political revolution that sought proselytes all the world over and applied itself as ardently to converting foreigners as compatriots.' Tocqueville viewed the total abandonment of the impetus of 1789 by the upper classes with a wistful nostalgia, but noted with considerable trepidation the headway it was making at the bottom of society:

Revolutionaries of a hitherto unknown breed came onto the scene: men who carried audacity to the point of sheer insanity; who baulked at no innovation and, unchecked by any scruples, acted with an unprecedented ruthlessness. Nor were these strange beings mere ephemera, born of a brief crisis and destined to pass away when it ended. They were rather the first of a new race of men who subsequently made good and proliferated in all parts of the civilized world, everywhere retaining the same characteristics. They were already here when we were born and they are still with us.

Wolin's formidable portrait of Tocqueville, overwhelmingly focused on *Democracy in America*, does not consider the significance of these later formulations, relegating *The Old Regime and the French Revolution* to the status of a late reactionary coda. Yet this work often gives a clearer indication of what would be entailed by a reactivation of the political than the earlier. The last lines of *Between Two Worlds* grimly convey the consequences of the total eclipse of popular sovereignty by its atomized simulacrum:

> Far from being valued as symbolizing an aspiration towards the democratization of power and a participatory society of political equals— democracy as subject—democracy would come to be regarded by late-modern power elites as an indispensable yet malleable myth for promoting American political and economic interests among premodern and post-totalitarian societies. At home democracy is touted not as self-government by an involved citizenry but as economic opportunity. Opportunity serves as the means of implicating the populace in anti-democracy, in a politico-economic system characterized by the dominating power of hierarchical organizations, widening class differentials, and a society where the hereditary element is confined to successive generations of the defenceless poor.

It is not clear whether Wolin believes Tocqueville will be the master-thinker of this post-democratic condition. Calls for a return of the political to the defining centre of a common life are commendable. But for politics to be a serious and urgent affair, there must the prospect of alternative social forms over which to contend. Tocqueville wanted the one without the other, and this still remains the dream of hopeful conservatives today. Marx may have lacked a comparable sense of the value of politics as free deliberation and will, but he did not make this mistake.

Addendum

Wolin's latest reflection on the political scene in America is a requiem for the democratic ideal. The last several years of Republican ascendancy have demoralized liberals and radicals alike. *Democracy Incorporated* eloquently articulates this experience of defeat, and belongs to a genre of contemporary lamentations on America's fateful passage from republic to empire.[2] Less beholden than many to the mythologies of a heroic age of America's foundation, Wolin sees the problem as going all the way back to the very composition of the Constitution itself—a document in which the word 'democracy' is not once mentioned. Madison's vision of a republic in which the demos would be held at bay is the point of departure for yet another genealogy of this post-political age, from a scholar whose work has defined the problem for two generations of Americans. But with the possible exception of the early 1930s, authentic democracy appears to have been a non-starter in the United States from the very beginning, and neither Reconstruction nor the 1960s interrupt the bleak uniformity of the story. In a paraphrase of both Tocqueville and Sombart, one could say that Wolin's question seems to be 'Why no democracy in America?'

While the title of the new volume evokes some familiar tropes, Wolin seeks to capture the recent darkening of the political skies

---

2　　Sheldon Wolin, *Democracy Incorporated, Managed Democracy and the Spectre of Inverted Totalitarianism*, Princeton, NJ: Princeton University Press, 2008; henceforward *DI*.

by depicting the current order in ways that do more than simply qualify the democratic ideal it is supposed to represent, but negate it entirely. Recalling the language of the Cold War, Wolin goes so far as to claim that American society is sliding towards an 'inverted totalitarianism'. How convincing is this characterization of post-Reagan America? While there are many today who would endorse his depiction of the US as a pseudo-consensual polity firmly in the grip of corporate elites, he himself concedes that its distinctive combination of neoliberal deregulation, mass apathy and multiculturalism strains any analogy to classical totalitarianism. Like 'fascism', 'totalitarianism' has a checkered career of polemical overextension, and the author's use of it is perhaps best seen as an attempt to index a disquieting intensification of long-standing trends, one that does not succeed, however, in bringing what is happening into sharper focus.

Where do the regressions of the American present fit into the larger sweep of modernity? Far from deviating from the mainline of development, America's political trajectory, according to Wolin, conforms to a metahistorical dialectic of enlightenment in which an advancing technological rationalism comes to undermine the conditions of self-determination and thus ends up reinstating the power of age-old myths. The latest, 'postmodern' phase of this story is characterized by the co-existence of religious–patriotic re-enchantment with the cynicism of atomized consumers and spectators. Although Wolin holds Cold War liberals responsible for the turn towards managerial-militarism, the real villain of the piece is the Republican Party, which from Ronald Reagan to Bush the Younger became an ever more ruthless vanguard of oligarchy. In this story of elite rollback, the Democrats fade into the background, absolved of all charges except perhaps that of having failed to protect their more vulnerable constituencies. This narrower, partisan account of the rightward lurches of the last thirty years sits uneasily within Wolin's understanding of the fate of the demos in the latter stages of modernity, where broader forces are at work. Symptomatically, *Democracy Incorporated* subscribes to a now widespread liberal understanding of the times in which Straussians—and their noble lies—appear at the forefront of this counter-revolution.

Wolin is cognizant of the larger structural logics behind the steady erosion of self-determination. So what explains his unwillingness to rise above the rhetoric of the moment? Tacitly, in his report the prospect of democratic renewal has become so unlikely that one must simply accept the ever more circumscribed understanding of the limits of politics that reigns today. We are told that the problem is the domination of the political by the economic—as if this division itself was not the very crux of the problem. The economic, he explains, is the realm of private interest and so always requires a healthy civic politics of the common good, whose outlines he describes as follows:

> Democratization is not about being 'left alone' but about becoming a self that sees the values of common involvements and endeavors and finds in them a source of self-fulfilment. Generic high school students can, before long, become principled lawyers, doctors, nurses, teachers, even MBAs who learn to behave, think, and speak according to ethical and demanding mores.[3]

Such are the forces marshalled against 'inverted totalitarianism'. For the many are fated to a life of labour, leaving them little time for politics. It follows that the only force that can check the depredations of the powerful would be 'a counter-elite' of highly educated public servants in the government sector, but more often today to be found in NGOs. 'The demos will never dominate politically', so it is perhaps only natural that 'the few' will remain at the helm. How far from the caricatured Plato of the Straussians is this faint-hearted Aristotelianism? The last

---

3   *DI*, p. 289.

line of the book perfectly encapsulates the horizons of our post-political world, which asks us 'not what new powers we can bring into the world, but what hard-won practices we can prevent from disappearing'.

8

Two on the Marble Cliffs

The publication of the correspondence between Carl Schmitt and Ernst Jünger is an intellectual event of some moment.[1] The letters collected in this volume span a full half century—from 1930, when the two first met in Berlin, to 1983, shortly before Schmitt died at the age of 97. Jünger survived him by over a decade, dying in 1998 at the age of 103. The care and skill with which this collection has been edited by Helmuth Kiesel makes it an impressive accomplishment: German literary scholarship at its best. Detailed notes and background information are provided on nearly every letter, ending with an authoritative afterword on the relationship between the two thinkers. In a handsome production, only an index is missing. The volume makes compelling reading. In range and level, it stands comparison with Benjamin's correspondence with Adorno or Scholem, or the thematically closer exchange between Leo Strauss and Alexander Kojève. The letters are usually more laconic, sometimes enigmatic, than such counterparts. But they are never dull or cumbersome. Schmitt and Jünger were in different ways masters of a German prose running against the grain of the language: terse, clear and elegant.

When the two men met in 1930, each enjoyed a distinctive eminence in Weimar intellectual life. Schmitt had risen from an

---

1   This article first appeared in *New Left Review* 2: 1, January–February 2000, and is a review of Ernst Jünger and Carl Schmitt, *Briefwechsel 1930–1983*, Stuttgart: Klett-Cotta, 1999.

obscure Catholic background in Westphalia to become one of Weimar's foremost legal authorities. But his wider reputation rested on a series of remarkable essays spanning a much broader range of themes: a political critique of German Romanticism; exploration of the theological background of Emergency Powers; portrait of the Roman Church as European bulwark against Bolshevism; diagnosis of the crisis of contemporary parliamentarism; and—not least—a theory of politics as a field constitutively defined by the distinction between friend and foe. Oscillating between moderate republicanism and counter-revolutionary decisionism, his main political links were with the Catholic *Zentrum*.

Jünger at this stage enjoyed a more dramatic notoriety. From a somewhat more respectable, though by no means elevated, Protestant background (his father was a pharmacist), as an 18-year-old he ran away to enlist in the French Foreign Legion. Brought home from Africa, he fought for Germany during the First World War on the Western front with such distinction—he was wounded seven times—that he was awarded the highest Prussian medal for courage, *Pour le Mérite*. His celebration of modern warfare in a coldly burnished, clinically exact prose, *Im Stahlgewittern* (*In the Storm of Steel*) was an immediate best-seller in 1920. An active participant in the paramilitarism of the Freikorps, he won further renown with works portraying the life-world of front-line soldiers as the model for a totally mobilized society of war and work to come. As a writer, Jünger was closely associated with ideas of a 'conservative revolution'; after a brief flirtation with the NSDAP in the mid-twenties, he moved towards the circle of 'National Bolsheviks' around Ernst Niekisch. His record was much more engaged with the far Right than was that of Schmitt. But in the vision of the latter's *Concept of the Political* he found reason to exalt. The correspondence opens with his salute to it, just after they became acquainted at Schmitt's initiative. 'You have invented a special technology of war: a mine that explodes silently. One sees as if by magic the ruins collapse; the destruction is over before it becomes audible.'

If the two were drawn together by similarities of style and outlook—both were adventurers, to some extent loners, in their respective milieux—their paths crossed over when the Nazis came to power. Schmitt, after spending the last years of the Republic as constitutional advisor and confidant to von Papen and Schleicher, and warning of the dangers of Nazism, rallied to the Third Reich and became a top figure in its legal establishment, under the protection of Goering. His adhesion to the regime, if it was certainly in part opportunistic—he was soon piling up honorary titles and strategic positions in a severely purged corps of academic jurisprudence—also answered to certain of his convictions. Hitler's regime seemed to offer a drastic solution to many of the problems of political order that Schmitt had posed so starkly in Weimar times.

Jünger, unexpectedly, took the opposite route. Initially an activist in the sub-culture of right-wing paramilitarism from which the Nazis had emerged, he later became detached from any organized movement, maintaining friendships not only on the Right but on the anarchist or deviant Left as well, in a spirit closer to literary bohemia than political faction. When Hitler came to power in 1933, he retired from Berlin to the provinces, where he was viewed with some suspicion by the new authorities. In these conditions, letters between the two men necessarily became allusive. Behind them, however, were more forthright and face-to-face political discussions. From the outset, Jünger warned Schmitt of any too close association with the new regime, whose inner circle he knew all too well. When Schmitt was offered a position on the Prussian State Council in 1933, Jünger advised him to leave the country and go to Serbia to live with his in-laws, as a scholar in voluntary exile, instead of accepting this poisoned chalice. In the following year, when Hitler staged the murderous Roehm purge and Schmitt publically defended the assassinations, Jünger told him he had committed political suicide and advised him to equip his domicile with machine-gun nests.

Two years later Schmitt was evicted from his niche in power, under a withering attack from the ss as a crypto-Catholic careerist who had no place in the regime. Confined to academic life again, he continued to be intellectually productive, with publications— on Hobbes; the structure of international relations; land and sea-power—which might help him recover the favour of the regime, without committing himself too expressly to its policies. Jünger, meanwhile, was writing his coded novel on tyranny, *Auf den Marmorklippen* (*On the Marble Cliffs*), published just before the war broke out in 1939. Shielded as a war hero by the Army High Command, he was awarded the Iron Cross for his part in the defeat of France, and posted to Paris as cultural attaché in the occupation regime. There, at the centre of literary and artistic life under the occupation, he knew Cocteau, Céline, Drieu la Rochelle, Brasillach, Sacha Guitry and many others; and in the autumn of 1941 arranged for Schmitt to be invited to speak at the German Institute, with a side-trip to Port-Royal on which the two exchanged reflections.

When the Officers' Plot struck in July 1944, narrowly failing to kill Hitler, the *Kommandantur* in Paris was deeply implicated, and leading generals shot. Jünger, aware of the plan to overthrow Hitler although not a participant, was lucky to escape into retirement. Schmitt, a close friend of civilian participants in the plot in Berlin, was not taken into their confidence. The two men ended the war in the humble capacity of air-raid wardens. After it, their fates diverged dramatically. Schmitt was arrested, jailed and interrogated for the better part of two years by American prosecutors, stripped of all academic positions, and released into ostracism—a forbidden figure in the Bonn Republic. Jünger, on the other hand, suffered no sanctions in the French Zone, and was soon publishing his Parisian Diaries to general acclaim. The next fifty years saw a brilliant second literary career, in which successive novels and essays established him as lucid ecological sage and counter-cultural anarch, whose passing was a national event.

The author who made his name by exalting the approximation of humans to machines became a writer calling for the protection of nature against humans—without great alterations of style; a unusual case in German, or perhaps any letters.

Schmitt was not without admirers in West Germany, and had back-door influence on the framing of the post-war constitution. But his reputation as a former Nazi jurist was too lurid for him ever to be able to re-enter public life again. His bitterness at this exclusion found often venomous expression in his diaries, where his jealousy of contemporaries who had survived the collapse of the Third Reich without damage is unconcealed. Here he gave way to a resentment of Jünger that he generally mastered when writing to him. Their correspondence—always formal, even when cordial—aims at a more dispassionate level. Contemporary political developments come into view, but rarely in the form of direct theoretical generalization. The letters written under Nazism, which comprise about two-fifths of the whole, approximate to what Leo Strauss thematized as the art of writing esoteric criticism without oppositional intent, under tyrannies. Sharp differences of outlook between the two men are apparent here that confound easy labelling.

The relationship between Schmitt and Jünger was based on an attempt to grasp and shape the often unfamiliar idioms of the other. Both were deeply dissatisfied with the intellectual traditions of German conservatism: it was this shared antipathy that in part gave them a preliminary rapport with each other. Jünger, not unaffected by Nietzsche or Spengler, had a more familiar background in this respect, but was willing to take his cues from Schmitt, who remained an inveterate enemy of the local intellectual scene. Schmitt guarded his prerogatives as a theoretical mentor, which Jünger calmly conceded to him from the beginning. This is all the more striking in that the letters are conspicuous for their consistently aesthetic points of reference. Innumerable exchanges focus on points of agreement or dispute over the significance of a wide range of writers held in shared esteem.

One strand here is a search for authentic representations of evil, maps that emplot the brutal coordinates of existence in an era of total civil war. Hiëronymus Bosch, Edgar Allen Poe and Herman Melville repeatedly come into consideration. Céline and Malraux figure as the latest representatives of the French moralist tradition, whose dispassionate literary pessimism is held superior to the German metaphysical variety of moralism and its obverse in Faustian amoralism. In these discussions, the heterodox Catholic fanatic Léon Bloy looms large—Schmitt introducing him as an antidote to Jünger's Nietzschean understanding of nihilism. Schmitt's tacit objective seems to have been to keep the exchange focused on literary topics, where he might influence Jünger's development as a writer, while preserving the division of roles between them, in which he held the more political and philosophical ground. Here, however, it is Jünger who lets drop the most arresting historical observation, when he remarks that the tragedy of modern German history stemmed from the absence of a strong nationalist Left. The argument, initially made in conversation with Schmitt in 1930, that Germany's core historical problem was the absence of a local Trotsky had an unsettling effect on Schmitt, who for decades repeatedly recollected it.

This idea, of course, came from Jünger's association with the circle round Niekisch, a sign of his more experimental political outlook. Schmitt, on the other hand, always had a deeper intellectual grasp of the challenge to traditional conceptions of politics posed by Marxism, after the victory of the Bolshevik Revolution. A similar pattern can be seen in their respective attitudes toward liberalism. Schmitt, more deeply implicated with the criminal regime, paradoxically had a much better understanding of the strengths of classical liberals, expressing sympathy and admiration for figures like Constant and Tocqueville. In a letter of 1934 he characteristically remarked that the most consequential liberal theorists—Hobbes and Constant, thinkers self-confessedly creatures of 'fear' and 'indolence', were cases in point—had a fundamentally illiberal vision of human nature. Traditions like these were not a reference for Jünger. Such differences, of course, were in part explicable in terms of intellectual interest and orientation.

They were also questions of temperament. From his Parisian vantage point, Jünger viewed the Nazi order with a frigid, caustic detachment. On occasion revulsion broke through, even to admission of his own role in helping to unleash an 'underworld of slave-drivers and murderers'. One of his most chilling letters reports a scene from hell—worthy, as he says, of Bosch—on the Russian front, seen from a cable-car while on duty in the Caucasus. But he gazed on moral condemnation and political resistance with the same general detachment. Fatalistically inclined to view Nazism as a force accelerating the nihilistic destruction of all Old European values, he would comfort himself with the belief that it might be clearing the ground for some transvaluation to come.

Common to Schmitt and Jünger, however, was a repression of the moral and political crisis of the time into metaphysical realms of parable and myth. As early as 1941, Schmitt was comparing himself to Benito Cereno, the Spanish captain of Melville's story, prisoner of a slave mutiny—whose image he made into the fable of his position under the Third Reich after the war.

The cloak of legend as medium of estrangement and exoneration fell, inevitably, over the fate of the Jews. In the Weimar period, Jünger had for a time brushed close to radical anti-Semitism; Schmitt, on good terms with Jewish colleagues and pupils, had shown no interest in it. But when Hitler came to power, their positions reversed. Jünger expressed disdain for official racism as a new Inquisition, while Schmitt moved to establish impeccable anti-Semitic credentials, organizing a campaign to root out Jewish influences in the legal world, though without convincing the ss. Driven back to the academic margin, he started for the first time to weave mythical motifs into his theoretical texts, taking Leviathan and Behemoth as Jewish monsters of sea and land in the Old Testament whose fateful after-life defined the direction and imagery of Hobbes's work. A giant pterodactyl of the air from Kabbalistic sources—'so powerful that an egg falling from its flight will shatter a thousand cedars of Lebanon'—appears in the letters soon afterwards. Cruelty and destruction are the marks of this Judaic bestiary.

Neither man had much doubt that the war was lost for Germany by 1943. By the end, it is clear that both were aware of the Judeocide, and each sought to distance themselves from it—not for the sake of the Jews, however, but for those who persecuted them. In the maelstrom of the final months of the Third Reich—February 1945—Jünger recalled Flavius Josephus's account of 'the obstinacy of the Jews in the siege of Jerusalem'. Nazi attacks on the ethics of the New Testament had profited only those of the Old: the extermination of the Jews was setting their morality loose in the world at large. Schmitt replied with a quotation from Bruno Bauer: 'But in the end God created the Jews, and if we kill them all, we will suffer the same fate.' The idea could be seen as a deranged corollary of Schmitt's argument in Weimar times that if an enemy always defines the horizon of a political project, he must be respected as such, since any attempt to annihilate him will destroy the project itself, politically annihilating the annihilator.

The enormity of these responses, as an odious casuistry of absolution, needs no comment. After the war, the differing circumstances of the two writers separated them. Paradoxically, if the sincerity—or intensity—of Schmitt's anti-Semitism as a subjective conviction can be doubted under Nazism, it is clear that once he was driven from public life after 1947, he became an unbridled anti-Semite, as the notebooks posthumously published in *Glossarium* (1991) make clear, since he now blamed Jews, from America or elsewhere, for his humiliation and expulsion. Jünger, now well adapted to post-war conditions, had no time for such phobias.

This led to the sharpest clash of their fifty-year correspondence. When Schmitt complained of Jünger's favourable portrait of the Jews, thinly disguised as Parsees, in his novel *Heliopolis* (1949) Jünger immediately issued him a 'friendly warning'—'you know the neuralgic point well enough'. Schmitt's reply was furious. Jünger then reminded him of their disagreement after the Night of the Long Knives: 'I have a right to advise you in this matter, as I showed at the most fateful decision of your life—you will recall the night I left you in Friedrichstrasse, in my distress', he wrote. 'If you had followed my advice and example then, you would perhaps no longer be alive today, but you would have the right in the highest court to judge me. If I had followed your advice and example, today I would certainly not be alive, either physically, or otherwise.' *Capisco et obmutesco*, Schmitt replied tersely. But in his notebooks he gave vent to a boiling rage, with virulent comments on Jünger. It was seven months before they renewed contact again. After Schmitt's death, Jünger, though shaken by the revelation of Schmitt's animosity, did not hold it severely against him.

If Jünger comes out well from this episode, this was certainly in part a question of character—he had many qualities Schmitt lacked. But it was also a symptom of the way events had treated them. By the 1950s, Jünger seemed to embody an image many Germans wanted of their lives under the Nazis: stoically performing the motions of duty, all the while living in internal exile. Schmitt, punished with post-war humiliation, when others—some with worse records—escaped unscathed, loomed by contrast as an uncomfortable reminder of the lost worlds of European fascism. It would be premature to think we have buried the legacy of either.

9

Overcoming Emancipation

Jürgen Habermas is the only contemporary philosopher whose *œuvre* could withstand comparison to the encyclopaedic accomplishments of German Idealism.[1] To all appearances, the ambition of the early Frankfurt School to transform this philosophical legacy into a social theory that would negotiate between the projects of Marx, Weber and Freud seems to have not only been realized, but exceeded in scale: the tradition of Horkheimer and Adorno now embraces a vast array of post-war agendas in linguistics, normative political philosophy, international relations, child psychology and bioethics. Running through this ongoing synthetic enterprise is a spirit of public engagement that has informed numerous highly visible interventions into the political debates of the Federal Republic of Germany, from the 1950s to the present. Habermas is arguably a unique case in intellectual history—a philosopher for whom *esprit de système* has rarely precluded deft adjustments to the prevailing trends.

Martin Beck Matuštík's profile offers the first critical overview of his entire career as a public intellectual in any language. A former Fulbright student of Habermas, Matuštík approaches his subject with an appealing combination of enormous respect and shrewd scepticism. The design of this biography is an unconventional

1   This article first appeared in *New Left Review* 2: 19, January–February 2003, and is a review of Martin Beck Matuštík, *Jürgen Habermas: A Philosophical-Political Profile*, Lanham, MD: Rowman and Littlefield, 2001.

present-tense narrative that scans the same life in three registers: an excavation of the political unconscious of the first post-war generation of young adults, indelibly marked by the German catastrophe; a meticulous story of topical evolution unfolding through successive conjunctures; and a more uneven account tracking the turning points in the development of Habermas's conception of critical social theory. Matuštík reconstructs the stream of his political interventions as a sequence of existential encounters with the decisive moments of post-war politics and of flawed translations of theory into practice. Written in an unpretentious, if somewhat over-italicized style, this portrait effectively captures the formative episodes of a figure who has persistently sought to define the boundaries of responsible opposition.

Born in Düsseldorf in 1929, Habermas was raised in the small town of Gummersbach, the son of a modestly affluent, politically conformist merchant, who—it is one of Matuštík's revelations—was a member of the Nazi Party from 1 May 1933 to the fall of Berlin in 1945. His son passed through the Third Reich without incident, briefly serving in the Hitler Youth near the end of the war. Catastrophic defeat—subsequently rendered as liberation—was the defining experience of his generation. The disclosures of the Nuremburg trials cast an eerie retrospective light on the normality of everyday life in this milieu. In interviews Habermas has described the early post-war years of occupation, re-education and tutelary democracy as a time of unrealistic hopes for a clean break from a suspicious, if still largely unexamined, national past. Before the dawning of the Cold War, Sartre, Mann, Kafka and even Brecht had begun to shape the outlook of a generational cohort that would strike periodic notes of cautious dissent in the restorationist atmosphere of the fifties. Habermas began a dissertation on Schelling under the influence of Heidegger, a looming presence in the intellectual landscape of the early Federal Republic. A sheltering silence still concealed the Nazi careers of many leading academics, including Habermas's own mentors at Göttingen, Erich Rothacker and Oskar Becker. Heidegger's decision to republish a text from the mid thirties sombrely referring, in passing, to the 'inner truth and greatness' of National Socialism (now rendered as 'the movement'), and his subsequent refusal to recant, elicited an anguished response from a now deeply disillusioned young admirer.

A change of orientation immediately ensued: while finishing his dissertation Habermas began to read seriously the Young Hegelians, early Marx and the Lukács of *History and Class Consciousness*. This experience opened his horizons to the intellectual world of the émigrés. The Nazi regime had effectively removed Marx and Freud from German culture; after the war they could initially seem like exotic fossils from another age. Personal contact with Marcuse was the initial point of entry into the orbit of the newly re-established Frankfurt school. The return of Horkheimer and Adorno to Frankfurt was part of the wider post-war restoration of sociology, a discipline which in short time revealed a familiar field of contrasts between schools of a more philosophical bent and those championing value-free social science. Habermas remembers that reading *Dialectic of Enlightenment* allowed him to appreciate for the first time the contemporary relevance of Marx—a rather surprising claim in that Marx, let alone the class struggle or socialism, features hardly at all in this work. To Horkheimer's alarm, Habermas also began to recover buried treasures from the archives of the pre-war Institute. But in sharp contrast to his elders, he was simultaneously attuned to the imported wares of logical positivism, empirical social psychology and pragmatism. Tensions between Horkheimer and Habermas began to rise, not over these newfound interests, but rather as a result of the younger thinker's first attempts to develop a critical theory that might inform a politics of opposition. Horkheimer, living in dread of fascist recidivism, saw no alternative to the American-guaranteed order in West Germany, and took umbrage at Habermas's participation in the campaign for nuclear disarmament. While punctually discussing this conflict, Matuštík does not explore the longer-term influence of Horkheimer and Adorno on Habermas as examples of political conduct. But Habermas's subsequent stance towards radical activism can be read as an unspoken tribute to their enduring authority, a relationship Matuštík's generational account tends to obscure.

Horkheimer's politically motivated rejection of the research that would become Habermas's dissertation, the groundwork for *The Structural Transformation of the Public Sphere*, prompted its author's departure from Frankfurt to Marburg, to work under Wolfgang Abendroth, at that time one of the Federal Republic's few Marxist professors. Published in 1962, today this work enjoys an international reception that has firmly established its reputation as a masterpiece of historical sociology. But though now probably the best-known of his writings, it has a strange status in contemporary estimations of Habermas's thought, recalling an earlier, more radical vocation for critical theory. At its centre is an ideal-type representation of the early modern 'public sphere'—a bourgeois milieu of coffee houses, salons, debating clubs, grub street publishing and learned correspondence, which formed the communicative infrastructure of the Enlightenment in France and England. After tracking the gradual decline of this multinational Republic of Letters into the depths of twentieth-century mass media and manipulated public opinion, Habermas held out the remote prospect of an Enlightenment to come, in which a critical democracy might not merely reverse the degeneration of liberal traditions, but develop a more egalitarian order beyond them.

As a stark sketch of the historical conditions of possibility for a cultural revolution in the advanced capitalist West, this text remains in many ways unsurpassed. Matuštík's study of Habermas's trajectory could profitably have taken more of its bearings from this doctoral opus, since it provides one of the few instances in his career where a political practice can be judged by a theoretical prognosis. Certainly, it is significant that Habermas, once he started to be published in English, seems for many years to have discouraged its translation, much in the spirit of Horkheimer's attitude to his own pre-war writings. For in Germany, its appearance in the early sixties electrified radical students, becoming a key reference for the SDS after its expulsion from the ranks of the SPD. It was not long after the completion of this work that Habermas's academic fortunes began to soar. With Adorno's support, he returned to Frankfurt in 1964 as a professor of philosophy and sociology, occupying the position that Horkheimer had held. Successive levies of increasingly dissident students now came to view him as a critical supporter of their causes.

Marcuse was a more central catalyst in this ferment; his notions of 'repressive desublimation', 'one-dimensional man' and 'the great refusal' captured more vividly the confluence of anti-imperialism, US ghetto upheavals and the generational discontents of affluent capitalism. By contrast, Habermas's writings from this period were always more sceptical about any ready translation of the Frankfurt legacy into a living politics. His 1963 collection of essays *Theory and Practice* offered a genealogy of positivist conceptions of social science, which held that politics hinged on the selection of value-free means to attain rationally unjustifiable ultimate ends. Against such doctrines, Habermas floated the idea of a self-reflexive social theory capable of overcoming the relativism entrenched in the different areas of a fractured society by formulating criteria for an emancipatory politics, without raising dogmatic claims to an Archimedean, holistic perspective. A more systematic work later in the decade, *Knowledge and Human Interests*, sought to anchor the possibility of such a reflexive methodological orientation in a quasi-transcendental human interest in lightening the load of man-made hardship, above and beyond our natural finitude. Commitment to this interest, he claimed, forms the horizon within which social relations can be conceptualized as the opaque screen of systematically damaged forms of life. Psychoanalysis rather than Marxism provided the model for the indicated diagnostics.

Matuštík sees the leitmotif of this emerging project as a

synthesis of the liberal-democratic reckoning of 1945 with the revolutionary aspirations of the sixties. When German students' increasingly militant anti-imperialism threatened to overstep the parameters of this mission, however, they were met with a hail of determined rebukes. From 1967 to 1969 the tense relationship between radical student groups and the elders of the Frankfurt School erupted into open hostilities. Matuštík re-creates a now legendary piece of political theatre in vivid detail. In 1967, within a few days of the killing of Benno Ohnesorg by the Berlin police during a demonstration against the Shah, Habermas stunned his admirers by denouncing a quite mild call by Rudi Dutschke for campus action as tantamount to 'left fascism'. The wildness of the charge sent shock waves through a non-violent, if raucous protest culture. Matuštík observes that this imprecation, more than anything Habermas was to write, came to define his relation to those on his Left. A more measured, if equally caustic verdict was issued in 1969: the rebellion of the previous year, he claimed, had been a phantom revolution, leaving society untransformed, but thoroughly on edge. Identification with revolutionary struggles in the Third World was the illusory compensation for an inability to come to terms with the democratic immobility of advanced capitalist societies. Such were the bitter parting comments of Horkheimer's successor. Adorno's death brought the demoralization of the previous few years to a head, leading to the final break-up of the Frankfurt School, and Habermas's departure for the Max Planck Institute at Starnberg.

In 1969 the first post-war German government of the Left under Willy Brandt had come to power with the slogan: 'dare more democracy'. But the reformist programme of the Social-Democratic government soon collided with the world economic downturn that began in the early seventies, setting off what would eventually become a permanent chorus of conservative alarm at the insupportable burdens of the welfare state and the malaise of an overly reflexive, liberated society. While Matuštík brings the cultural-revolutionary drama of 1968 admirably to life, he fails to register the impact of this later material conjuncture on Habermas's conception of critical theory. For this is the moment when his scepticism towards the classical agenda of social emancipation became programmatic. Habermas spent most of this decade working on what is arguably his magnum opus, the two volumes of his *Theory of Communicative Action*, published in 1981. In it he exhibits a polymathic fluency in nearly every language of social theory from the late eighteenth century to the present. But whereas Marx and Freud had previously provided the major coordinates of his vision of a dialectic of enlightenment, here it is the systems theory of Talcott Parsons that discloses the architectonic shape of modernity, outlining more circumscribed boundaries for the rational critique of society. By not exploring its conclusions, Matuštík fails to track the conservative drift in Habermas's theoretical outlook, as the civil restoration of 1945 effectively eclipsed the Fronde of 1968, now visible only as a luminous—or alternatively ominous—fringe of the *Grundgesetz*.

Resuscitating a venerable trope of sociology, modernization was now presented as the differentiation of society into separate spheres—administration, markets and a more fluid realm of communicative fellowship—each governed by distinct standards of performance. Culture, in this account, is divested of its traditional legitimating function as a comprehensive world view, and is recast on a grid of specialization where science, law and art develop distinct, immanent norms of judgment. Habermas maintains that this autopoesis of rationalization requires ongoing enlightenment in the nebula of the life-world, if the human face of modern society is to be preserved. Embedded in the performative conditions of human utterance is a normative expectation that consensus will arise out of unimpeded communication. This principle provides a vantage point for a critique of the vast, intricately intertwining operations of money, administration and technical expertise that tend to thwart such unforced agreement. As opposed to a critique of political economy, focusing on the exploitation or emancipation of reified labour-power, the norm of undistorted communication traces the only realistic horizon of improvement in advanced societies. But a politics informed by it must stay within the limits set by the impersonal orders of bureaucracy and money, as any attempt to overstep them in upsurges of would-be self-determination can only cancel the achievements of social rationalization. The remote prospect of a radical assertion of popular sovereignty that Habermas held out in *Structural Transformation of the Public Sphere* has been definitively retracted. The salvageable core of a politics of emancipation is no more than a civilized balance between money, power and solidarity.

Habermas offered, however, no optimistic gloss for liberal-democratic capitalism. Although a constitutional welfare state energized by protest politics coming from alternative lifestyles is presented as the final form of social rationalization, *Theory of Communicative Action* ends with the bleak observation that capitalist crisis had effectively checked the forward march of this process, and was setting in motion trends that now threatened to reverse post-war advances through a long, demoralizing attrition. This disconcerting conclusion, in which the severity of the predicament is aggravated by the impossibility of any concerted political solution, recapitulates the uneasiness the late Hegel felt before a modernity that had failed to settle into its purportedly comprehended, architectonic form. But in Habermas's case it is not the tremors of popular sovereignty that disturb the stately edifice of objective reason, but the attenuation of what has come to stand in for them.

Meanwhile another, more ominous phantom revolution was threatening civil peace in Germany. While Habermas was still writing these tomes at the Max Planck Institute, the Federal Republic was rocked by a series of spectacular assassinations of prominent politicians and businessmen, carried out by underground cells of the Red Army Faction. The political reaction that had failed to materialize in the aftermath of 1968 now went into full swing.

Yellow journalism, academic black lists, loyalty oaths and prison deaths recalled states of emergency from other times. Matuštík explores Habermas's courageous response to the Hot Autumn of 1977, when he stood his ground before counter-terrorist panic, while defending the Frankfurt School from accusations that it had planted the seeds of violence in the previous decade.

Confounding expectations of a long era of Social Democratic ascendancy, a Centre-Right coalition came to power in 1982 with the defection of the FDP under Genscher to the side of the CDU. Christian Democratic rule would demonstrate a more solid grasp of the organic formulae of government in the decade of the Second Cold War. Habermas's return to Frankfurt in 1982 coincided with massive protests against the Kohl government's welcome for the installation of Pershing missiles by the US. Habermas saw in the ensuing campaign of civil disobedience a healthy manifestation of resistance from the life-world to unaccountable power and— overcoming previous inhibitions—defended its compatibility with the authentic spirit of the Basic Law. Despite these expressions of sympathy, he did not question West Germany's allegiance to NATO. Matuštík passes over Habermas's tense relationship with the newly formed Green Party, a political formation drawing on the still intact sub-cultures of 1968. The philosopher sternly reprimanded the early Greens for their 'lunatic' antics in the Bundestag, 'irresponsible' anti-Americanism and nostalgic vision of a divided nation, trapped between nuclear power blocs.

Matuštík offers instead a detailed account of Habermas's battles with a resurgent neo-conservatism, which he feared might reverse the Federal Republic's fraught passage into the comity of Western culture. The prospect of Reagan and Kohl commemorating the casualties of the Second World War before SS graves at Bitburg raised the spectre of an unsettling revisionism in which Germany's role in the post-war Alliance could be represented as a continuation of its wartime efforts on the Eastern Front. Just this implication was developed in the historian Ernst Nolte's incendiary thesis that

Nazism in Germany should be seen as a pathological response of bourgeois society to the annihilating threat of the Red Terror in Russia—and as such calling for potentially more empathetic comprehension. The Historians' Debate that broke out in 1986 around this, and other attempts to offer an allegedly more balanced retrospective judgment on the historic predicaments of the German Reich, captured international attention, as Habermas weighed in to attack the suggestion that there was anything salvageable in this geopolitical legacy. Intermingled with his powerful rebuttals, however, was a curt dismissal of any attempt to revive the anachronistic agenda of national reunification. The like-minded Hans-Ulrich Wehler complained that conservative nostalgia for such unity did more to endanger the Federal Republic's allegiance to the West than even the foolish prattle of the Greens. Habermas declared that the only viable form of collective identity that remained for the Federal Republic was a constitutional patriotism, voided of all retro-nationalist vestiges.

While no one could foresee that within three years the GDR would be erased from the map, Habermas's blindness to the division of the country compared poorly with the record of others on the Left less fixated on Bonn, and more sensitive to historical realities likely to outlast the Cold War. It is greatly to his credit that when reunification came in 1990, Habermas argued against immediate *Anschluss* of the East, calling instead for a new constitutional settlement to be approved by a referendum in both parts of the country, in accordance with Article 15 of the *Grundgesetz*. But the force of his appeal was weakened by his prior failure—in common with virtually the whole liberal–Left mainstream in the West, which uncritically celebrated 1945 as a year of Allied deliverance— to respond with any imagination to the consequences of post-war partition.

Not long after, anti-immigrant pogroms erupted in old and new *Länder* alike, and the Basic Law's generous asylum provisions, an émigré legacy of the post-war settlement, came under broad attack. Here too Habermas spoke up with commendable clarity and vigour against the dangers of incipient racism, expressing his long-standing commitment to a vision of political order grounded in humanitarian norms. German reunification could be reconciled to these, he argued, only with an unequivocal disavowal of any intention to flex new muscles in Europe, and a determination to pursue ever-greater integration into the EC. Developing the conception of a post-national democracy, he warned that return to the old capital in the Berlin Republic encouraged a complacent verdict that normal nationhood had at last been attained. At the very moment when world history had slated the nation for down-sizing, neo-conservative nostalgia was muddying the waters of cultural understanding, deferring a mature engagement with the times.

In such interventions—over Bitburg, the Historians' Debate, Reunification, the Asylum Law—Habermas has played the role of a vigilant intellectual guardian, alerting the public to the omnipresent dangers of political amnesia. It is a balance-sheet Matuštík understandably honours. But it cannot be separated so easily from the side of Habermas that came to disturb him. For it was in this capacity too that Habermas, in an extraordinary display of indifference to historical accuracy that took even close friends on the liberal Left aback, hailed Daniel Goldhagen's grotesque distillation of modern German national identity prior to occupation into a psychotic anti-Semitism. The trashiness of this American best-seller was apparently less important to him than its serviceability as political grist to his mill. Spectres from a haunted past, always threatening to return, could be exorcized only through abjuring forever the temptation to become an autonomous state. Self-dissolution into a European—and eventually world—federation is a way of working off this debt to other countries, which can set their own timetables for entering into the post-national age. Matuštík is reluctant to challenge Habermas's lofty perch in the watchtower of the nation's conscience, but it is from just this position that an anachronistic anti-Fascism would pass judgment on the fate of Belgrade and Baghdad.

For this was the moment at which Matuštík entered Habermas's circle in Frankfurt, an experience that left an indelible impression on him. Despite his respect for the philosopher, he could not follow him in endorsing America's wars in the Gulf and the Balkans. Most painful of all, in this association with 'cluster-bomb liberals', was the glaring contrast between Habermas's intemperate denunciation of the unarmed student protests of 1968 and his complacence towards the raining down of high-tech military violence by the most powerful state machine in the world—'his fear of student street activism and revolutionary aspirations' on the one hand, and his 'support for extreme levels of the state monopoly of violence and killing', on the other. The passion of Matuštík's reproaches is all the more impressive for the sincerity of his attachment to Habermas. Nor can he shut his eyes to other signs of adherence to the Atlantic status quo. Commenting on *Between Facts and Norms*, he writes:

> The need for economic democracy exists in Habermas's theory neither as a theoretical nor a practical possibility. Existing capital, labour and investment markets are left undisputed: they are designed for efficiency by the market economists and utilized by entrepreneurs since efficiency cannot be translated into the language of social justice and vice versa . . . In sum, capitalism and democracy are not a contradiction, since there is nothing undemocratic about efficiency and nothing economic about democracy.

These are criticisms of an admirer whose good faith is beyond question. They are prompted by a conviction that Habermas— the living embodiment of critical theory, in Matuštík's view—has in such cases failed to understand the political logic of his own theoretical project. But if one accepts the premise that its origin lay in a deep-going attempt to bring to light the hidden potentials for emancipation in the present, it is more reasonable to conclude that Habermas has now abandoned this agenda for another. The problem today is how to universalize and institutionally anchor the norms of liberal-democratic civilization with due regard to the diversity of human cultures, ultimately grounded in the symbolic remnants of world religions. In the light of this contemporary preoccupation, the classical conception of popular sovereignty as the constituent power of a self-determining society can be rejected as a primitive national metaphysics. Archaic fantasies of collective emancipation—Habermas has explained he no longer uses the term—are being superseded by a nascent geopolitics of human rights.

According to this prospectus, a clear view of the horizon of modernity can emerge only when we abandon the figment of a sovereign people as a collective subject for a proceduralist constitutionalism, rooted in inter-subjective rules of unforced mutual agreement. Misgivings that such consensus might still be an artefact of some opaque impersonal coercion are now relegated to the occasional aside. The new Habermas is an essentially establishment philosopher, with little taste for the hermeneutics of suspicion. The task of criticism is simply to clarify the intuitions underlying the existing constitutional dispensation, blocking the path to any regressive majoritarianism. Where older theories of democracy mistakenly conceived of individual rights as checks on the will of a hypostasized collective subject, Habermas argues that a radical democracy must on the contrary conceive such rights as the necessary condition for the formation of a true consensus; though why this is more radical, and not less, is not itself explained. Historically, those who denounced radical democracy—fearing the coercive power of sovereign multitudes to dissolve property rights and introduce a more sweeping equality—have with good reason identified it with the former, not the latter conception.

For Habermas, by contrast, modern constitutions are open to their own supersession, not by any insurgency arising out of the depths of an endangered life-world, but through governments dissolving the jurisdiction of their own states into an overarching, cosmopolitan legal order. Europe is the first stop for Germany, supposedly en route to a world federation. This passage, we are reminded, is fraught with risk, as the trend lines of globalization are extremely difficult to extrapolate. A mood of 'enlightened helplessness' is rampant on the mainstream Left, but that is unwarranted in Habermas's view, because as solidarities of national welfare *Gemeinschaft* dry up, new ones are emerging in the milieu of a multicultural *Gesellschaft*. Habermas offers his revised understanding of democracy as a guideline for managing the ensuing ethno-religious frictions in a society of strangers. But the rhetoric of multiculturalism also provides a convenient idiom for a certain way of disposing of the legacies of colonialism. He writes in *The Inclusion of the Other*:

> *Eurocentrism and the hegemony of Western culture* are in the last analysis catchwords for a struggle for recognition at an international level. The Gulf War made us aware of this. Under the shadow of colonial history that is still vivid in people's minds, the allied intervention was regarded by religiously motivated masses and secularized intellectuals alike as a failure to respect the identity and autonomy of the Islamic-Arabic world. The historical relationship between the Occident and the Orient, and especially the First, to the former Third World, continues to bear the marks of a denial of recognition.

The turn towards discourse ethics allows a curtain of mystifying euphemism to be drawn across the enormity of contemporary imperialism.

But what calculations of real forces lie behind Habermas's redefinition of democracy? In the twenty years since the publication of *Theory of Communicative Action* the power of capital has taken a Great Leap Forward. Habermas concedes that this development threatens to negate the formula of modernity as a balance between money, power and solidarity. Unleashed, uncomprehended money appears to be cancelling the autonomy of the state, and overwhelming one outpost of the life-world after another. Do we now move from Talcott Parsons back to Karl Marx? Not at all. For the time being, there is no political solution to our predicament. Certainly no nationalist closure or secession from the world market can be considered, but seen in the light of twentieth century attempts to exercise this option, that is nothing to regret. For according to Habermas modernity is precisely this process of periodic 'expansion' of the life-world through waves of creative destruction. We stand in the midst of another Great Transformation, and like the one that unfolded from the mid-nineteenth century to the Belle Époque, it is reshaping the social order through the unregulated agency of money so rapidly that only those riding in the fiery chariots of world finance have the wind in their banners.

But this Polanyian account inevitably leads to an unsettling parallel that Habermas chooses not to draw. For in this reckoning, the first era of globalization led to the horrors of world war and fascism before the Bretton Woods order neutralized the volatility of world capitalism. Habermas argues that the defining moment of the twentieth century was not the defeat of Communism but rather the vanquishing of Fascism, as this is what made possible the democratic welfare state and decolonization—the two decisive advances of post-war history. But he does not consider, in turn, whether the end of the Cold War, whose significance is reduced to a second installment of victory over totalitarianism, has set into motion a trend in the opposite direction—towards a new form of laissez-faire imperialism. Following the Polanyian narrative one could conclude that we are once again heading to the brink of catastrophe.

The horizon of this second era of globalization seems dark but Habermas implies that we can see this process through to another era of social regulation without an intervening time of catastrophes.

The danger is that this Great Transformation, even more than the first, seems to be uprooting the solidarities needed for a future democratic response. Where is the refuge of optimism on this blighted landscape of inequality and atomization? The unstated premise that follows is paradoxical: the decline of older communities of fate is precisely what makes possible two major advances in the rationalization process—the euthanasia of nationalism in the lands of its origin, and an irreversible, ongoing feminization of society. For the German historian Lutz Niethammer this bizarre juxtaposition of progressive and regressive developments forms the distinguishing pattern of an age of identity politics—a world all too liable to break apart in Hobbesian culture wars. Habermas appears to be more sanguine. But if multiculturalism and feminism will not suffice to stave off catastrophic meltdowns and nationalist backlashes outside of the OECD zone, what is the force that will hold the world together in the coming time of transition?

Habermas is counting on the rationalization of inter-state relations going into high gear. Unlike the first half of the twentieth century, the second reveals a trend, in his view, towards the pacification of inter-state relations. First, completely breaking with historic precedent, all the developed capitalist countries became liberal democracies, locked into an American-dominated security framework that has made war between them unthinkable. Second, the collapse of the Soviet empire has eliminated, for the time being, the threat of nuclear war that previously hung over this internal rationalization of Western state and society. For Habermas the post–Cold War era offers the prospect that Kant's vision of historical progress towards a world federation is finally on the agenda. In this perspective, open season on rogue states is a spring-cleaning of the historical debris left over from the era of nationalism.

Throughout the nineties Habermas developed this conception of a new world order crystallizing around humanitarian norms, undaunted by the cavalier legalities and collateral damage of neo-imperial warfare. The historical experience of the last half century, he has suggested, affords a revision of the essential premises of Kant's sketch of the unfolding of international law within the world of war, commerce and diplomacy. According to Kant, state power would be compelled by an emerging European-wide sphere of public opinion firstly to conform to constitutional limitations, then to renounce war against other constitutional states and, finally, to leap into irrevocable federation with them. Kant steadfastly opposed the idea that any one state could ever be entrusted to establish this condition on its own terms. The result, Habermas observes, is that 'he must rely exclusively on each government's own moral self-obligation. But such trust is scarcely reconcilable with Kant's soberly realistic description of the politics of his own time.'

What has changed in the world since Kant's time that now warrants a less soberly realistic description of international affairs? Habermas claims that in the era of globalization, '"soft power" displaces "hard power" and robs the subjects to whom Kant's association of free states was tailored of the very basis of their independence'. As a result, a global 'civil society' that provides the political setting for a human-rights agenda has emerged. Even a world media domain divided between multinational giants and postmodern robber barons offers episodic coverage of human-rights violations, famines and other calamities of interest. Habermas seems to think that had Kant lived to see the beginning of the Second American Century, he might also have thrown caution to the winds and embraced a republican empire with the power to vault over the threshold of sovereign statehood and establish a new kind of world polity.

While Habermas expressed the hope that this process would unfold within the framework of a reformed United Nations, it was clear from the establishment of the Anglo-American no-fly zones over Iraq, and certainly from the time of the Rambouillet diktat, that the outlines of another world order were emerging, reducing the General Assembly to absolute irrelevance, and the Security Council to the undignified role of providing, when solicited, legal cover for the sovereign decisions of the White House. Habermas, like many on the European Left, has difficulty perceiving the United Nations as it is. But in a time of transition between old and new inter-state regimes, his normative political theory can perform an essential ideological function. It offers a method for bridging the interpretive no-man's-land between the increasingly defunct norms of the Charter and the imputed ideal structure of obligations under a supposedly nascent international law— that is to say, a legal order that has yet to come into being, but whose humanitarian norms can be invoked by the most powerful state in the world to authorize any departure from the Charter framework. The incipient soft norms of human rights turn out to require an emergency regime of hard steel and high explosives to come into being.

Confronted with current us assertions of America's eternal supremacy, as the Pentagon gears up to seize Baghdad, Habermas has not been moved to revise his confidence in the West's new *mission civilisatrice*. While expressing conventional European misgivings about the dangers of 'unilateralism', he has deplored Schroeder's declaration that Germany would not join an invasion of Iraq, even were the Security Council to mandate one, as failing to display 'unreserved respect for the authority of the un'. The more loyal attitude of Foreign Minister Fischer—a favourite of both the State Department and the philosopher—was preferable. For Habermas, once again, the decisive question is the *language* to be used in justifying the latest state of exception, as if this is what determines the final architecture of world politics. Here is the distinction with which (in a recent *Nation* interview) he garlanded motives for the Balkan War:

> In Continental Europe, proponents of intervention took pains to shore
> up rather weak arguments from international law by pointing out that

the action was intended to promote what they saw as the transition from a soft international law toward a fully implemented human rights regime, whereas both US and British advocates remained in their tradition of liberal nationalism. They did not appeal to 'principles' of a future cosmopolitan order but were satisfied to enforce their demand for international recognition of what they perceived to be the universalistic force of their own national 'values'.

The shell game of principles versus values defines the parameters of the only debate that the later Habermas considers worthwhile. Conversations with Rawls and Rorty—'the heirs of Jefferson'— boil down to justifying the writ of liberal democracy in different idioms. Acknowledgment that 'the idea of a just and peaceful cosmopolitan order lacks any historical and philosophical support' does not deter Habermas from concluding that there is no alternative to striving for its realization, even if its military expressions, for all their good will, so far leave something to be desired. The suspicion that such wishful thinking might preclude historical and philosophical comprehension of the real world has been successfully kept at bay. Habermas recently wrote of Herbert Marcuse that he believed he had to introduce a vocabulary that could only open eyes clouded to realities that had grown invisible 'by bathing apparently unfamiliar phenomena in a harsh counterlight'. But reconstructing this forgotten language, and learning how to speak it, is the sole vocation of a theory that is genuinely critical.

10

The Age of Identity

Over the last quarter of a century, the deflation of the radical agendas of the generation of 1968 has in many quarters generated a nervous sensibility, jumpy at any hint of large hypotheses.[1] But in the wider movement away from epic theories of historical development, the German scene has exhibited persistently distinctive features. One of these has been the local variant of micro-history, which has sought to refurbish the traditional craft pretensions of the discipline, while avoiding older positivist obsessions: a typical research agenda involves anthropological decipherment of enormous quantities of variegated documents, often with the objective of recapturing concealed textures of daily experience. The concluding formulations to these exercises typically call into question the value of writing histories organized around misleading canonical categories: capitalism, industrialization, the state—all construed as residues of discredited philosophies. Much of this work exhibits a populist temper that has earned its authors the affectionate local sobriquet of 'barefoot historians'.

Within this field, the contributions of Lutz Niethammer have been distinguished by both range and originality. A prolific oral historian, in cohort and sensibility Niethammer might in some

1   This article appeared originally in *New Left Review* 2: 16, July–August 2002, and is a review of Lutz Niethammer, *Kollektive Identität: Heimliche Quellen einer unheimlichen Konjunktur*, Hamburg: Rowohlt Verlag, 2000.

ways be compared to Raphael Samuel, though the national differences are as significant as the methodological similarities. Most notably, Niethammer's version of history from below has been shadowed by a wary respect, even fascination, for the imperious theorizations he rejects in the name of a critical empiricism. His best-known work, *Posthistoire*, published in English in 1994, is an intellectual study of a theme which, in his judgment, brought to a head the follies of this whole genre: the End of History. It is a taut masterpiece, a 160-page excavation of an uncanny, yet sharply delineated topos.

Niethammer's latest enterprise is a sprawling genealogy of a term which, by contrast, designates no coherent theme: 'collective identity', traced from its obscure origins to its present status as the signature master category of our times. The initial focus is on a cluster of writings from the first half of the twentieth century. Niethammer's methodological premise here is that 'collective identity' eludes any stringent conceptual determination: prevailing definitions, invariably vague, oscillate meaninglessly between essentialism and constructivism, alleged facts and spurious norms. The conventional methods of the historian cannot take us into the murky underside of intellectual life where this floating signifier acquired its first, sundry meanings; here, research has to take its cue from shrewd guesswork and quirky intuitions. For Niethammer the original locutions of 'identity' in the works of some of the leading intellectuals of this period are to be read as symptoms of an attempt to conceal an uncanny alterity haunting their life projects. This traumatic layer of experience running through their works can be brought to light only by psychoanalysing their politico-intellectual commitments. Niethammer suggests that an inquiry into the incipient connotations of this terminological cipher, in formulations from Carl Schmitt, Georg Lukács, Carl Jung, Sigmund Freud, Maurice Halbwachs and Aldous Huxley, reveals the range of its later ideological functions across the political spectrum of the post-war era. For the micro-historian attuned to the irreducible manifold of human experience, the inflation of such a blatantly homogenizing discourse at a time of ongoing social fragmentation and dissolution of traditional modes of life is deeply puzzling.

The narrative Niethammer offers is intended to counter what he sees as the German legend of the origin of the contemporary preoccupation with identity. According to this account, the democratic project of American ego psychology was re-imported back into Germany after the Second World War. The founder of this school, Erik Erikson, famously upheld the ideal of a well-balanced personal identity—an anodyne image of modern subjectivity, well suited to the Adenauer era. Subsequently, so the fable goes, its range was extended into the theorization of collectives, at a time in which its origins in German idealism were rediscovered. Niethammer directly challenges the progressive credentials implied by this account by tracing the inception of the term 'collective identity' back to the inter-war era, when it made its first flickering appearance, in his view, as a token signalling the psychopathologies of an age of extremes.

This is not a genealogy in the Nietzschean sense. Indeed the claim that 'the origin of a thing and its eventual utility, its employment in a system of purposes, lie worlds apart', is diametrically opposed to the methodological maxim of this book. Niethammer unabashedly defends what he calls the prejudice of the historian: that the origin invariably reveals the structure and meaning of a phenomenon and contains the secret of its subsequent development. Not all historians have shared this conviction, of course, but here it is firmly upheld, even as one suspects it is leading the author to questionable conclusions. With many of the inter-war figures he discusses, the term appears only once or twice in their entire œuvre, often in the remote margins of a little-known text. Acknowledging the often tenuous status of his interpretations, Niethammer suggests that the difficulties encountered in taking this approach to the origins of 'collective identity' reveal no flaw in the method, but rather that there is something constitutively indeterminable about the meaning of the term. As he puts it, what is essential about the term is that the essential—or what he imputes it to be—is concealed. For Niethammer the bare presence of the word 'identity' provides the occasion for ingenious symptomatic readings: the burden of his argument is that it is the neuralgic point at which the writer under consideration attempted to exorcize the disconcerting implications of his own conception of the nature and boundaries of a particular collective, at a time in which these were radically called into question by civil war, the erosion of traditional religion and the catastrophic resolution of the Jewish Question.

The interrogation begins with Carl Schmitt, in what seems an arbitrary choice to establish the ominous valences of identity language. Born on the eve of the Wilhelmine era into a Catholic provincial milieu, Schmitt made his debut on the Weimar intellectual scene with a series of startling diagnoses of the post-war meltdown of the German state. Niethammer accepts the conventional characterization of Schmitt as a counter-revolutionary, an anti-Semitic Catholic nationalist who made opportunistic adjustments to the Weimar order, while persistently labouring to discredit it, before throwing in his lot with the Nazis in 1933. Schmitt's enigmatic claim from 1922 that democracy should be understood as a relationship of identity between rulers and ruled is interpreted as a nationalist metaphysics licensing violent exclusions of racially defined enemies. Niethammer's suggestion that, for Schmitt, the enigmatic heterogeneity of the Jewish diaspora disrupted the possibility of imagining a smooth identity of rulers and ruled is intriguing, but implausible: there are no discernable traces of anti-Semitism in Schmitt's works prior to 1932, and the term 'identity' is simply absent in his authentically anti-Semitic formulations from the Nazi era. There is considerable textual evidence to suggest that Niethammer's portrait is a caricature, which leads him to drastically misinterpret Schmitt's earlier use of the word. Leaving aside the portrait, the fact that Schmitt explicitly rejected ethnic conceptions of nationhood in his Weimar era texts is simply not acknowledged. Normally discriminating and sensitive, Niethammer here reveals the dangers of unfalsifiable symptomatic reading. More persuasive is the claim that Schmitt's definition of democracy as identity points to the coercion and mystification inherent in a mass mobilization of the general will. In this register, the difference between direct democracy and plebiscitary dictatorship is eclipsed by the frontal antithesis of each to parliamentary liberalism.

A recognizable semantics of collective identity only emerges in the post-war decades of affluent capitalism. The sixties' revival of political life in West Germany set off an apparent diffusion of Schmittian definitions of democracy across the political spectrum, from the far Right to moderate conservatives, and social-democracy to the far Left. Paradoxically, it now assumed a salience in public discourse that it never occupied in Schmitt's work, though how deep this went is another matter. But it is possible that it was the resonance of a formula in a political milieu oblivious to its origins which prompted Niethammer to explore the possibility that identity jargon, in all its variants, entered into post-war German intellectual life with false papers, covering up a shady past. In fact, Schmitt is in many respects the paradigmatic case for Niethammer's claim that 'collective identity' is the negation of the democratic project, a featureless emblem of its capture and neutralization. The appropriation of this elastic formulation by the Left, according to Niethammer, resulted in a dulled awareness of the real predicaments of post-war democracy, and provided a handy idiom for the conservative backlash that followed.

Next in the line-up is Schmitt's partisan double on the other side of the European civil war, the Hungarian Communist Georg Lukács. The story of his rapid and total metamorphosis from romantic aesthete to revolutionary ideologue is retold here, with an emphatic insistence that the political is the personal: a recently ennobled family of the Jewish haute bourgeoisie of the Austro-Hungarian empire, a psychological impasse brought on by an essentially aesthetic retreat from this world, a flight forward into Bolshevism. Niethammer argues that *History and Class Consciousness* is only superficially an attempt to recover the promise of a dialectical reason extinguished by the Second International. A more sober reading of the work reveals a double construction of 'collective identity': the proletariat as the identical subject–object of an eschatologically solved riddle of history; and the imputed identity between the consciousness of the revolutionary vanguard and that of the proletariat, concealing a tacit awareness that the proletariat never achieves self-determination and remains essentially an object of mythological projections. According to Niethammer these formulæ can only be interpreted as symptoms of an attempted self-negation of Lukács's own experience of alienation—'status insecurity'—amidst the ruling classes of Belle Époque Hungary. At times the historian seems to accept the essential maxim of identity politics, which enjoins us never to deny our origins.

Niethammer points to a number of intriguing parallels between the psycho-dynamics of this decision for the Revolution and those behind Schmitt's option for the opposite cause. Born at the antipodes of the Central European cultural world, both were drawn to religiously tinged aesthetic critiques of bourgeois society, stances they later violently disavowed at the onset of an age of war and revolution, but which persisted in the displaced form of totalizing solutions to the divisions of modern society. The parallels between them were actually acknowledged by an older Schmitt—moved, he claimed, upon hearing the news of the death of his intimate enemy. In Niethammer's assessment, their respective constructions of collective identity transformed earlier philosophies of consciousness into ideologies of total mobilization. Although Lukács subsequently retracted his conception of the proletariat as the subject–object of history, even more so than in the case of Schmitt, his identity formulation was a visible presence on the theoretical horizons of post-war radicalism. Niethammer considers the vagaries of this later reception, but leaves it open as to whether he sees any Lukácsian moments in contemporary identity politics.

The next figures Niethammer scans for identity terminology come from the ranks of the early psychoanalytic movement— the rival pair of Sigmund Freud, its founding father, and Carl Jung, the designated successor and later apostate. The reliance on symptomatic reading becomes even more conspicuous as references to identity become extremely scant; and—in contrast to the work of Schmitt and Lukács—the significance of these references in the later reception of their thought slopes down to zero, as the texts in question went unpublished and remain largely unknown. It could be asked why they are included in his account. The answer seems to be that in the relevant passages from Jung and Freud the term 'identity' appears in closer proximity to the nerve centre of their estrangement, their hidden thoughts on the Jewish Question.

Symmetrically, it might be argued that it is this issue that lends its energy and length to Niethammer's preoccupation with the semantics of identity. His approach to it is an arresting variation on a Young Hegelian theme: the problem of collective identity emerges out of encounters with the Jewish Question in a secularizing society alternately fascinated and provoked by the persistence of the Jewish people. The universalistic bourgeois state, which Marx claimed would relegate their religion to the private realm, remained residually Christian, throwing up opaque barriers to the inclusion of residually Jewish minorities. In the age of assimilation, an older religious grudge lurked under the surface of the new racial anti-Semitism. How was it possible that such a people—from most angles indistinguishable from their gentile counterparts—could even be considered as members of a different race? Isaiah Berlin thought that assimilated Jews in this era were a source of unease to the societies in which they lived as well as to themselves, an anxiety taking shape in racial phantasms. Niethammer suggests that this now receding experience is the key to understanding why the post-war literature of collective identity in large part consists of studies on Jewish identity, written by Jewish authors. Antedating this now massive body of work, two contributions by early Zionist publicists—Israel Zangwill and Horace Kallen—also established the fundamental metaphors for American talk on ethnicity: the melting pot and the salad bowl.

Niethammer sketches these anticipations as the thematic backdrop for his interpretation of the relationship between Freud and Jung. Born in 1875 in Basle, son of a minister with a scholarly knowledge of Old Testament scripture, but drawn to a mother with amateur interests in mythology and mysticism, Jung was the first 'Aryan' adherent to psychoanalysis—and as such the great white hope of a movement insecure about its reputation as a strictly Jewish affair. Groomed as Freud's successor, Jung began to branch out in directions that departed from the master's strict focus on sexuality, developing mystical motifs incompatible with the scientific pretensions of psychoanalysis. Niethammer stages the break between the two as a tense Oedipal dynamic, played out in the form of competing formulations on the *differentia specifica* of Jewish identity.

Again the word appears only once in the writings of each, which does not prevent Niethammer from making it the pivot of the whole story. Jung was actually the first to coin the term 'collective identity', in an early version of a text—never subsequently published—from 1916. Niethammer reads it as an elliptical attempt to come to terms with the meaning of the Great War, envisioned as the descent of the West back into the primordial sea of the collective unconscious. The later ascent of fascism prompted Jung to consider the possibility that this *ricorso* might occasion a great transvaluation under the guidance of a new breed of spiritual chieftains. This vision of a rejuvenating barbarism led to a brief flirtation with National Socialism, and a sharpening of latent anti-Semitic themes—an episode that ended abruptly, with more introspection than was typical of those intellectuals who had shared these illusions. In the standard German account of the origins of the term 'collective identity', it was Erikson who provided the impetus for its later articulation. But Niethammer argues that in fact Freud himself had used the arcane phrase in a speech delivered to the Vienna branch of the B'nai B'rith as he grappled with the uncanny experience of belonging to a group under erasure. Assimilation had left a psychic remainder, an alarm bell activating memories of millennia of tribulations. It was this honourable stance, an impulse to endure the worst, that moved Freud from scepticism to sympathy for the Zionist project. Niethammer's evaluation of the latter displays some of the characteristic inhibitions of Germany's post-war generations.

Erikson was the first actually to coin the term 'national identity' as a substitute for the more stolid notion of national character, arguing that it better conveyed the dynamic and plastic qualities of modern mass psychology. With considerable finesse, Niethammer suggests that Erikson's identity conception emerged out of a concealed, unconscious attempt to synthesize Freud and Jung; a formal adhesion to Freudian orthodoxy with an openness to a collective problematic purged of Jung's reactionary mysticism. Erikson quietly assented to Jung's claim that Freudianism was bound to the bourgeois private world of his neurotic clients, suffering from the tics of assimilation. He sought to bring psychoanalysis into the American century, by harnessing it to a project of establishing positive role models for the nation. Niethammer registers the irony of this commitment, seen through a gap in the biography: a troubled relationship to his Jewish origins in the Old World, overdetermined by divided allegiances in the internecine struggles of the psychoanalytic movement, inspired this proponent of the ideal of the healthy personality to change his name from Homburg to Erikson.

The next figure Niethammer considers lay altogether at a tangent to the predicaments of Central European culture. Maurice Halbwachs came from an Alsatian family, which after 1871 opted for France. Born in 1877 and raised in a liberal Parisian milieu, nominally Catholic, Halbwachs was a partisan of Dreyfus and moderate socialist, somewhat to the left of his mentor Émile Durkheim. After Durkheim's death he became the leading light of French sociology, which he opened to the stimulus of selective German interlocutors: Simmel, Sombart and Bernstein were taken on board, while Marx was held at bay. His reputation rests on a pioneering project to theorize the social dimension of memory, directed against Bergson's claim of the interior causalities of the life of the mind. A series of investigations into unexplored realms of memory had led to a sea change comparable to the impact of the philosophy of consciousness in the early nineteenth century. Halbwachs's work unfolded on this recently discovered terrain. The writers who shaped this new problematic—Proust, Bergson, Freud, Warburg, Cassirer and Benjamin—were all Jewish, with the exception of this Alsatian. But even here Niethammer is at pains to detect the traces of a complex engagement with the Jewish question in a work on the history of Christianity. Portrayed as an ethical revolution, establishing a novel universalism in morality, Christianity appears as a prefiguration of a modern socialism, transcending differences of nation and race. It followed that the persistence of Judaism, by contrast, was animated by a primitive spirit of ethnic particularism enjoying affinities to contemporary reactionary nationalisms, even those of the most anti-Semitic variety. This was, of course, a rather widespread conception, not in any way peculiar to Halbwachs.

For Halbwachs, all collective memories were social constructs which preserved a feeling of continuity through history; the veracity of these memories was not a problem for sociology. But for Niethammer, his occasional use of the word 'identity' actually suggests the possibility of the erasure of those memories that resist mythologization. Niethammer points out that the initial objective of this project was a demystification of the fictional nature of collective identity. But the retreat of the French Republic in face of an advancing National Socialism precipitated a dramatic turn from critique to myth-making. Before he was interned and executed in a German concentration camp, an elderly Halbwachs posited the possibility of constructing a new, republican collective memory, as an ideal impervious to the recent humiliations of the actual republic. This was a proposition that could retrospectively be taken to prefigure the possibility of concealing the experience of collaboration, with myths of Resistance. Although sympathetic to Halbwachs's institutionalist scepticism, Niethammer argues that all attempts to mould a plurality of memories into a uniform shape must fail. His claim that the nation is never a community of memories comes out of a long engagement with this problem in the German post-war context. The traumatic traces of the Judeocide in memories of 'ordinary Germans' are, he maintains, irreducibly fragmentary.

Aldous Huxley stands at the end of this series of inter-war fashioners of the rhetoric of identity. A figure oblivious to ferments at work in the zone between Strasbourg and Budapest, Huxley was an eccentric on the more insular, yet nonetheless variegated turf of British intellectual life. Best known as the author of *Brave New World*, Huxley had previously been sympathetic to the idea of a Platonic caste society on a global scale, before this image of eugenic modernity capsized into a dystopia, turning an earlier, near-Wellsian biotechnophilia into its opposite.

Even by the standards of the book's own improvisational method, the readings of this chapter defy the protocols of evidence. The word 'identity' appears, without any subsequent elaboration, in the bold staccato of the novel's first few lines announcing the official slogan of the new world order: Community, Identity, Stability. It is never mentioned again, in the novel or in anything else Huxley wrote. This satirical transvaluation of the French Revolutionary motto is in turn satirized, but from an unnamed perspective—hostile to equality and fraternity, affirming liberty, but strangely illiberal. In Europe this stance was better defined, expressing conservative disillusionment with fascism in power, but simultaneously an unwillingness to return to an allegedly obsolete liberalism. There are audible echoes of the language of certain strains in the 'conservative revolution' on the Continent in an earlier work by Huxley, entitled *Proper Studies*. No gloomy counter-enlightenment prophecy, this optimistically foresaw the replacement of democracy by a regime of social engineering which would not only recognize natural inequality, but genetically manufacture it. Huxley held that the primary task of such a regime was not the breeding of an aristocracy of the spirit but rather a class of cheerful drones, moving to the rhythms of Fordist production. Niethammer suggests that the 'identity' of Huxley's satirical motto conjures up the possibility of a total absorption of each individual into a function—a society whose defining document is the ID card. He arguably misses a more disconcerting possibility: the identity that he denies is even possible between human beings might, in the future, become real enough through cloning.

Total mobilization, euphemisms of an uncanny cultural difference, politics as collective commemoration and a dystopian, bell-curved society: are these imputed connotations of the floating signifier elements of a later synthesis? Niethammer's story of faint anticipations is taken up to the present, but the proof that this is the case is never marshalled. The second half of the book adopts a more conventional mode of contextual interpretation, enlivened by periodic attempts to read the inter-war palimpsest between the lines of more recent writings on collective identity. The diagnosis Niethammer advances oscillates between afterthoughts on a harmless, multicultural fragmentation and grim prophecies of deadly culture wars. The pathos of the work stems from a sense that the latter scenario is more likely: multiculturalism as a prelude to a renaissance of xenophobia. This is an assessment he shares, of course, with a quite different kind of historian of the Left, Eric Hobsbawm.

Niethammer sees three waves of post-war identity semantics: a progressive, a reactionary, and a contemporary, hyper-inflationary moment that is oddly both at the same time. These are global phases of a post-war political culture with an emphasis on European variants. The progressive wave emerged out of the confluence of reformist social psychology, challenges to the American colour line, and Third World decolonization. In Germany, left Hegelianism and an unacknowledged Schmittianism were added to the mix. In the subsequent regressive wave, collective identity became a mantra of the new right, registering the overlapping anxieties of neo-conservatism and the skinhead scene. Across the OECD zone, social welfarism based on optimism about unlimited growth gave way to a Malthusian consciousness of scarcity, in an atmosphere of pervasive insecurity and malaise. This set the stage for a largely successful recapture of intellectual hegemony by the right. The achievement of the latter was to orchestrate an endless conversation on an endangered collective identity, as a surrogate for the creeping erosion of collective self-determination. Finally we witness today the contemporary inflation of collective identity as a ubiquitous signifier of academia, politics and the media. Although Niethammer claims that he leaves out contemporary feminist and minoritarian discourses because they contribute less to the prevailing intellectual mystification, one senses in the very term he uses to designate this last wave—'progressive regression'—a certain irritation towards the subaltern variants of identity claims.

The concluding chapters of the book survey a number of recent American and European additions to this centennial episteme which are closer to his central concerns, bearing on nationalism, immigration and European integration. Fukuyama, relegating ethnic difference to the harmless private sphere of a universal state, is counterposed to Huntington, theorist of a national-security version of identity politics and the coming global clash of fundamentalisms. Niethammer's perturbation at these swashbuckling visions from the right is conventional enough. More unexpectedly, he adopts an equally caustic tone in treating recent works by figures of the liberal Left. Bluntly noting the unlikelihood of any real democratization of the European community, he offers a sceptical overview of Habermas's turn from a democratic public sphere to Eurocratic identity politics. The claim that Europe is a culture whose values have been shaped by centuries of experience with tolerance and compromise is given short shrift. There is an echo of Benjamin in his insistence that one must always remember that vast pool of humanity purged and excluded from Europe, in all its thematic articulations, past and present. Passerini's affectionate portrait of Europe as a theme of courtly love and longing, transcending national borders, is dismissed as an ingenuous concealment of this simultaneously more prosaic and more disturbing historical reality. Even worse is Sloterdijk's cheeky defence of Germany's post-1968 brand of negative national identity: the view that one's own nation has forfeited the privilege—dubious anyhow—of a national agenda. For Sloterdijk, the world has much to learn from this experience of masochistic neutralization of the will to power. For Niethammer, these pronouncements are a frivolous attempt to posit a new national destiny, dangerous even when delivered in the playful tones of cosmopolitan irony. He concludes his overview by considering a representative sample of national-identity writing in the aftermath of German reunification—from triumphalist neoliberals in the West, to nostalgic defenders of an arrogantly devalued experience in the East. Niethammer, based in Jena, expresses only very mild criticisms of the latter, recommending a less self-righteous way of venting regional grievances, and more detachment from the PDS.

The book's conclusion—its title question reads: 'Should Something be Smaller?'—offers, without qualification, a lurid verdict on any notion of collective identity. Only one hard core lurks in this fatal magma: a demarcation [*Abgrenzung*] against what is not-identical, predestining it to conflict. In the escalation of such conflict, collective identity can find an ultimate foundation in religion and race alone. 'To that extent the impulse to fundamentalism and violence is inherent in collective identity.' Law provides no safeguard against its ravages, since it moves in a realm intermediate between culture and violence, beyond legal norms. Schmitt, Lukács and Huntington, who endorsed this nexus, saw deeper than its seemingly more innocuous champions, who repressed it. 'Is there any safeguard against the unconscious slippage of apparently harmless demands for cultural and political identity into legitimation of violence? My answer is: no.'

Against the catastrophic spread of this virus, Niethammer proffers an antidote. His 'modest proposal' is to eliminate the category of identity from contemporary discourse, and use the term 'we' instead. The first-person plural, he thinks, may not be free from mystifications of its own, but as a form of address it is weaker, more variable, and inclusive—allowing for diverse and mutable affinities, rather than the rigidly objectified fixations of identity, with its inherent dynamic of violence. We-speech will discourage us from confecting enemies and make it easier for us to come to understanding with others in practical affairs, in the knowledge that all large groups actually break down into lesser ones, themselves composed of individuals. Eschewing fictive totalizations, the safe little pronoun should allow us to think more realistically about political problems today.

The whimsicality of this ending suggests the need for Niethammer's own characteristic tools to understand it. On the plane of theory, he makes scant attempt to explain the spread of the identity rhetoric he deplores: the question of why it has become so prevalent cannot be bypassed merely by invoking its uncanny opacity. It is striking, in a work of such capacious scope, treating at length authors many of whom scarcely used the term 'identity' at all, that the most substantial exploration of the category—Adorno and Horkheimer's famous tracking of it as an expression of the cultural logic of a social order in *Dialectic of Enlightenment*—is barely mentioned. Nor does Niethammer offer much grounds for thinking that a rejection of collective reason as radical as his has any logical stopping-place short of an all-too familiar methodological individualism of Anglo-American stamp. Clearly, this is not Niethammer's intention. But the strange aporia with which the book ends raises, inescapably, the question of its political bearing.

In a work of formidable and ingenious erudition, Niethammer always maintains a directly political note. His sketch of the post–Cold War world, of triumphant neoliberal capitalism, is sharp and unforgiving, and he has no hesitation in taking Habermas to task for offering a 'bourgeois [*bürgerliches—sc.* citizens'] programme for the New Centre', fit 'for Schroeder's guest-book'. No one could doubt the decency of his sympathies. But the rhetoric of a 'weaker, more vulnerable and sober form of thought' that would supposedly be the salve for sores of collective identity, is a now long-standing German trope: the value of a quiet, modest, provincial yet hospitable outlook that has learnt from the cataclysm of the Third Reich to shun all big ideas and grand ambitions. However understandable, this always involved an element of self-deception—what Lukács once called *Illusionspolitik*—since, if the Federal Republic was a province, it was, from the start, one of the American imperial order. Once the only two rebellions against its military carapace were beaten down—in the early seventies and early eighties—the logic of Left humility and self-limitation was not long coming.

No German writer or thinker more eloquently expounded

the modesty and sobriety Niethammer recommends today than Hans Magnus Enzensberger, whose *Ach Europa!* (1987) decried all dreams of a European super-state, found truth in the neglected peripheries rather than the overbearing Franco-German core of the Community, and looked forward to a *Kleinstaaterei* that would leave imperial follies to the Americans. Within a short space of time, as Desert Storm was under way, he discovered that Saddam Hussein was another Hitler, whom the United States and its allies must fight with all their might. A few years later, at a lesser intellectual, but more prominent political level, Joschka Fischer and the domesticated Greens took the same route, saluting the American attack on Yugoslavia as the path of humanity and progress, and brigading Germany into NATO's campaign in the Balkans—to the applause of Habermas, regretting only that UN cover for the bombardment could not be procured in advance.

Niethammer's book appeared before the current operations in Afghanistan and the Middle East, but after the Gulf War, the Balkan War and the outbreak of the second Intifada. What does it have to say about this dominating context of the world-political scene, which has scarcely spared the newly reunited Federal Republic? There is a deafening silence. In a work that finds Jewish preoccupations or sources, however imperceptible, in every nook and cranny of the destructive discourse of collective identity, is there a single mention of Israel? Not one. This is not because the book moves on a higher plane than current affairs. In the same modest spirit of German self-limitation, it finds time to commend European acquiescence in the American extension of NATO to Russia's borders as 'progressive'.

Side-lights such as these cast a disquieting glow on Niethammer's final plea for the first-person plural. For as any glance at editorials, columns or perorations throughout the West makes clear, it is not the language of collective identity that rules the world, but—precisely—we-talk: the language of the 'international community'. Niethammer's fixation on a dynamic of identitarian exclusion has blinded him to the far greater power of the rhetoric of coercive inclusion. Today, every overweening lunge of the American predator—and the assorted pack of European scavengers that comes in its wake—floats in the hypostasized pronoun he lauds. No better motto for the time than *Le Monde*'s famous declaration: *nous sommes tous américains*. Is it an accident that Niethammer should begin his book with one misdescription of Kofi Annan—mysteriously exported from his native Ghana to the Ivory Coast—and end with another, more pregnant one? We are told—of the major-domo picked by the White House to do its will in the UN, who has covered every arbitrary or illegal action of the US and its allies, from the planting of emissaries of the CIA in UN inspection teams in Iraq to the bombardments of Yugoslavia and Afghanistan—'he represents no ideology that either wishes to legitimize violence or represses the perception of it.' Solemnly warning against the dangers of collective identity, the international community scarcely ever leaves his lips.

The violence Niethammer detests is not escaped by burying one's head in Thuringian sands. Collective identity is not a notion with much place on the left—its imputation to Lukács, whose usage of the Hegelian senses of 'identity' has virtually nothing in common with it, is an act of force—but to fetishize it as the main discursive enemy today is the theoretical equivalent of the inflation of ethnic and religious violence in Yugoslavia into the spectre of 'a new Holocaust', the standard Green justification for the NATO war in the Balkans. Contrary to Niethammer's assertion, collective identity as a historical phenomenon is by no means always a deduction from race or religion. Class and sex offer other bases for it. The workers' movement, whose legacy Niethammer at one point reproaches Habermas with forgetting, would have been impossible without it. The 'conflict potential' Niethammer so dreads had another name then, which has disappeared from these pages—class struggle. A general anathema on any conception of collective identity means, inevitably, a rejection of collective mobilization. Niethammer's dictum that we should never forget 'how hopelessly rare it is that a commitment moves and how much its failure petrifies' [*wie hoffnungslos wenig oft ein Engagement bewegt und wieviel sein Versäumnis versteinert*] is an invitation to an elegiac quietism. Should 'something be smaller'? The way of the world does not allow it. *Kleingrupperei* today, like the *Kleinstaaterei* of yesterday, leads straight into the arms of Grand Strategy.

11

The Politics of Piety

The discourse of multiculturalism, often regarded as characteristically American, has in recent years steadily gained ground in Europe.[1] This can be seen as a belated response to the often striking transformation of the metropolitan *Lebenswelt* by the inflow of millions from Asia, Africa, the Antilles and the Middle East. Decades of friction between majorities and minorities in the streets, on the labour market, in public housing, over access to welfare and in schools have thrown up fractured ethno-landscapes all across the continent. At a time when the orthodoxies of the market have all but eliminated any alternatives from the political field, both admirers and detractors of multiculturalism insist on the increasing centrality of a new axis of group differentiation and the problems that it poses to inherited conceptions of national identity. The presence of large immigrant communities in the EU, often dating from the twilight era of colonialism, acquires a more pregnant significance—it is often felt—in an era of globalization, as the main vectors of economic development, geopolitics and mass culture all seem to point to a feature-less horizon beyond the nation-state. Immigrants from the

---

1   This article originally appeared in *New Left Review* 2: 7, January–February 2001, and is a review of Bhikhu Parekh, *Rethinking Multiculturalism*, London: Macmillan, 2000.

non-European world appear to introduce an extra element of uncertainty into this transition, perhaps threatening to derail the train to Euroland altogether.

In *Rethinking Multiculturalism* the eminently establishment figure of Bhikhu Parekh—vice-chancellor of Baroda University, deputy chair of the Commission for Racial Equality in the UK, and peer in the British House of Lords—attempts to relate such European issues to North American and Indian experiences. His aim is to propose a comprehensive normative framework for addressing ethno-religious and racial conflicts in liberal democracies. The practical objective of securing a peaceful and inclusive civic life overrides any temptation on Parekh's part to dwell at length on incommensurable values. His construction of multiculturalism eschews any deep theory of culture, using the term to refer simply to communal modes of being in the world that generate complex but manageable problems of inter-group communication and cohabitation. The communal cultures he discusses usually emerge out of a fusion of ethnicity and religion. Loyalty to the way of life they prescribe is represented not as an adhesion to transcendental imperatives, but rather as the expression of an irreplaceable quotidian experience.

But if such cultures are rich in themselves, they are also multistranded, like pieces of rope, and by weaving together certain strands from each, a durable and colourful fabric of society can be made. Since cultures of this sort tend to be most palpable when they exclude outsiders, it might be objected that multiculturalism—however good for keeping the peace—is unlikely to be quite so good for the integrity of the cultures themselves. But Parekh is confident that an open-minded dialogue between majorities and minorities will not only preserve, but refine the ethno-religious traditions of each. Conceding that too much mixing might dilute what is valuable in any particular culture, he insists that doctrinaire universalism and its opposite, chauvinistic culturalism, are worse. By way of demonstration, he takes the reader on a flat-footed tour through the gallery of Great Philosophers—from Plato to Rawls—stopping here and there to explain to what degree a given thinker failed to grasp the mellow verities of the middle ground, either because he leaned too far in the direction of universalistic monism, or alternately too far in the direction of relativism.

Ostensibly, Parekh's book sets out to offer a critique of contemporary liberals who fail to recognize the impossibility of public neutrality between different conceptions of the good life, according surreptitious priority to their own values of autonomy, human rights and distributive justice. Granting without difficulty a minimum of universal prohibitions—against slavery, torture, and the like—he contends that liberals illegitimately expand the empire of rights in ways that often violate the customary norms of traditional communities. This looks like the stuff of a sharp philosophical conflict, but when Parekh elaborates on it, the upshot is little that really departs from actually existing Anglo-American liberalism. Indeed he maintains that, at least in Western countries, a public commitment to liberal values must be accepted since a thoroughgoing neutrality between liberal and non-liberal conceptions of legitimacy is impossible. This turns out to be more than just a matter of expediency: for all practical purposes Parekh appears to believe—though he does not say so—that liberal values are closest to what we all know to be universally valid.

His principal objection to mainstream liberalism is simply that it does not have a theory of cultural groups and the rights that they can legitimately claim. But the criteria he suggests for recognition of such groups prove to be a confused medley of the conservative, the sentimental and the completely evasive, embracing traditional communities, social pariahs, or just those who contribute something valuable to society: Orthodox Jews, Untouchables, African Americans and any legitimate claimant to special status. Unwilling to yield to 'postmodern' conceptions of fluid and hybridized identities, Parekh seeks to be both firm and flexible here, distinguishing between multiculturalism proper—that is, relations between 'communal' cultures—and mere subcultural diversity. Although he introduces other criteria to allow for affirmative action, his theory of group entitlements is heavily biased towards more traditional cultures. The same list is visible in his treatment of current inter-cultural controversies. Most of the cases he discusses involve divisions between European national majorities and Muslim, Hindu or Sikh minorities over public symbolism and the allocation of public resources. The issues on which he focuses are scarves, turbans, funerals and funding of religious schools. On these he sides with immigrant communities, while at the same time explaining that Western societies can legitimately accord priority to their own traditional institutions, creeds and symbols. By extension, Parekh expresses muted approval for the Israeli Law of Return as a culture-preserving measure.

When it comes to ethno-religious practices or rules governing the position of women, Parekh has little hesitation in appealing to universal moral norms, and though he rhetorically sides with protesters against Rushdie's *Satanic Verses*, maintaining that the Indian government was right to ban the novel, he ends by concluding that it would probably be sensible to abolish blasphemy laws altogether. The sum of his recommendations could, in effect, be accepted by virtually any right-thinking upholder of Westminster values. Billed as a critical reconsideration of liberal premises, the objective of *Rethinking Multiculturalism* could be more accurately described as the de-Westernization of liberalism—a stealth liberalism capable of integrating variously devout immigrants into unevenly secular European societies. Reform of too-extreme dogmas or customs, of course, he believes essential, to bring the culture of traditional religious communities into line with the requirements of the modern world. The end result would, in a best-case scenario, be a continent in which all could take a modest pride in their ethnic or religious patrimonies, untainted by aggressive fanaticism or corrosive cynicism.

Multiculturalism, so understood, is an unobjectionable extension of contemporary liberalism, for which Parekh—who makes no claims as a radical—cannot be faulted. It is quite another matter for the Left to make this outlook its own. A glance at the differing situations in Europe and America is enough to make this plain. In both, the idea of multiculturalism appeals to a certain sensibility on the Left, as a higher form of anti-racism that meshes with the culturalist common sense of the time: that the order of human things is a cultural artefact and therefore that the fundamental conflicts within it are fought over representation, identity and lifestyle. One corollary is that a good society can be established without any coercive redistribution of property. Another is that religion is neither obscurantist nor an opiate, but rather a form of identity and a way of life—just like class, nation or sexual preference. In Europe, it is the latter deduction that is politically most salient, as the critical stance of the Enlightenment towards religion has been widely jettisoned. It is now standard for religious protectionism of one kind or another to be dressed up as anti-racism. A paradigm case is the denunciation of any criticism of Judaism or Zionism as anti-Semitic, or of Islam as arabophobic. Religious faiths may, in fact, offer defensive identities for vulnerable immigrant communities. But the same creeds can be weapons of vicious repression in their homelands—and that there can be links between the two the followers of Khomeini or Kahane amply demonstrate.

Across the Atlantic, on the other hand, in a country accustomed to hyphenated identities and with no recent history of ethno-religious exclusion, multiculturalism arose in an academic setting of inveterate professions of pluralism. Where the European debate reflects a context in which long-standing national identities have suddenly been put into question, this has almost never been at issue in the US, let alone in the second Gilded Age we enjoy now. The discourse of ethnic difference is as American as apple pie. Here, however, it is race—most centrally the legacy of slavery—and not ethno-religion that overdetermines the problematic of diversity. Crime, welfare and the work-educational ethic are the essential coordinates of nativist obsession. Foreign immigrants, of the most diverse religious and ethnic backgrounds, often enter into regions of the labour and housing market where blacks are still kept out, as they have done in the past. The disproportionate number of Asians at US universities and the growing preponderance of Latinos at the bottom end of the workforce, however, represent a break in the history of the White Republic. The identity jargon of multiculturalism is, on the one hand, a distorted ideological expression of the possibility of a momentous, incipient de-racialization of US society. On the other, it is a fairy tale of upward mobility in which the harsh world of the black and brown underclass is abolished by institutionalizing cultural diversity on college campuses, as if the problem was one of the lack of role models. In this guise multiculturalism is simply an ideology of affirmative action, incapable of imagining what it would take to achieve real social equality. The multicultural schema transforms a whole gamut of inequities into mere demands for tolerance of difference. The binary oppositions of this discourse—universal/particular, majority/minority, closed/open, homogeneity/heterogeneity—cannot bring massive and growing inequality of wealth into conceptual, let alone political, focus. Its treacly pieties are incompatible with any polemical élan against the established order.

In its lack of critical spirit, today's multiculturalism is the antithesis of what once could more rightly have claimed the name. The possibility of gaining a critical vantage point on one's own society by learning about an alien one, the true vocation of a philosophical anthropology, is almost entirely foreclosed by its complacent cult of difference. More than four centuries ago, Montaigne, recounting the reception of three savages from America by the King of France in Rouen, taught another lesson. Having witnessed the splendour of a society so utterly unlike their own, they were asked what they found most remarkable in it. 'They said in the first place that they found it very strange that so many tall, bearded men, all strong and well armed, who were around the King, should be willing to obey a child, rather than choose one of their own number to command them. Secondly— they have a way in their language of speaking of men as halves of one another—that they had noticed among us some men gorged to the full with things of every sort, while other halves were beggars at their doors, emaciated with hunger and poverty. They found it strange that these poverty-stricken halves did not take the others by the throat or set fire to their houses.'

12

From Florence to Moscow

The posthumous publication of Louis Althusser's reflections on Machiavelli offers an unsettling occasion to return to both thinkers.[1] If we except the more limited cases of Della Volpe and Colletti, Althusser was the only figure in the Western Marxist tradition to engage with a number of the classics of Western political theory. But his writings on Montesquieu, Rousseau and Hegel—remarkable, even at times coruscating, as they could be—were still beholden to the idea that such theorists might be judged by how closely they came to anticipating the discoveries of historical materialism. His unpublished text on Machiavelli, dating from a later period, exhibits a different spirit. Here relations are if anything reversed—the Florentine figured as a more radical and original theorist than any successor in the Communist tradition. According to his pupil Emmanuel Terray, he once confessed that Machiavelli was 'without doubt the author who has most fascinated me, much more so than Marx'.

Althusser began to sketch lectures on Machiavelli in 1962, less than a year after a formative first encounter while on holiday in Italy; a draft took shape around 1971–2 in preparation for another course, and was largely completed by 1975. This version was periodically revised up through the mid-eighties, but left unpublished at his death in 1990. Overtly, none of the major

---

1   This article first appeared in *New Left Review* 2: 3, May–June 2000, and is a review of Louis Althusser, *Machiavelli and Us*, London: Verso, 1999.

events of post-war Communism left any mark on these pages. De-Stalinization, the Sino-Soviet split, the Cultural Revolution, May 1968, Eurocommunism are visible only through extremely oblique allusions. Unmistakably, however, Althusser intended *Machiavelli and Us*—his own title—as a philosophical reflection on the short twentieth century defined by the legacy of the Russian Revolution.

Only indirectly topical, the text is also only subliminally exegetical. Althusser not only avoids conventional quotation from Machiavelli. Even more conspicuously he ignores nearly all of the great multinational landmarks of twentieth-century Machiavelli scholarship. It seems likely that Althusser came to know of this body of work only when he read *Le Travail de l'œuvre*, a massive study of Machiavelli by Claude Lefort published in 1972 which discusses a number of scholars—Gerhard Ritter, Rene Koenig, Ernst Cassirer and Leo Strauss, amongst others—far removed from the French intellectual scene of the time. The only influence he acknowledges, if still somewhat perfunctorily, is Gramsci. His own glosses are often cavalier, scanting issues others have reflected on more clearly and carefully. Althusser's philological indifference finds revealing expression in his comment that Machiavelli can only be made interesting if he is 'utterly transformed' by reading his ideas in the light of contemporary concerns.

The primary concern of Althusser's study is to establish Machiavelli's significance as a unique figure in the history of philosophy. His central claim is that Machiavelli's writings inaugurated a completely original materialism—one that is neither a monistic ontology, nor a claim about the primacy of the economic in history, not even in the last instance. More captiously, Machiavelli is defined as a materialist because he is a theorist of 'concrete conjunctures', who brings concealed vectors of strategic action to light, exposing the immanent possibilities of the present as a moment in history. 'Matter' under this meaning is too complex and ductile to allow for any general laws: it is simply the ungrounded, emergent causality of open-ended transitions.

Marxists have classically argued that historical materialism is the science of the systemic compulsions and counter-finalities of the struggle between groups fought out under conditions of scarcity. Although in the whole tradition of Western Marxism there was no one who had a more positive view of science, Althusser actually subscribed to an extremely modest view of the knowledge that a Marxist science of history could offer; as a field of contradiction and over-determination, history was a process structured only in a distant last instance by economic modes of production. Here, however, dismissing the stereotype of Machiavelli as the founder of a coldly realistic analytics of power, Althusser tacitly relinquishes his own distinctive conception of class struggles too. For the flux of conjunctures now precludes any law-like regularities. What Machiavelli offers us instead is an art of thinking focused wholly on the conditions of undertaking tasks immediately to hand, without anchorage in any underlying movement of history: a supposedly deeper, albeit more unstable kind of knowledge. The purpose of his rhetorical construction of exemplary cases was, Althusser argues, to offer a repertoire of scenarios for transformative agency. This was an optic designed for sharp focus on those faint interstitial possibilities that only become 'events' through great, improbable awakenings of the down-and-out. Indeed, according to Althusser, the problem which defined the horizon of Machiavelli's thought was how a new political order could be established in wholly unfavourable circumstances. The utopian energy of his writing springs from an impasse: while the possibilities of a new state were being realized elsewhere in Europe in the form of absolutism, the Italian city-state was unable to reinvent itself on the enlarged national scale necessary for a successful transition to capitalism.

But despite the fact that the examples and distinctions deployed in his texts are often embedded in the contentions of a distant era, Machiavelli remains actual today as the inventor of a new genre of writing about politics, whose potential has yet to be grasped. The most significant moments in his work speak to an interlocutor who is not ultimately a valorous individual, but rather the masses whose possibilities of agency are represented in the form of such a figure. Machiavelli's writings establish roles for potential actors on the political stage and interpellate subjects who will play out those roles. It is the presence of these empty spaces, to be read and occupied by anonymous partisan subjects, that make it so difficult to decipher the agendas lurking beneath his deceptively clear prose. This indeterminacy is constitutive and ineradicable. By way of parables, stories of the concrete, Machiavelli broke out of the generalizing format of the classical treatise, and invented the prototype of the manifesto. The rhetorical novelty of the latter is that it is a text which inserts itself into the space of agency that it has itself identified. Machiavelli, unlike Marx, leaves these spaces open: more cognizant of the aleatory dialectic of political conflict, he does not seal them with any ideological closure. Machiavelli addresses the masses via the silhouette of a resolute ruler only because, conceived in that form, decisive action can begin at any time. The Prince, unlike the proletariat, is 'the pure possibility of the event', 'agency out of the void', 'absolute new beginning'. Machiavelli's writings analyse 'the conditions of an impossible event', blasting open the continuum of history. It is as if we overhear at this point an uncanny, voluntarist echo of Benjamin.

Shifting from the plane of this unearthly general 'materialism', Althusser's text moves to a more specific question, the object of a long-standing controversy, to which he returns an over-coded answer. How is it possible to reconcile Machiavelli the patriotic republican with Machiavelli the counsellor of princes? Althusser argues that there is no conflict between the political agenda of *The Prince* and that of the *Discourses* because the former simply explores the violent agency required to found a new state which will, over the course of time, eventually become the national-republican polity which Machiavelli was ultimately aiming for. Here Althusser develops Gramsci's idea that Machiavelli was, even as a counsellor to princes, a proto-Jacobin attempting to shape the construction of an emergent popular will by pointing out courses of appropriate action to those for whom this could never be a conscious goal. *The Prince* is the handbook for a would-be founder of a new state, who must work alone, purging and liquidating his enemies. The *Discourses*, by contrast, offer a more panoramic vision of the longer-term work of incorporating the masses into the new state through laws, and mobilizing them though representative institutions.

By this account *The Prince* is the more 'revolutionary' of the two works because it lays bare the violence involved in the foundation of the new state, and gazes unperturbed at the horrors of this origin. Unlike theorists of natural law and the social contract, who saw consent at the origins of government, Machiavelli was 'a man who, even before all the ideologists blocked out reality with their stories, was capable not just of living, or tolerating, but of thinking the violence of the birth-throes of the state.' In this sense Machiavelli was not a theorist of political conjunctures in general, but of a particular, recurring phenomenon: the traumatic revolutionary moment of 'primitive political accumulation'. This is what a return to the 'absolute beginning' means: the restoration of the primordial vulnerability and plasticity of human beings. But Machiavelli's insights extended further. For he saw the necessity of building up a new citizen-army not just as a condition of survival in the predatory world of war and diplomacy, but also as a way to liquidate old social hierarchies and fuse new groups. It is in this context, Althusser suggests, that we should grasp the significance of Machiavelli's notorious, unfairly ridiculed belief in the superiority of infantry to cavalry and artillery. What underlay this conviction was a vision of epic mass mobilizations, comprehensively subordinating animal and mechanical power to human purposes.

These are inventive notations, if marred—as so often in Althusser—by the absence of any controlled exegesis. Nonetheless many of the points on which they turn are contestable. The claim that Machiavelli was a theorist of the conditions of absolutist state formation in the early modern transition from feudalism to capitalism is not plausible. For his conception of the state so emphatically accentuated the personality of the ruler or ruling body that it failed to capture or anticipate the dual nature of early modern absolutism, characterized at once by a hypostasization of the figure of the monarch, and an incipient depersonalization —'bureaucratization'—of the structure of feudal jurisdiction. Likewise, his strenuous attachment to a citizen militia stood in stark opposition to the whole pattern of absolutist state formation. These discrepancies between Tuscan concerns and European trends found repeated expression in his judgments of contemporary polities. Machiavelli had no premonition of the impending involution of the Holy Roman Empire of the German Nation, whose ornate medieval federalism he viewed in a highly positive light. France, the early modern state that loomed largest for him, he esteemed not for its absolutism—which had not yet really taken shape—but as a kingdom based on a legal framework of estates representation. The Swiss Federation, which he admired in Tacitean fashion as an intact relic of ancient Teutonic simplicity, was the polar antithesis of Renaissance proto-absolutism. In his critique of *The Prince* written more than two centuries later, Frederick the Great of Prussia showed without difficulty how remote Machiavelli was from any understanding of the territorial scale, institutional architecture and aristocratic ethos of the dynastic world of absolutism, an order everywhere erected on the foundations of a quiescent and unarmed populace of peasants and burghers.

It is clear, however, that behind Althusser's claim that Machiavelli can be seen as a theorist of emergent absolutism, understood as the resolution of the problem of state formation in the epoch of transition from feudalism to capitalism, lay an obsessive contemporary projection. Throughout *Machiavelli and Us*, Althusser's ultimate theme was plainly a problematic from his own time—the foundation and evolution of the Soviet Union, as the state form of a transition from capitalism to socialism. This was the conjuncture that defined the horizon of world politics for him. Machiavelli's quotation from Virgil in *The Prince* could in this light be read as a maxim of an emergency regime attempting against all odds to build socialism in one country: 'Harsh necessity, and the fact that my kingdom is new, oblige me to do these things and amass armies on the frontiers.'

Appeal to the authority of such Latin precedent is pervasive in Machiavelli. It raises a perennial question: What is the significance of the classical world in his thought? Was it an expedient cover concealing an entirely new structure of thought, or did he actually seek to restore an ancient political prudence? Althusser's modernization of Machiavelli is no isolated act of force. It reflects a recurrent pattern in reception of the Florentine. Gramsci's interpretation of him as a precursor of Saint-Just poses some of the same problems. Was Machiavelli then forced to represent the prosaic content of the emerging absolutist state in 'Roman costume and with Roman slogans', as Marx said the Jacobins had done, in order 'to maintain their enthusiasm at the high level appropriate to great historical tragedy'? In this light, Machiavelli could be seen as the founding father of a bourgeois revolutionary ideology. But if this were the case, he would be a figure of limited relevance in approaching the problems of a proletarian revolution, an enterprise that, according to Marx, no longer needs to cloak its objectives in robes borrowed from a mythical past. Gramsci, representing the disciplined collective parties of the Third International as a 'New Prince', discontinuous in nature from the old, in his own way acknowledged this. A classical frame of reference is not out of place in his portrait of Machiavelli.

Althusser's image of Machiavelli, as seer into a farther Stalinist distance, faces more radical difficulties. By the mid-seventies, he had little or no attachment to what had become of the USSR. In Machiavelli he wanted to find the shapes of an alternative history, encompassing the need for a moment of founding violence as Lenin accepted it, but modulating towards a different, less murderous and conservative outcome than the regime built by Stalin. Hence the two-stage theory he puts forward to resolve the apparent conflict of political purpose between *The Prince* and the *Discourses*—the former is to the violent foundation of the new state what the latter is to its duration and eventual 'democratization'. But this schema does not capture the spirit of the *Discourses*, often mistakenly thought to be less ferocious in their representation of politics. Although he notes that the distinction between the two fundamental types of regime Machiavelli theorizes—principality and republic—more or less collapses as he moves to the climactic middle of his free-wheeling 'commentary' on Livy's history of the origins and later development of the Roman Republic, Althusser does not recognize the problem this poses for his interpretation of the difference between the two texts.

For what it suggests is the fluidity and imprecision of the names we give to regimes and the fierce tyrannical core of any *pouvoir constituant*, which manifests itself not just at the outset of a new state but also in periodic conditions of emergency. It is in the *Discourses* that Machiavelli writes: 'he who proposes to set up an absolute power, or what writers call a tyranny, must renovate everything.' He is not pointing to an evil to be thwarted by civic republicans, but to figures by no means viewed as execrable despots—coolly suggesting the example of the Biblical King David 'who filled the hungry with good things and the rich sent empty away'. He who wishes to make a new beginning must be ready 'to build new cities, to destroy those already built, and to move the inhabitants from one place to another far distant from it; in short to leave nothing of that province intact, and nothing in it, neither rank, nor institution, nor form of government, nor wealth, except it be held by such as recognize that it comes from you'. He concedes that 'such methods are exceedingly cruel and are repugnant to any community, not just a Christian one, but to any composed of men', but excludes any alternative. The most sacred figures of the Christian tradition could not do otherwise: 'He who reads the Bible judiciously will see that Moses was forced, in order that his laws and orders should prosper, to massacre innumerable human beings who, moved by nothing but envy, opposed his designs.'

Biblical examples, of course, weighed less for Machiavelli, who was prepared to envisage the end of Christianity as an all-purpose moral code, than the experience of the Roman Republic. It is this that Althusser seems to have had in mind when thinking of the Soviet Union. But here too his two-stage solution to the apparent opposition of *The Prince* and the *Discourses* shows its limits, since there was no one founder of the Roman Republic, whose political structure emerged out of a continuous sequence of innovative acts, few or none exempt from force. Machiavelli's conception of the violence of beginnings must be put into historical perspective. He was after all no revolutionary in the modern sense of the word. His vision of history was cyclical, every epoch ending in the same drastic puncture: 'when every province is replete with inhabitants who can neither obtain a livelihood nor move elsewhere since all other places are occupied and full up, and when the craftiness and malignity of man has gone as far as it can go, the world must be purged in one of these three ways [floods, pestilence, famine] so that humankind being reduced to comparatively few and humbled by adversity, may adopt a more appropriate form of life and grow better.'

Machiavelli was a theorist of transitions, of fresh beginnings, but the opposite of a utopian. He never imagined the possibility of something truly new: a progressive amelioration of scarcity, bringing a universal emancipation through the transformation of nature. Like Goethe's Mephistopheles he was an old-world devil, who hoped only to unleash virtuous cycles of conflict, negation and liberty, fully realizing that they would eventually become vicious cycles. But his reflections on this dismal sequence are infused with a sense of gallows humour. He declined to see it as a tragedy. Althusser's memorial on Machiavelli traces, in its plunge to indeterminacy and contingency, the dissolution of his own theoretical system, on the eve of the historical disappearance of its practical referent. He dismissed the satirical side of Machiavelli from sight. But this is the legacy that may count most for any future Enlightenment. If Marxism is to play its role in the daybreak to another era of upheavals, it will have to be a gay science.

Envoi

13

Machiavelli and the Reawakening of History

Nietzsche once wrote that the modern European was compelled to live ironically, 'in a historicizing and, as it were, a twilight mood', leading him to fear that 'in the future he will be totally unable to rescue any more of his youthful hopes and powers.'[1] Contemporary culture is no longer captivated by this nineteenth-century presumption of the historicity of life forms, nor are we burdened by the accompanying anxiety that we are fated to live as epigones. But the study of the history of political thought persists, still honouring the faded ideals of its founders. In keeping with them, twentieth-century scholarship on Machiavelli began with the assumption that his writings can be understood only in the context of the republican and courtly politics of his times, whose topics and semantics belong to a world that is no longer continuous with our own. Anachronism, in this view, is the main obstacle to an understanding of artefacts from a lost political world. Attempting to surmount it is a now vast body of work devoted to the careful investigation of the older meanings of 'fortune', 'virtue' and 'glory'. Why does Machiavelli—more than any other figure in what still might be called the canon—invite this broadly historicist approach? One reason may be that his ideas now seem familiar even to those who are new to Machiavelli. His observations and proposals are the common currency of politics, and it is no longer obvious how one might read his works for

---

1   Friedrich Nietzsche, 'On the Uses and Disadvantages of History for Life', *Untimely Meditations*, Cambridge: Cambridge University Press, 1997, p.107.

politico-historical instruction, as Bacon or Rousseau once did. Leo Strauss observed that not even Machiavelli's most truculent proposals disturb contemporary interpreters. From a historicist perspective, this is as it should be. A mature understanding of the past only comes to those who recognize that it was organized according to commitments that later historians are not in a position to judge.

It follows that to paraphrase his arguments and conclusions always risks creating a mere litany of commonplaces, of hackneyed ideas garnished with classical references. On reflection, we might wonder why this is so, as incisive summaries exist of the works of Aristotle, Hobbes and Hegel that provide at least an adequate first approach to the core concerns of these thinkers. In such cases, thought appears in a more manifestly systematic form, in the recognizable genre of 'philosophy', with its established rules of reading and interpretation. Machiavelli was not a philosopher in this sense; nor are his two major political works histories in the classical mould. There is then an unresolved, preliminary problem of classifying *The Prince* and the *Discourses* on Livy that highlights the strangeness of these books, and explains, in part, some of the abiding confusion in interpretation.

This impasse might also have arisen because the object of these studies has not yet cooled; Machiavelli's books resist their reduction to the status of artefacts. As there remain unresolved problems of the manner in which Machiavelli's writings are divided between past and present, the salutary historicist desire to exhume old contexts might profit from a mode of reading that estranges us from our own political universe of elections, money and hand-wringing over the decline of public virtue. From a podium in Barcelona in 1929, Carl Schmitt claimed: 'We can no longer say anything worthwhile about culture and history without first becoming aware of our own historical situation.'[2]

---

2   Carl Schmitt, 'The Age of Neutralizations and Depoliticizations', in *The Concept of the Political*, Chicago: University of Chicago Press, 2007, p. 80.

Scholars often conceive of the historicity of political language from the vantage point of an unhistoricized, indeed unproblematic, present. I would like to propose that we adopt the opposite stance towards this problem of the historicity of thought forms by recapturing the perspective of a writer facing a future—without, however, assuming that this means us, or any static posterity. Thucydides and Plutarch wrote for posterity, presuming the kind of lucidity of what comes after that only a fixed, classical civilization can provide. By contrast, Machiavelli seems to have foreseen, and manifestly wanted to begin, a history of new beginnings, of the periodic opening up of paths 'as yet untrodden by anyone'.[3] It would be tempting to thematize this newness and the desire for it in terms of what is called 'modernity', but as that comes laden with mythologies concerning the origins of a much later condition—roughly our own—it might be advisable to keep that category in mind, without, however, too quickly subsuming his predictions under that imposing term. Leo Strauss's conception of Machiavelli as the founder of modernity depends upon a teleology that arguably contradicts Machiavelli's own understanding of a new kind of newness. I would like to suggest that an essential historical dimension of Machiavelli's major writings can only be grasped in terms of the formal structure of their attempted transcendence of the present, and the whereto of this manoeuvre. By retrieving the traces of this horizon in his writings, its projective intention, we might be in a position to get a better understanding of its notorious opacity, for, so conceived, there would be no determinate receiver of these messages, no one whose assumptions could be taken for granted. One might go so far as to conclude that they were written in anticipation of a new state of uncertainty regarding the relationship between the short and the long term.

---

3   Niccolo Machiavelli, *Discourses on Livy*, Preface, Chicago: University of Chicago, 1996, p. 5.

In 1941, fleeing the advancing fascist storm, Bertolt Brecht
wrote in his journal that

> to equip a work to stand the test of time, on the face of it a 'natural' aim,
> becomes a more serious matter when the writer has grounds for the
> pessimistic assumption that his ideas may find acceptance only in the long
> term. The measures, incidentally, that one employs to this end must not
> detract from the topical effect of the work. The necessary epic touches
> applied to things that are 'self-evident' at the time of writing lose their
> value as estrangement effects after that time. The conceptual autarchy
> of the works contains an element of criticism: the writer is analyzing the
> transience of the concepts and observations of his own times.[4]

Even political writers who see things from the point of view of
the *longue durée*, 'in terms of continents and epochs', experience
historical transience through the existential categories of victory and
defeat. The narrative of the rise and fall of individuals and groups
of men was, of course, traditionally organized around the tropes
of tragedy and comedy. But, as already noted, neither *The Prince*
nor the *Discourses* are histories in any conventional sense; while
they may share a vision of history—one also organized around
these categories of victory and defeat—this vision is arguably
neither comic nor tragic.[5] What kind of texts are these then, and
by what mode of emplotment do they become intelligible?[6] In
addressing these problems of literary interpretation, it might be
useful to consider that unconventional genres of political writing
arose in the sixteenth century that envisioned a radical break from

---

4   *Bertolt Brecht Journals*, trans. Hugh Rorrison, New York: Routledge, 1995,
p.145.
5   Fredric Jameson, 'From Tragedy to the Dialectic', in forthcoming
Valences of the Dialectic, London: Verso, 2009.
6   Hayden White, *Metahistory: The Historical Imagination in Nineteenth-
Century Europe*, Baltimore: Johns Hopkins, 1973. Many of the ideas of this essay
arose out of conversations with the author of this work.

the status quo in new narrative forms. Thomas More's *Utopia* is the first of a genre that is still with us, at least vestigially. Radical difference in the utopian form is presented spatially, that is, as another, indeterminate place. By contrast, following Althusser's remarkable suggestion, *The Prince* might be read as the first of another new genre, the manifesto. The obvious element of projection involved in reading this tract as an antecedent of *The Communist Manifesto* need not detain us. The claim is suggestive because it brings into focus a novel rhetoric of radical, or absolute, difference. In both *The Prince* and the *Discourses*, a de-linking from the present, from the status quo, appears not in a spatial but rather in a temporal register, as the conditions of possibility in bringing forth 'the new'.

The point of raising these problems of genre and literary form is not to substitute classification for interpretation, but rather to consider some of the rhetorical devices by which the author makes it possible to conceive of the wholly new state. In this regard, the first thing to notice is those points where the author posits a very specific orientation towards time, as if it were a generalization about human nature to which anybody, at any period, might give their assent: 'men are desirous of new things, so much that most often those who are well-off desire newness as much as those who are badly off.'[7] Perhaps, but as we are informed elsewhere, it is very difficult for the belief in new things to be maintained in the volatility and fog of their inception, and this withholding of belief prevents these things from coming into existence. A naturalizing judgment establishes, then, the enabling premise, a condition of possibility for theorizing an event that does not yet have a foundation in experience. If one were then to go on to ask what the unthematized historical condition of this premise's articulation was, the problem of its immediate context could be reframed in terms of the historical experience that made it possible. The following is

---

7   *Discourses*, Book III, Chap. 21, p. 263.

offered as a speculative description of this context, or condition, of the origination of a novel outlook on newness. The particular site of this experience might be visualized as a radically endangered pocket of stasis, an enclave within the prevailing order of time, a moment and a place from which the figure of an absolute departure from the status quo came into view. Just as the monasteries, right before their dissolution, formed a humanist eddy in the flood tide of rampant privatization and absolutist consolidation from which Utopia could be thought,[8] the terminal crisis of the Florentine commune might be seen as having set the stage for a figuration of the new, as a repetition of antiquity with a difference. I would like to propose that in Machiavelli this conception of a new state folds back into an attempt to think about historical time itself—of discontinuities, of points at which an older order of things come to an incomprehensible end, displaced by an unprecedented impetus.

The figuration of the hereditary principality is constructed in the second chapter of *The Prince* as a counterpart to the text's central theme. Such a state can be thought to embody a traditional understanding of time in which each successive generation takes its place in a lineage, building on an already existing foundation. Perhaps this is the reason why the author seems so insistent on the necessity of 'extinguishing the bloodlines', a vivid image of the violent breaking open of a customary, even natural, order of generational succession, in which nothing new ever emerges. *The Prince* is perhaps better suited to foregrounding the conditions of this moment of rupture, because by addressing a single, resolute ruler, the onset of action can begin at any time, blasting open the continuum of bloodlines, of posterity. A people's origins and their first steps towards self-rule are, by contrast, always more difficult to narrate as a story of timely beginnings. As a result, *The Prince*, in its focus on 'the new', arguably lacks the historical depth of the *Discourses*, despite its resemblance to certain already existing

8   Fredric Jameson, *Archaeologies of the Future: The Desire Called Utopia and other Science Fictions*, London: Verso, 2005, pp. 23–26.

literary forms. Nonetheless, the concluding formulation of this above-mentioned chapter from *The Prince* on hereditary lineages offers a striking figuration of a new dimension of historical time that takes the form of a return to the foundations, a reactivation of a concealed and dormant potential that was present at the inception of an order within whose walls one still resides:

> In the antiquity and continuity of the dominion the memories and causes of innovations are eliminated; for one change always leaves a dentation for the building of another.[9]

Why are the root causes of a new order so difficult to recollect? To help us understand this complex architectural metaphor, we might reflect upon the current inconceivability of figures of political action that could change our own modes and orders, even in the midst of a mounting disorder. But *The Prince* does not just provide a figuration of history as a process of innovation and its subsequent forgetting; it offers some actual categories for thinking about the logic of origination.

The first category is 'occasion'. Beginning presupposes an occasion: what is the consistency of this given, this precondition of an act? When looking at the greatest examples of founders (all of whom turn out to be semi-mythological individuals—Theseus, Romulus, Moses, even Cyrus), it would seem as if an occasion was a near complete absence of what we would call all an opportunity. At least for the cases that Machiavelli calls the greatest, the occasion, paradoxically, seems to take the form of a liberating, if also disquieting, realization that a would-be founder must start

---

9   Niccolo Machiavelli, *The Prince*, Chicago: The University of Chicago Press, 1998, Chap. 2, p. 7. The Chicago edition provides the following gloss on 'dentation': 'a toothed wall left on the side of a building so that another building may be attached to it. NM's metaphor compares the hereditary, or "natural", principality to a row of houses continually added to but never finished and, as it were, not begun from the beginning.'

from scratch, from next to nothing. Innovation presents an almost philosophical problem, for new things do not exist in a clear-cut form: 'the incredulity of men who do not truly believe in new things unless they have come to have a firm experience of them'.[10] Machiavelli's writings are reflections on a politico-ontological problem regarding how to bring new things into being and make them endure. It can be framed as follows: why does origination depend upon what he calls imitation? After all, to think of newness as imitation, as the repetition, or recurrence of the greatest examples, is very difficult: 'For the greatness of the thing partly terrifies men, so that they fail in their first beginnings.'[11]

He writes that all contemporary things have their counterpart in ancient times. It is interesting to note, even though the reason seems obvious, that for Machiavelli the formal historical structure of the most difficult, because in a specific sense groundless, form of innovation is, first and foremost, the imitation of the ancients by the moderns. For this act involves a kind of giant leap. The formal structure of contrast in Machiavelli's writings might be compared to the parallelism of Plutarch's *Lives*, and this immediately emphasizes that the disjunction between ancient and modern cases in Machiavelli's commentaries and histories is framing a distinction in the form of a more fundamental historical caesura.

This complex relationship of modern to ancient times is reflected in the strange preface to Book I of the *Discourses*, which in a sense begins twice, with formulations that point in opposing temporal directions: the first paragraph, with a modernist declaration of an intent to accomplish the equivalent of the discovery of unknown lands and waters; the second, in sharp contrast, with a call to restore an authentic knowledge of ancient politics through the study of its historians. The following passage captures the formal structure of this disjunctive relationship between ancient and modern epochs:

10   Ibid, Chap. 6, p. 24.
11   *Discourses*, Book I, Chap. 55, p. 112.

> So it is an easy thing for whoever examines past things diligently to foresee future things in every republic and to take the remedies for them that were used by the ancients, *or, if they do not find any that were used, to think up new ones though the similarity of accidents.*[12]

These unforeseeable accidents will turn out to be the essential ones, for a new history begins by transforming such an unclassifiable moment into an incomparable occasion, the setting for a potential beginning. An accident can either be an event, a surprising development, or the larger context of a time and a place, a whole site. In the problematic conjunction of ancient and modern sites, Machiavelli establishes two essential modes of historical change, of the new coming out of the old. The first is relative and dialectical, where the names, the appearances of ancient modes are retained, while being hollowed out. This vision of change is put forth in Chapter 25 of Book I of the *Discourses*. The next chapter introduces the absolute and disjunctive form of change, in which everything is made new, names included:

> To make in cities new governments with new names, new authorities, new men; to make the rich poor, the poor rich . . . to build new cities, to take down those built, to exchange the inhabitants from one place to another; and in sum, not to leave anything untouched.[13]

Was it actually possible to forge new peoples in this manner? First he tells us: 'I do not know whether this has ever occurred or whether it is possible.' Then, that it would be a 'very cruel enterprise or altogether impossible'. Next, how it could be done. As Rousseau once wrote: 'He who dares to undertake the establishment of a people should feel that he is, so to speak, in a position to change

12   *Discourses*, Book I, Chap. 39, p. 84; italics added.
13   *Discourses*, Book I, Chap. 26, p. 61.

human nature.'[14] When can such a figure of radical agency come into existence? The answer must take into account the immense variability in the potency and knowledge of men in different times and places: 'the weakness of men at present, caused by their weak education and their slight knowledge of things, makes them judge ancient judgments in part inhuman, in part impossible.'[15]

These reflections frame a historically specific, and contemporaneous problem, which according to Machiavelli is close to insoluble: namely, how to build a civil way of life in a Europe corrupted by lordly and clerical idleness. What he calls 'these corrupt centuries of ours' form an unprecedented accident—a hybrid of Christian effeminacy, urban involution and a post-classical feudal barbarism. The outlines of this *monstrum* only take shape as things happen that open up a horizon, making this condition seem transcendable—the rise of the French Kingdom, the successes of Swiss arms, the onslaught of the Turk, the open corruption and impending scourge of the Roman Church, all in an atmosphere charged by the ongoing revival of ancient learning. The hypothesis I will advance here is that the occasion, or condition, of possibility for a new state—or in epochal terms, a new political civilization—is the accident of the European *monstrum* grasped in the moment of its potential transcendence. To reiterate, the desired destination of this imagined transport, its *whereto*, is perhaps impossible.

These observations raise a question regarding a fundamental historical category: namely, what is an epoch? Periodization is always fraught with the problems attendant on identifying some definitive breaking point—how much more so when what's at stake is the temporal identity of one's own times. Machiavelli's historical thought is organized around an

14   Jean-Jacques Rousseau, *The Social Contract*, Book II, p. 163; from *The Basic Political Writings*, trans. Donald A. Cress, Indianapolis: Hackett Publishing Company, 1987.
15   *Discourses*, Book III, p. 275.

opposition, a partly concealed rivalry, between ancient and modern times. Everyone knows the story of the long historical passage from a time when the relative eminence of ancients and moderns was a matter of controversy to the later conclusion that the past was simply different. While there seem to be no traces of this latter implication in Machiavelli's writings, at least in the preface to Book II of the *Discourses*, the author seems to have entertained an extreme scepticism regarding the reliability of ancient sources, and the radicalization of this scepticism at least opens up the space for another, if more circumscribed, kind of historical relativism. But we should not anticipate too much. Machiavelli asked another question, one that partly conceals a rivalry with ancient times: why, he asks in the preface to Book II of the *Discourses*, are we partisans, enthusiasts for the past? First of all, it is not at all clear that men are always as Machiavelli will now describe them; indeed, one could say that he posits a very specific experience of how men relate to time in Storm and Stress, as if it were a fact about human nature. Human beings, we are informed, feel discontent, disgust, boredom with the things they possess: 'This makes them blame the present, praise the past and desire the future, even if they are not moved to do this by any reasonable cause.'[16]

If we were to take this formulation literally, it would force us to ask why the ancients did not judge their own times inferior to a period more ancient still. Why does Machiavelli's claim only work as an observation about modern Europe? I would propose that thinking through this duality underscores the following: at least some ancient peoples had a free beginning, because what preceded their history was an obscure, that is to say non-historic, mythological past. But modern Europeans, like the city of Florence itself, had an unfree beginning, ultimately because they remained

---

16 *Discourses*, Book II, Chap. 1, p. 125.

dependent upon the example of other historical times for any new beginning. Of course, the rebirth of virtue is made easier by ancient precedents and judgments, but such ease, for Machiavelli, is always fatally tainted, for repeaters find it nearly impossible to make a new example, that is to say, a new absolute of themselves. But, and here's the twist—it would then follow that overcoming this condition of coming after, of being the epigone, would be the most virtuous, most praiseworthy act of all.

In a very complicated analogy from the same preface, Machiavelli compares those who now praise antiquity to old men trying to recall their youth: they remember the past, but not what was truly youthful, what was new in it then. Reading this, one might recall Stendhal's definition of the classical as the modernity of the past. The analogy is meant to raise the question of how our corrupt times—unprecedented and thus of an indeterminate age— might become youthful. Leo Strauss proposed that modernity could be seen as a youth movement, devaluing prudence as a corrupt and inverted historical conception of past and present. But given this emphasis on rejuvenation, why do the *Discourses* end on such a grim note: the mass executions of Bacchanals, the quarantining of foreigners? Here I think we might consider a parallel to Lucretius's *De Rerum Natura*, which begins with a tribute to love and ends with a disturbing portrait of a city in the grip of devastating plague: what vision of history does this ending suggest? Is there an ecological finitude that turns back the forward thrust of civilization? The seventeenth-century Englishman Thomas Burnett, haunted by this Lucretian thought, imagined that 'we are living amidst ruins, evidence of a world in decay, the dawn of a new disorder, an unforeseen and negative intention on the part of nature.'[17] Machiavelli does not seem to have entirely accepted such corollaries of the Lucretian view, and it would be interesting to explore the reasons why. I think his thoughts on this

---

17   Paolo Rossi, *The Dark Abyss of Time*, Chicago: University of Chicago Press, 1984, p. 55.

matter are perhaps most clearly formulated in *Discourses*, Book II, Chapter 5, where he asks: 'Whence arises the oblivion of things?' This next chapter begins with a brief consideration of what was then a long-standing problem of whether the world was eternal or, alternatively, had a beginning in time. Here we should ask what is meant by a world. Perhaps there is a more than formal parallel to explore between these moments in Machiavelli, and Lucretius's poem in which worlds are presented as chance combinations of atoms, periodically drying up, like the soil of Italy itself, depleted by the latifundia. I think this might provide a hint as to why the *Discourses* end as they do.

Of course, the Machiavellian oblivion of worlds is historical and not cosmological, and is articulated as a problem of not just the finitude of all human modes, but also of the destruction of the very memory of them—why doesn't historical memory ever go back more than five thousand years?[18] Accounts of times beyond this threshold are fabulous, even mendacious, he writes. I would like to propose that Machiavelli's historicization of the Lucretian vision is the basis of a distinctive vision of civilizational change that is interesting on its own terms, as well as for the fact that it anticipates the later theme of European exceptionalism. He was of course familiar with ancient conceptions of 'the malignity of time', in which nature periodically extinguishes corrupt worlds, leaving behind a coarse remnant of mountain men, and indeed this provides the point of departure for his own treatment of the inevitable recurrence of what Russians call 'a time of troubles', when the centres of civilization are destroyed and a new order emerges after an indeterminate span of time from hitherto marginal areas. This cyclical vision is very different from that which informs the Western idea of a Middle Ages, a period in its own right,[19] based on an unprecedented synthesis of remnants

---

18   *Discourses*, Book II, Chap. 6.
19   Fredric Jameson, 'From Tragedy to the Dialectic', in the forthcoming *Valences of the Dialectic*, London: Verso, 2009.

of classical civilization with barbarism, all made possible by the rise to imperium of a very unusual sect. I would like to propose that the author of the Discourses is working out the beginnings of a non-cyclical vision of civilizational change that arises out of reflections on this wholly new form of corruption, at a moment when its transcendence has become conceivable. For in this case alone, ancient learning was preserved as if in a time capsule. This hypothesis might allow us to better understand a current in the formation of a later historicism. It might be tempting then to conclude that a modern historicism comprehending Machiavelli, encountering a Machiavelli exploring new depths of temporality, might form something like a hermeneutic circle, albeit of a wholly unfamiliar kind.

The Machiavelli that emerges is one for whom the essence of a way of life is concentrated in its experience of finitude, and in its modes of confronting and overcoming it. Like Heidegger, Machiavelli was attempting to formulate the conditions under which this experience of finitude becomes explicitly historical. Of course this new experience of the historicity of existence should not be identified with some holistic world picture of an age, but rather with new modes of fixating on the manifestations of vast structural changes and continuities, of defeat turning into victory, and vice versa.

Before concluding I would like to consider one of these temporal modes, as it plays a very significant role in the argument of the Discourses: hope. The drift of Book III and its grim conclusion raise the question of what one can hope for after the defeat of causes that aspired to rejuvenate the human race. As I suggested at this chapter's beginning, the political enlightenment that comes from recognizing the ultimate finitude of all modes and orders is neither tragic nor comic. The following reflection from Machiavelli on the temporality of a resolute hope is unsurpassed:

> men can second fortune, but not oppose it, they can weave its warp but
> never break it. They should indeed never give up, for since they do not

know its end and it proceeds by oblique and unknown ways, they have always to hope and since they hope not to give up in whatever fortune and in whatever travail they may find themselves.[20]

In our corrupt times, we often hear that attempts to wholly transform the world were a catastrophic failure, and that we must therefore reconcile ourselves to prudential limits, to liberal democracy, and the like, as if the experience of a generation or two was somehow definitive on this the highest of all problems. Machiavelli reasoned differently when confronting his own experience of defeat, in a few lines from that disquieting Book II, Chapter 8 of the *Discourses*, where change is identified with corruption: 'It is impossible that the life of one individual be enough to corrupt an order so that he could draw benefit from it.' Or, as he elsewhere put in the form of an imperative: 'it is the duty of the good man to teach others the good that you could not work because of the malignity of the times or of fortune, so that when many are capable of it, someone of them more loved by heaven will be able to work it.'[21] As the great historical movement from defeat to victory begins anew we see that 'little by little, and from generation to generation' the wickedness of change comes. Machiavelli's stance towards this ebb and flow is captured in a now well-known line from Samuel Beckett, another great thinker of repetition and change: 'Try again, fail again, fail better.'

---

20 *Discourses*, Book II, Chap. 29, p. 199.
21 *Discourses*, Book III, Chap. 8, p. 238; Book II, Preface, p. 125.

Index

Index